The **Amerasia**
Spy Case

The Amer

asia
Spy Case

Harvey Klehr
&
Ronald Radosh

Prelude to
McCarthyism

The University of

North Carolina Press

Chapel Hill and

London

© 1996

The University of North Carolina Press

All rights reserved

Manufactured in the United States of America

The paper in this book meets the guidelines for permanence and durability of the Committee on Production Guidelines for Book Longevity of the Council on Library Resources.

oo 99 98 97 96

5   4   3   2   1

E
743.5
K55
1996

Library of Congress Cataloging-in-Publication Data

Klehr, Harvey.

The Amerasia spy case : prelude to McCarthyism / by Harvey Klehr and Ronald Radosh.

p. cm.

Includes bibliographical references and index.

ISBN 0-8078-2245-0 (cloth : alk. paper)

1. Amerasia. 2. Espionage—United States—History—20th century. 3. Internal security—United States—History—20th century. 4. Anti-communist movements—United States—History—20th century. 5. Communism—United States—History—20th century. 6. Press and politics—United States—History—20th century. 7. United States—Relations—China. 8. China—Relations—United States. I. Radosh, Ronald. II. Title.

E743.5.K55   1996

973.918—dc20   95-22320

CIP

*In memory of
Professor Sidney Wise of
Franklin and Marshall College,
a teacher and friend*
HARVEY KLEHR

*For my wife Allis,
and my children Michael,
Daniel, and Laura*
RONALD RADOSH

Contents

Illustrations

Acknowledgments

This project began more than a decade ago. We are grateful to the many people who continued to have faith in our ability to finish it. First and foremost, we thank the foundations whose generous support enabled us to complete much of the research. We are especially grateful to Hillel Fradkin and Michael Joyce of the Lynde and Harry Bradley Foundation, David Kennedy of the Earhart Foundation, Leslie Lenkowsky of the Institute for Educational Affairs, and Devon Gaffney of the Smith Richardson Foundation.

We also owe an enormous debt of gratitude to Joyce Milton, who worked with us on the book for some time. Her skill and insights were extraordinarily valuable; we regret that other commitments made it impossible for her to continue as a coauthor.

A number of people with firsthand knowledge of the *Amerasia* case gave us substantial amounts of their time and energy, not only agreeing to interviews but also making available private papers for our examination, even when they were not sure what we would make of their role in the affair. We especially appreciate the help of Robert Crowley, Lauchlin Currie, Ralph de Toledano, Fred Field, Agnes Jaffe, Minister Ji Chao-shu, Robert Lamphere, Thelma Larsen, Ruth Levine, Robert Morris, Andrew Roth, John Stewart Service, and William Youngman. Stephen Koch generously shared his own research with us.

The staff of the Special Collections Department of the Robert W. Woodruff Library, Emory University, particularly the director, Linda Matthews, and Ginger Cain, the archivist and assistant department head, helped obtain the FBI files that unlocked most of the mysteries surrounding the *Amerasia* case and made going through the tens of thousands of pages less onerous than it would otherwise have been.

Finally, we deeply appreciate the faith in this project shown by our editor at the University of North Carolina Press, Lewis Bateman, and thank Paula Wald for her skillful copyediting.

Abbreviations

The following abbreviations are used throughout this book. Additional abbreviations are listed in the notes.

BAT   British-American Tobacco Corporation

CCNY   City College of New York

CPUSA Communist Party of the United States of America

DID   Domestic Investigations Division

FBI   Federal Bureau of Investigation

FCC   Federal Communications Commission

FEA   Foreign Economic Administration

GRU   Chief Intelligence Directorate of the General Staff

HUAC   House Un-American Activities Committee

IBRD   International Bank for Reconstruction and Development

ILD   International Labor Defense

IPR   Institute of Pacific Relations

KGB   Committee for State Security

KMT   Kuomintang

ONI   Office of Naval Intelligence

OSS   Office of Strategic Services

OWI   Office of War Information

UN   United Nations

Introduction

June 1945. For Americans, it was a time of buoyant optimism mingled with anxiety. The war in Europe was over, but the shape of the new era that was dawning was not yet apparent.

In Bavaria, a delegation of American officers began the month by making an inspection tour of Berchtesgaden, the Führer's abandoned mountain retreat, and a baby-faced lieutenant named Audie Murphy was awarded the Legion of Merit, leaving him just one medal short of becoming America's most-decorated war hero.

In Moscow, a "high Russian military source" announced that a corpse found in the rubble of occupied Berlin had been identified "with fair certainty" as that of Adolf Hitler. On the same day that this conclusion was made public, the Soviet Union released a map indicating that it planned to occupy fully half of the territory of the Reich. The news, commented the *New York Times*, "came as a surprise to London" and would mean that the U.S. Army might have to pull back as far as 150 miles from the front it had established in southern Germany.[1]

In San Francisco, delegates to the World Security Conference were listening to testimony about antidemocratic practices in Argentina. The delegates would eventually vote to approve the charter of a new international peacekeeping organization, the United Nations (UN). But the Allied entente that had made the conference possible, the much-touted Spirit of Yalta, was already strained.

Franklin Delano Roosevelt had been dead for six weeks. Although Roosevelt's passing had come as a shock to the public, his rapidly deteriorating health had been an open secret in Washington for months, contributing to the controversy over his unprecedented bid for a fourth term. During his autumn 1944 campaign, Roosevelt had been unable to stand to deliver his speeches, even with the aid of his crutches and leg braces, and in cabinet meetings, he was occasionally, and uncharacteristically, inattentive and misinformed. The Republican candidate, Thomas Dewey of New York, had wanted to raise the question of the president's fitness for office but was dissuaded by advisers who warned that such a tactic would only generate sympathy for the ailing chief. Instead, Dewey chose to take up the charge that Communists were "seizing control of the New Deal," even going so far as to suggest that Roosevelt's fourth term was only a prelude to an attempt to overthrow the Constitution and dispense with free elections entirely. In Dewey's mind, the rising tide of Communist influence was exemplified by the presence of labor leader Sidney Hillman among the inner circle of Democratic campaign organizers. The voters rejected this argument, and Dewey as well.[2]

Revered by many, despised by some, Roosevelt was the only president many younger Americans could remember. Now his place had been filled by an unknown quantity, the dapper machine politician from Missouri, Harry S (for nothing) Truman. The new chief executive, inexperienced in foreign affairs, was doing his best to coax Joseph Stalin into agreeing to meet with him and Winston Churchill at a Big Three summit conference, in which the United States and Great Britain could discuss their apprehension over the Soviet Union's actions in Eastern Europe. In the meantime, on May 31, Truman had told Congress that within the coming year, 7 million Americans would be fighting in Asia against "the eastern enemy."[3]

The Sixth Marine Division, after advancing across the muddy hills of Okinawa, was even then fighting for control of the Japanese military airstrip at Naha. Kōbe, on the Japanese mainland, was bombed on June 5, and by mid-July carrier-based planes of Admiral William Halsey's Third Fleet would be strafing airfields on the outskirts of Tokyo. Nevertheless, American strategists had no confidence that they would be able to compel an orderly surrender. If the Japanese military refused to accept defeat, American troops could be forced to reconquer the archipelago, island by island, and to reclaim Japanese-occupied China, square inch by square inch.

On June 7, the Soviets' plans for the occupation of Germany and the identification of Hitler's remains shared space on the front pages of the morning newspapers with a domestic news story—the arrests of six individuals on charges of conspiracy to commit espionage. Three members of the group were government employees—Emmanuel Larsen and John Stewart Service, both State Department officials, and Lieutenant Andrew Roth, a Navy reserve officer who, according to the *New York Times'* account of the arrests, "has not recently been on active duty." Two others, Philip Jaffe and Kate Mitchell, were editors of a pro-Communist magazine called *Amerasia*, described by the *Times* as a small-circulation journal printed on good quality glossy paper and selling for 15 cents a copy. The sixth suspect was Mark Gayn, a journalist whose articles on the war in Asia appeared regularly in *Time* magazine and *Collier's*.

The investigation that led to the arrests of the six suspects had begun the previous February when Kenneth Wells, chief of the Southern Asia section of the Office of Strategic Services (OSS), picked up the January 26, 1945, issue of *Amerasia* to read an article entitled "British Imperial Policy in Asia." One section dealt with British activity in Thailand, a subject Wells had researched as part of his own work. He had received a tip from his counterpart in British intelligence that the views of *Amerasia*'s editors on the subject would be of more than routine interest. Wells soon discovered that the British agent had been right—and not because the content was new to him. To his astonishment, Wells found himself reading his own words, lifted almost verbatim from a highly classified report on British-American relations in Southeast Asia that had been circulated only among top Asia experts in the State Department and the military intelligence agencies. In a few places, Wells's original language had been lightly paraphrased and some of the fifteen points he enumerated in his article had been rearranged, but the plagiarism was glaringly obvious to anyone familiar with the original.[4]

amerasia

a fortnightly review of america and asia

January 26, 1945

BRITISH IMPERIAL POLICY IN ASIA

Part II

Britain's Postwar Plans • The Views of
Leading Spokesmen • Differences in U.S.
and British Attitude Towards Thailand
Colonial Economics—the Postwar Model

DUTCH, FRENCH POLICY

FIFTEEN CENTS

Cover of the January 26, 1945, issue of *Amerasia* that first alerted the OSS to a security leak.

Wells had good reason to be alarmed. A portion of his report discussed the existence of an anti-Japanese resistance movement headed by Thailand's prince regent, Nui Pridi Phanomyong. Pridi's anti-Japanese activity had been a well-kept secret so far. Even though this particular section of the report had not been published in *Amerasia*, it seemed likely that the author had been working from a complete copy of the document.[5]

The survival of the prince regent, indeed of the entire Thai resistance movement, was imperiled. OSS security chief Archibald Van Beuren was determined to track down the source of this dangerous breach of government security. An OSS agent was stationed outside *Amerasia*'s New York City headquarters, a modest suite located in an office building at 225 Fifth Avenue. The neighborhood was normally deserted after business hours, and initially, the OSS planned to wrap up the operation quickly. But it seemed that even though the rest of the building emptied promptly at 5:00 P.M., someone was always putting in overtime at the *Amerasia* office. It was not until a Sunday evening two weeks later on March 11, during a blustery winter rainstorm, that the OSS lookout found the suite empty.

Minutes after the lookout called his superiors and gave them the all-clear signal, a five-man team led by OSS director of investigations Frank Bielaski entered the suite. Although at first the OSS had assumed the report had merely been leaked accidentally to an inquiring scholar or journalist, Bielaski suspected by now that more was involved. What he found exceeded even his wildest speculations. Opening the door of a small room near the front of the shabbily furnished suite, he found a well-equipped darkroom—a surprising discovery in itself since *Amerasia* did not contain photographs. At the end of the corridor, in the small private offices of the editor-publisher and his assistant, the team came upon evidence that someone had been working in the darkroom earlier that evening. Photographs, still damp from the developing solution, were spread out on the desk in one of the offices. A quick examination revealed that these were photographed pages from perhaps twenty different government documents, several of them stamped "Top Secret."

On the desk in one of the offices were two briefcases and a cheap, bellows-type suitcase, all locked. One member of the team, an officer from the Office of Naval Intelligence (ONI), picked open the locks and found that the bags were stuffed full of documents from government sources: army and navy intelligence, British intelligence, the State Department, the Office of Censorship, and the OSS. In the meantime, Bielaski and his assistant Olaf Oleson had entered a large room off the main corridor that was used as a combination library and work room. The library table was piled high with documents, both originals and copies.

Oleson picked up one envelope from the table and showed it to his boss. The name of John Hersey, the well-known author and journalist, was scrawled across one corner. Inside were six typed copies of "Top Secret" documents. One of the documents, dated October 1944, set forth the

.locations of the ships of the Japanese fleet. Another described American plans for the bombardment of the Japanese mainland.[6]

Overwhelmed by the magnitude of his find, Bielaski made a snap decision. There were so many government papers strewn around the offices that he concluded it ought to be possible to retrieve a few as evidence without tipping off the *Amerasia* staff to the break-in. Hastily, the team gathered several dozen documents that had originated with the OSS, including six copies of the Wells report on Thailand, then carefully relocked the briefcases and the suite's front door and left.[7]

Surprisingly, Bielaski's gamble paid off. Although, presumably, the documents his team made off with were eventually missed, Philip Jaffe, the editor and publisher of *Amerasia*, did not immediately suspect that his offices had been entered and searched. During the next two and a half months, he and his assistant, Kate Mitchell, continued to do business as usual, not realizing that they were being watched day and night by a team of Federal Bureau of Investigation (FBI) agents. The surveillance, eventually expanded to cover several of Jaffe's associates and alleged sources, kept seventy-five of the bureau's most experienced agents busy in round-the-clock shifts.

This intensive spy hunt revealed evidence of a massive penetration of the government's wartime security measures. Nearly every agency that dealt with classified information was represented in the cache of papers eventually seized in connection with the investigation—the War Department, the State Department, the OSS, the Office of Postal and Telegraph Censorship, and the ONI, among others.

To the newspaper-reading public, unaware of the magnitude of the sensitive information in the possession of the defendants, the tersely worded press release that reported the arrests of the *Amerasia* six had an unfamiliar ring to it. Although a number of Hollywood movies had dealt with the theme of espionage, for several years the public had heard little hard news about spies. Following a series of spy scares just before and after the attack on Pearl Harbor, the FBI had changed its policy. Hoping to avoid the spy hysteria that had swept the nation during World War I, it had made a decision to limit publicity about its efforts to search out pro-Axis agents. Although the bureau had quietly organized an extensive network of informants among defense plant workers to spot possible sabotage, a nationwide publicity campaign was launched to discourage amateur sleuthing by the general public. Posters and trailers shown in movie houses encouraged watchful citizens to "leave it to the FBI."[8]

Now, within weeks of V-E Day, an active Washington spy ring had allegedly been uncovered, but it was not pro-Axis in character. Instead, several of the defendants were sympathetic to America's Communist allies. Moreover, the suspects were not the shifty-eyed foreign agents or disgruntled fifth-column saboteurs that dock and defense plant workers had been warned to look out for but a group of well-educated, highly presentable professionals. Despite Dewey's campaign rhetoric about Communist infiltration, the very idea that the Soviet Union was actively engaged in spying on the American government was a novel proposition to most Americans, and even many well-informed observers dismissed such claims as a right-wing fantasy.

Predictably, the breaking news of the *Amerasia* arrests was hailed by conservative pundits such as Hearst columnist Howard Rushmore. A former Communist and *Daily Worker* drama critic who had broken with the party after he was disciplined for giving a favorable review of the movie *Gone with the Wind*, Rushmore pronounced the case "sensational proof that Communist organizers had access to highly confidential files of vital government agencies." Others, from left-wing commentator I. F. Stone to writers for the *New York Herald Tribune*, the voice of moderate Republicans, wondered if the case was really about espionage at all, or, as the *Herald Tribune* put it, a simple case of "Red-baiting." Either way, the Justice Department's resolve to bring espionage charges against a publisher and an established journalist raised important constitutional questions about the conflict between freedom of the press and the government's need to keep sensitive information secret, especially during wartime. Everyone expected that the issue would be thrashed out in the course of a sensational and highly publicized trial.[9]

That trial never took place.

From the first, the government prosecutors in the *Amerasia* matter were dogged by disappointments and bad luck. The results of the FBI's investigation proved unexpectedly meager and unconvincing. Within six months of the arrests, the chief prosecutor went on record as agreeing with Philip Jaffe's attorney that the defendants were guilty of nothing more than an "excess of journalistic zeal."

The prosecutor's statement, apparently proving that the suspicions of the liberal press had been correct all along, has been accepted by most historians as the final verdict on the *Amerasia* affair. Philip Jaffe, in this view, was merely a somewhat eccentric left-wing publisher with a penchant for collecting and squirreling away official papers in his personal brary. As David Caute summarized it in his survey of the McCarthy years, *The Great Fear: The Anti-Communist Purge under Truman and Eisenhower*, the *Amerasia* case "revealed how quick-fingered politically committed government servants could be"; nevertheless, the defendants were engaged in leaking, not espionage—"neither he [Jaffe] nor his sources had in mind to pass information to a foreign power."[10]

A few conservatives and anti-Communist zealots refused to accept this explanation. On the right, it became an article of faith that a "whitewash" or cover-up of the scandal had occurred—and that unknown persons in high places had conspired to fix the case. In 1950 these charges were taken up by Senator Joseph McCarthy, who cited the *Amerasia* affair as proof of his contention that the Department of State had been infiltrated by a clique of "card carrying Communists." To McCarthy and his allies, the government's failure to send the *Amerasia* defendants to jail was just the tip of the iceberg, the visible proof of the existence of a vast conspiracy of underground Communists and their liberal dupes that had already resulted in the "loss" of China to the Communists and was ultimately aimed at destroying the American way of life.

McCarthy's charges brought *Amerasia* back into the headlines and led to a Senate investigation. The Tydings Committee, as it was informally known, concluded that charges of a cover-up in the *Amerasia* affair were baseless. But in the long run, the committee's verdict failed to settle the issue.

Loyal Democrats insisted that there had been no whitewash—and no connection between the *Amerasia* defendants and Soviet espionage. Even to suggest otherwise was to endorse the conspiracy theories of McCarthy and his China Lobby allies.

On the other hand, a cloud of rumor and suspicion continued to hang over the case. The chief prosecutor soon became a partner in a law firm founded by an uncle of one of the defendants. Another key figure in the case left the country permanently, hounded by charges that he had been a Soviet agent. Justice Department spokespersons missed no opportunity to insist that no crime had been committed in the first place and that the prosecution had been misguided from the beginning, leading skeptics to wonder just what the department was attempting to hide by making these uncharacteristic claims to incompetence.

Suspecting that McCarthy was onto something, conservative and even some moderate Republicans continued to support him despite their growing distaste for his tactics. In the meantime, other congressional committees rushed to investigate charges that America's failure to throw its full support behind the Nationalist government of Chiang Kai-shek in its struggle against the Reds was the work of a pro-Communist clique inside the State Department. A generation of Chinese-area experts were forced to defend themselves before a succession of congressional committees and State Department Loyalty-Security Board proceedings. Most were eventually driven out of the foreign service, their careers and reputations in ruins.

The *Amerasia* case was the first of the great spy cases of the postwar era. Unlike the Alger Hiss case or the Rosenberg case, it did not lead to an epic courtroom confrontation or the imprisonment or execution of any of the principals. Today it is far less well known or remembered than the others. Nevertheless, its importance should not be overlooked. It prompted several congressional investigations, stirred up a major partisan controversy, and threatened to destroy the political reputations of several important government officials.

It was the first public drama featuring charges that respectable American citizens had spied for the Communists. The refusal of many liberals to believe that the Rosenbergs or Alger Hiss had actually spied was, in part, conditioned by the peculiar circumstances and outcome of the *Amerasia* case. The *Amerasia* case contributed mightily to the creation of McCarthyism in American life. The rancorous debate about the federal government's employee loyalty program was linked to the case. So, too, was the debate about who had "lost" China.

It is striking that no full-scale study of the *Amerasia* case has been undertaken. It has, of course, been discussed in broader histories of the period, in the memoirs of some of those involved in the affair, and in accounts of Soviet espionage in the United States. But unlike the Hiss and Rosenberg cases, there is no consensus about the meaning of the whole affair or, indeed, just what took place. Espionage or leaking? Treason or political manipulation? A government plot or Communist subversion?

At long last, thanks to the availability of long-closed government documents, most of the *Amerasia* story can be uncovered. It has few heroes, many villains, and more than a few knaves. None of the participants emerges with an unscathed reputation. It prompted several prominent government officials not merely to dissemble but even to commit perjury. The *Amerasia* case sheds light not only on America's China policy, Soviet espionage, McCarthyism, and the loyalty program but also on the bureau-cratic intricacies of anti-Communism in Washington, involving brutal battles among the FBI, the White House, the Justice Department, and other government agencies in their efforts to take credit for accomplish-ments and avoid blame for disasters.

The China Hands

Few Americans were familiar with the name John Stewart Service at the time of his arrest in 1945, but he would eventually emerge as the key figure in the *Amerasia* case. Service was among several of the State Department's foreign service officers—the "China Hands"—who were accused of favoring the victory of Mao Tse-tung's Communists and of working to undermine Chiang Kai-shek's Kuomintang. Because of his involvement, the *Amerasia* case would forever be linked to the triumph of Communism in China.

If ever a man seemed destined to rise through the ranks of the diplomatic corps to a position of influence, it was Jack Service. To correspondents like Brooks Atkinson of the *New York Times*, who got to know him in China during World War II, Service was the epitome of everything a career foreign service officer should be. Everything about him was right, including his lean good looks, his reserved manner, his fluent command of the Chinese language—even, by one of those startling and inexplicable coincidences, his surname, which prompted Madame Chiang Kai-shek to quip the first time they were introduced, "We hope you will be of service to China."

That such a dedicated and effective public servant could be forced to spend his most productive years defending himself against charges of disloyalty has often been cited as evidence that something had gone drastically wrong with the fabric of political debate during the early 1950s. In 1970 Barbara Tuchman singled out Service's arrest in the *Amerasia* case as the "first step" toward the "tawdry reign of terror soon to be imposed with such astonishing ease by Senator Joseph McCarthy."[1] To others, like William F. Buckley, Jr., and L. Brent Bozell, writing in 1954, Service's involvement was proof that the *Amerasia* affair was not just another grubby espionage case but evidence that "conspiratorial forces operating on the highest levels of the U.S. government" had labored to swing U.S. foreign policy "to the side of the Chinese Communists and helped to establish them in power." The day Service was finally dismissed from his government job, after being investigated for six years by the FBI, the State Department Loyalty-Security Board, the Civil Service Commission's Loyalty Review Board, and congressional committees, was, Buckley and Bozell concluded, the day "McCarthy was . . . vindicated."[2]

Of these two judgments, the viewpoint that singles out Service as the first victim of the cold war comes closer to the truth. Yet it fails to explain how a man who was considered one of the best and brightest young diplomats of his generation could have been quite as naive and unsuspecting as he portrayed himself as being in his own testimony.

John Stewart Service was born in 1909 in Ch'eng-tu, in the Szechwan province of China, where his father was an administrator of the Young Men's Christian Association's mission program. Robert Roy Service was not an ordained minister. Nevertheless, he and his wife Grace, both graduates of the University of California at Berkeley, were typical of the American missionary community in China. Conservative to the point of austerity in their personal habits, they were social gospel Christians, enlightened and internationalist in outlook. Having come to China to save souls, they had been converted into ardent admirers of Chinese art and culture.

Although the American missionaries who went to China during the late nineteenth and early twentieth centuries failed to transform the Middle

Kingdom into a Christian nation, they were quite successful in introdu
ing a generation of young Chinese intellectuals to American values a
customs, from basketball to democracy, and even more successful in
spreading their enthusiastic but often highly romanticized portraits of
Chinese life to Americans at home. Crusading in favor of rewriting unfair
treaties and eliminating special privileges for foreigners, the missionaries
were natural antagonists of the foreign businesspeople, who lived mainly
in Shanghai's extraterritorial enclaves and dealt with their customers
through the medium of Westernized middlemen called comprador Chinese.

As early as the 1920s, the conservative George Rea, publisher of the
business-oriented *Far Eastern Review*, toured the United States, lecturing
on the insidious influence of the "YMCA missionary lobby" whose impractical liberalism would, he charged, have the effect of discouraging
foreign investment, thus obstructing China's emergence into the modern
world. Rea, who eventually left a post as adviser to the Chinese government to work for the Japanese puppet regime in Manchuria, was typical of
businesspeople and traditionally educated diplomats who felt more com-
fortable with the disciplined, growth-oriented Japanese. Even those recognizing that Japanese militarism was a threat to peace in the Pacific basin
still found the aggressive chauvinism of the Empire of the Rising Sun
preferable to the chaos of Chinese politics.

Compared to the foreign business community, missionary families like
the Services had much closer ties to the mainstream of Chinese life. Still,
they were hardly immersed in it. Growing up in Ch'eng-tu, Jack Service
and his two younger brothers had few Chinese playmates. Life in his
parents' large, rambling house, filled with a museum-quality collection of
Tibetan artifacts, was pleasant but isolated. Service was tutored at home
by his mother, who ordered correspondence courses from the Calvert
School in Baltimore, and he and his brothers often played alone. Missionary parents, fearful of communicable diseases and crime, often limited
their children's contact with Chinese children. And in the Services' case,
other American families, like the Davies family, whose son John Paton
would become Service's State Department colleague, lived too far away
for their children to see each other on a daily basis. Except for his parents'
sabbatical year in Cleveland in 1915, when Jack was enrolled in a public
first grade, he did not attend school with other children until age eleven,
when he entered an American boarding school in distant Shanghai.

In 1924 Robert and Grace Service again returned to the United States on furlough, where Jack finished his senior year of high school in Berkeley, California. He then briefly returned to Shanghai, traveled in Asia and Europe, and earned his bachelor of arts degree at Oberlin College, followed by a year of graduate study in art history. In 1933 he passed the foreign service examination, but because there were no immediate openings, he did not receive an official appointment until October 1935.[3]

Although Service began on the bottom rung of the diplomatic ladder, his exceptional abilities were obvious and advancement came rapidly. Posted to Peking as a language attaché in 1936, Service witnessed the outbreak of war with Japan. In January 1938, he was reassigned to Shanghai. In 1940, with the Chinese military situation deteriorating rapidly, the dependents of American diplomats were evacuated, among them Service's wife Caroline and their two young children. A year later—as the Nationalist government withdrew inland, one step ahead of the Japanese army's advance up the Yangtze—he found himself joining the crush of Chinese and foreign officials thrown together in the wartime capital, the seedy, overcrowded provincial town of Chungking. By now, he was serving as a political officer, a post that required him to make fact-gathering tours in the provinces and in trouble spots as far away as the Burmese border, acting as the eyes and ears of the ambassador, Clarence Gauss.

Along with John Paton Davies, his childhood acquaintance from Ch'eng-tu, Service was part of a small group of young men whose fluency in the Chinese language and understanding of Chinese culture proved invaluable to their superiors. Even among this talented group, Service stood out. Tall and thin—at five feet eleven inches tall, he weighed only about 126 pounds—Jack Service had been a long-distance runner in college and kept in shape by sprinting up and down the hills of Chungking, which were so steep that less fit Americans occasionally resorted to being transported in sedan chairs. His quiet manners set him apart in the small American community of diplomats and journalists whose propensity for hard drinking and practical jokes had been sharpened by the long separation from their families and the difficult wartime conditions. Service became a particular favorite of Ambassador Gauss, who later said, "I don't know of any officer in my whole thirty-nine years of service who impressed me more favorably . . . and I have had an awful lot of young officers with me." Gauss was particularly impressed that a individual who spent so much of his life abroad had managed to remain essentially American in outlook—"right down the middle of the road as an American," as Gauss put it.[4]

Young, vigorous, and scholarly—which they had to be to master the more than 1,500 characters of written Chinese—the "China Hands" were understandably a bit contemptuous at times of their bosses, men such as Stanley Hornbeck, who orchestrated Chinese policy from his desk in the State Department even though he had not visited China for a decade. In turn, Hornbeck, who was himself well known for writing high-handed and peremptory memoranda, sometimes found the tone of the junior political officers' reports immature and arrogant. For some reason, Hornbeck was particularly irritated by Service's reports; after reading one of them he fumed, "Seldom if ever have I seen a document prepared by a responsible officer of the Department or of the Foreign Service, of no matter what age or length of experience, expressive of such complete self-assurance on the part of the author that he knew all the facts and that he could prescribe the remedy."[5]

Hornbeck's irritation deepened as America's relations with the Nationalist regime of Chiang Kai-shek deteriorated. By 1942, the Nationalist government was awash in corruption. The loss to Japan of its industrial base in eastern China had sparked rampant inflation. The peasants, overtaxed and angered by the army's brutal conscription methods, were fast turning against the government. A major famine that would eventually claim more than a million lives was developing in the Hunan province. Chiang's personal behavior was increasingly bizarre to the point of megalomania; the influence of his relatively moderate Soong in-laws was waning as members of a more reactionary and corrupt clique came to dominate his entourage. Moreover, although the Nationalists had fought hard at the beginning of the Japanese advance, they were now on the defensive, determined above all to preserve their army in preparation for an eventual civil war with the Communists.

All this was bad news that policy makers in Washington did not want to hear. American strategy was predicated first of all on keeping China in World War II and, second, on enabling the Nationalist regime to survive into the postwar era so that China would not fall to the Communists by default. There would be time, later, to worry about democratic reforms. But Gauss's career aides on the scene saw that events were unfolding more rapidly than anyone in Washington seemed to realize. Chiang's Kuomintang (KMT) party was in disarray, while the Communists were daily extending their influence, even managing to organize villages in areas officially controlled by the Japanese.

Chiang, meanwhile, had reacted to America's entry into the fight against Japan by demanding $1 billion in Allied military aid. Washington saw the sum as the price of propping up a troubled ally, but Ambassador Gauss, a rather saturnine, withdrawn individual who disliked dealing with the Chinese one-on-one, was already disenchanted with Chiang, and his subordinates in the embassy were passionately against the aid deal. A report on the subject, drafted by the embassy's first secretary, John Carter Vincent, predicted that the sum, far too large for the KMT government to use effectively, would simply vanish into the black hole of corruption. Inflation would be exacerbated, and many weapons would no doubt end up in the hands of the Japanese. Vincent further argued that American military planners' expectations that Chiang would be willing to risk his army in the defense of the Burma Road were purely fantasy. Fortunately, he went on, the European theater was where the war would be won or lost, and American aid to Russia would be more effective. Finally, Vincent recommended that any aid package should be contingent on Chiang's agreement to institute economic and human rights reforms immediately.

Chiang Kai-shek and his svelte, Wellesley-educated wife, the former May-ling Soong, had always been highly conscious of their image in the United States, and as the war dragged on, they became increasingly adept at bypassing the embassy and pressing their demands on Washington via a series of personal emissaries sent to Chungking by Roosevelt. Each new mediator was invariably enveloped in a cocoon of flattery during his brief stay in the wartime capital, while the Chiangs went as far as they dared in communicating their distrust of Gauss and his staff.

Among the first to get a taste of the Chiangs' hospitality was Roosevelt's economic troubleshooter, the Scottish-born Keynesian economist Lauchlin Currie. A former lecturer at Harvard University and professor at the Fletcher School of Law and Diplomacy, Currie first came to China in the summer of 1941 to set up a program billed as the Chinese version of Lend-Lease. A theoretician known for his grasp of international monetary policy, Currie was anything but a man of action. He had never been on an airplane before coming to Chungking, and according to a profile published in *Current Biography* in 1941, his usual method of working was to lie on a sofa with his eyes closed while dictating his thoughts on abstruse economic matters to a secretary. To his admirers, Currie was a brilliant economist who went out of his way to act as a mentor to a circle of younger men in government, mostly intellectuals with liberal to distinctly leftist political views. But his detractors, a number of whom are quoted generously though often anonymously in the FBI's thick background file on him, painted a darker picture, describing him as a "manipulator" and a "conniver" as well as a shallow thinker—in the words of one source, "a busybody who had more damned ideas than a dog had fleas."[6]

Currie was royally feted on his first visit to Chungking, and he impressed the Chiangs as sympathetic to their demands. Madame Chiang was so sure of Currie's support that during one dinner party shortly after his departure she took John Carter Vincent aside and suggested to him that "whenever you want to communicate in complete confidence with Dr. Currie, you can do it through me." Vincent, indignant, reported this overture in a letter to his wife Betty. "It means I am invited to double-cross the Ambassador. . . . To my sensitive nostrils, it stinks."[7]

In spite of this visceral reaction to Madame Chiang's request, Vincent did eventually become friendly with Currie. Betty Vincent happened to be part of the same Washington social circle as Currie and his wife, and during a subsequent visit to Chungking, Currie had an opportunity to get to know both John Carter Vincent and Jack Service, who soon learned that the presidential aide was far less sympathetic to the Chiangs than they had been led to believe.

Unlike Service and John Paton Davies, John Carter Vincent had not been brought up in China. A Clemson University graduate, Vincent had joined the U.S. Consular Service in 1924 hoping to be posted to Copenhagen but had been sent to the Hunan province instead. Nineteen years later, having spent most of his career in China, his chief ambition was to get out of Chungking, and in May 1943 he managed to be transferred back to Washington, where he temporarily left the State Department to work under Currie, taking over the commodities desk at the Foreign Economic Administration (FEA). Service, meanwhile, began a personal correspondence with Currie, keeping him posted on the latest KMT scandals.

A few months after Vincent's departure, in August 1943, Service was detached from the embassy for temporary duty as chief political officer to General Joseph Stilwell, the commander of the Far East theater of operations. Although still technically a civilian, Service wore an army uniform. His duties, much the same as they had been under Gauss, consisted largely of supplying the general with political analysis, gleaned from frequent visits to remote areas as well as personal contacts with individual Chinese.

Service's view of the KMT was as unrelievedly critical as ever, and besides chronicling disasters far and wide, from famine conditions in Hunan to the reluctance of KMT generals to engage the Japanese, he occasionally passed on gossip about Chiang's inner circle. In one May 10, 1944, report entitled "Domestic Troubles in the Chiang Household," he noted that due to her anger over the Generalissimo's carryings on with his latest mistress, Madame Chiang Kai-shek was barely on speaking terms with her husband. Madame Chiang, Service added, was by now so unpopular that stories about her husband's infidelities were eagerly circulated and were regarded by the Chinese "as a joke at her expense." She was also said to be suffering from a disfiguring skin ailment, so serious that she was avoiding photographers. As for Chiang's behavior, Service concluded, "Critics of the Generalissimo regard it all as evidence of the hollowness of his Christian and New Life moralizing, and another indication that he is after all not far from being an old fashioned warlord."[8]

The stream of negative reports Stilwell received from Service probably did not improve his opinion of the Nationalists, but Stilwell did not need Service to remind him of all that he disliked about Chiang Kai-shek and his government. "Vinegar Joe" Stilwell had been a military intelligence attaché in China after World War I, and as early as 1936, when he made an inspection tour of Chinese military installations, he had concluded that Chiang was an incompetent commander with no concept of the requirements of modern warfare. When Chiang refused to place KMT units in Burma under Stilwell's direct command, the stage was set for a full-scale feud. The crusty Stilwell conceived an intense hatred for the Generalissimo, whom he nicknamed "Peanut."

In June 1944 another of Roosevelt's special emissaries arrived in Chungking. Vice President Henry Wallace was accompanied by his personal translator and adviser, Owen Lattimore, and by John Carter Vincent, now back with the State Department and sent along on the trip to act as the department's liaison for the mission. Chiang Kai-shek used the occasion to lobby for the recall of Stilwell, and Wallace, on his part, managed to get Chiang to agree to an American plan to send a team of military observers to the Communist stronghold in Yenan.

Chiang was assured that the U.S. presence in Yenan—code-named the Dixie Mission because the Chinese Reds were the "rebels"—was purely for purposes of intelligence gathering. No doubt he knew better. Frustrated in its dealings with the Generalissimo and impressed by the success of the Communists' guerrilla operations against Japanese forces in the north, the United States was beginning to reconsider its policy of avoiding direct dealings with the Reds.

Jack Service, along with John Davies, had been an early advocate of sending observers to Yenan, and in July he became the first American civilian to visit the Communist stronghold as part of the Dixie Mission. Landing in Yenan on July 22, Service's group found Mao Tse-tung, General Chu Teh, and the other members of the Red Chinese high command living austerely in mud-daubed caves carved out of the cliffs that lined the Yen River. In order to alleviate the shortage of food, everyone, even Mao himself, raised vegetables and tobacco to meet their personal needs. Like the journalists Edgar Snow and Agnes Smedley, who spent time in Yenan in the late 1930s, Service was immediately struck by the high morale, the sense of purposefulness, and the spirit of egalitarianism. Six days after his arrival, he reported that "all of our party have the same feeling—that we have come into a different country and are meeting different people. There is undeniably a change in the spirit and atmosphere. . . . Bodyguards, gendarmes and the claptrap of Chungking officialdom are completely lacking. To the casual eye there are no police in Yenan. And very few soldiers are seen. There are also no beggars, nor signs of desperate poverty." Lest all of this seem too good to be true, he added: "To the skeptical, the general atmosphere in Yenan can be compared to that of a rather small, sectarian college—or a religious summer conference. There is a bit of the smugness, self-righteousness and conscious fellowship."[9]

In later years, it would often be charged that Service, along with other China experts of his generation, had tried to sell the State Department on the notion that the Chinese Reds were not "real" Communists at all but merely "agrarian reformers." Service's defenders have been equally quick to deny that he ever made such a claim. In fact, a February 1945 dispatch coauthored by Service and Raymond Ludden did say something of the sort, proposing that the "so-called Communists" were merely the most prominent manifestation of a broad movement for "agrarian reform, civil rights, the establishment of democratic institutions."[10]

Nevertheless, Service's views on China were hardly so simplistic. In an analysis of the Communist political program dated August 3, Service stated plainly that the Communists considered themselves Marxists, and he suggested that their moderate land policies and willingness to cooperate with the KMT armies in the defeat of Japan might well be only temporary expedients. However, he did raise the possibility that, given China's underdeveloped economy, the party might be content with a gradual transition to a socialist economy: "Their Communism, therefore, does not mean the immediate overthrow of private capital—because there is still almost no capitalism in China. It does not mean the dictatorship of the proletariat—because there is as yet no proletariat. It does not mean the collectivization of farms—because the political education of the peasants has not yet overcome their primitive individualistic desire to till their own land."[11]

Subsequent developments in Chinese history would demonstrate how little respect the Communists had for the "primitive individualistic" desires of the peasantry. Yet, undeniably, since their arrival in northwest China after the Long March, the Communists had carefully cultivated the support of the peasants in the areas they controlled. Although Service's suggestion that the Reds had no immediate plans to collectivize the Chinese economy may have been the height of naïveté, the main thrust of the reports he sent from Yenan was grounded in realpolitik considerations. After the defeat of Japan, he argued, there would be a civil war that the Communists would win. Continued American support for the KMT was a dead end that could only result in defeat, wasted resources, and the sacrifice of any possible influence with the future rulers of China.

Yet by no means did all Americans in China agree that the time had come to write off the Nationalists. On February 24, 1945, Service ran into Joseph Alsop, who was serving as public relations aide to Claire Chennault, the commander of the KMT air force. No admirer of Stilwell, Alsop began the conversation by claiming that the American insistence that the KMT risk its armies by aggressively pursuing the war against Japan was "naive." Since the war would be won or lost in Europe anyway—and on this point, Alsop agreed with John Carter Vincent—it made sense to look to the future and the coming struggle for control of Asia. "Any American commander who put his immediate objective, and his own personal desire to make a name for himself, ahead of fundamental long-range American interests should be flogged from his post," Alsop argued.

Anyone who believed that the Chinese Reds were not mere pawns of the Soviet Union was "idiotic," he added heatedly. And he went on to predict that once Japan was defeated, the United States would need to commit land troops in substantial numbers to help the KMT defeat the Reds. "Of course, magazines like the *New Republic* will work themselves into a frenzy," Alsop concluded, but the American public would support the effort once it understood "the true picture."[12]

By the time this conversation took place, Service's work for Stilwell, his anti-Chiang views, and his wide-ranging intelligence contacts had made him a subject of some interest to the KMT secret police. The Nationalist police were already gathering allegations that would later be circulated against him. Ironically, while they concentrated on his meetings with officials in the Chungking liaison office of the Communists—which were part of his job—the police were apparently unaware of a situation that would have been of far greater interest to them.

During 1944 Service was sharing a house in Chungking with Solomon Adler, an employee of the U.S. Treasury Department whose Communist sympathies would later land him in serious trouble. Upstairs, in a separate flat, lived Chi Ch'ao-ting, an economist educated in the United States who was the confidential secretary of H. H. Kung, the KMT minister of finance and husband of Madame Chiang's sister Ai-ling, widely regarded as the brains behind the Soong family's rise to wealth and power. Unknown to the KMT police, the respected Chi was leading a double life.

A member of radical student groups in his youth, Chi had received a Boxer Indemnity fellowship to study at the University of Chicago, where, in 1926, he became the first Chinese student to join the Communist Party of the United States of America (CPUSA). In 1927 he attended the Comintern's International Congress of Oppressed Peoples in Brussels, then worked as a translator in Moscow and served as a Chinese delegate to the sixth Comintern congress. In 1929 he returned to the United States to pursue graduate studies in economics at Columbia University, where he began to compile a distinguished resume as a scholar and teacher.[13]

In 1940 Solomon Adler and Frank Coe, another Treasury Department employee who was a member of the CPUSA, introduced Chi to K. P. Chen, the Nationalist government's agent in Washington. Chi became Chen's assistant, participating in negotiations to obtain American military aid. A year later, he returned to China, where he rose quickly in government and financial circles, serving as secretary-general of the American-British-Chinese Currency Stabilization Board. Later, as H. H. Kung's secretary, he attended the Bretton Woods United Nations Monetary and Financial Conference.

Chi's father had been a good friend of Kung, who, in sharp contrast to his wife, possessed a third-rate mind and an unsuspecting nature. Once he had Kung's patronage, Chi's Communist past was either forgotten or written off as a youthful indiscretion. Considering that some observers rated Kung's grasp of finance as no better than the average twelve-year-old's, Chi no doubt exercised considerable influence over the KMT's disastrous monetary policy. After World War II, Chi became a representative of the Nationalist government in Washington, and after the Communists' victory in the Chinese civil war, he surprised everyone by choosing to return to

Peking to join the new government. Not until after his death in 1963 was it definitely revealed that he had been a covert agent of the Communists all along, working secretly on their behalf during his years as a KMT functionary.[14]

Service apparently knew nothing about Chi's activities as a spy, though considering their mutual friendship with Sol Adler, he must have had some idea where his sympathies lay. Of course, in steamy, intrigue-ridden Chungking, where public dissent was ruthlessly persecuted by the KMT secret police and competing factions and cliques energetically pursued their private vendettas, divided loyalties were hardly unusual. Service, meanwhile, had other things on his mind. Chiang and Stilwell were constantly at odds, and desperately needed Lend-Lease shipments regularly vanished, leaving nothing behind but a trail of falsified paperwork.

After 1944, Service also had personal problems. He had fallen in love with a Chinese woman, a young actress. Such affairs were hardly unusual among American officials who had been separated from their wives and children since the beginning of the war, but Service had a conscience. While he tried to decide what the involvement meant for his future, KMT secret police were already taking note of the situation, which could later be used to his embarrassment.[15]

As for Stilwell, he managed to hang on to his post despite the demands for his removal relayed to the president by Henry Wallace, but by the fall of 1944, his feud with Chiang had become a universally recognized disaster. Not even Alsop could deny any longer that Chiang Kai-shek was thoroughly corrupt. Nevertheless, as Alsop later noted, Chiang's belief that it was the Americans, through Stilwell, who were driving him to the brink of disaster was somewhat justified. The Nationalists' best troops were siphoned off to Burma, to be sacrificed in the unsuccessful campaign to keep the Burma Road open, while the Communists were using their guerrilla war against Japan to prepare themselves for the coming civil war. The United States, as Alsop put it, "kicked a drowning friend briskly in the face as he sank for the second and third times."[16]

And, indeed, Stilwell did take an almost perverse pleasure in bullying and humiliating Chiang. After one interview, in which he pressed his demands for military control, the general wrote, gloatingly, that the experience was "like kicking an old lady in the stomach." After another, during which Chiang was handed a sternly worded telegram from Roosevelt taking him to task for his past failures, Stilwell returned to his quarters and dashed off a bit of doggerel to celebrate the occasion. It read, in part:

The old harpoon was ready
    With aim and timing 'true,
I sunk it to the handle,
    And stung him through and through.

The little bastard shivered,
    And lost the power of speech.
His face turned green and quivered,
    As he struggled not to screech.[17]

The 1944 confrontation memorialized in these lines was witnessed by still another of Roosevelt's special emissaries, Patrick J. Hurley. An Oklahoma Republican who had served as secretary of war under Herbert Hoover, Hurley arrived in Chungking in early September with instructions to "promote harmonious relations" between General and Generalissimo. Within a week of this incident, he concluded that the task was hopeless.[18] Like Wallace before him—not to mention Lauchlin Currie, who had suggested replacing Stilwell after his second trip to China in late 1942—Hurley concluded that Stilwell had to go. By securing an agreement from Chiang that Stilwell's successor would have direct command over Chinese ground forces, he made Washington's approval of the change inevitable. On October 19, Stilwell was informed that he was being replaced by General Joseph Wedemeyer.

Not surprisingly, given the tone of some of Stilwell's private comments, he was hustled out of China before he had a chance to talk to the press and, once back in Washington, placed under a gag order that forbade him to write or give interviews. Never at a loss for words, even if he could not publish them, Stilwell described himself as "a fugitive from a Chiang gang."[19]

Service was in Yenan, unaware of the worsening situation, when an American colonel arriving from Chungking tipped him off to the rumor that Stilwell was about to be relieved of his command. Distraught, he wrote the general an emotional memo expressing his support. "Our dealings with Chiang Kai-shek apparently continue on the basis of the unrealistic assumption that he is China and that he is necessary to our cause," he wrote. And further:

We need not support Chiang in the belief that he represents pro-American or democratic groups. All the people and all other political groups of importance in China are friendly to the United States and look to it for the salvation of the country, now and after the war. . . . The parallel to Yugoslavia has been drawn before but is becoming more and more apt. It is as impractical to seek Chinese unity, the use of the Communist forces, and the mobilization of the population in the rapidly growing areas by discussion in Chungking with the Kuomintang alone as it was to seek the solution of these problems through Mikhailovitch and King Peter's government in London, ignoring Tito.[20]

The memo, which went on for several pages in this vein, was not seen by Stilwell, who had already left China. But a copy Service had dutifully forwarded to the American embassy did reach the eyes of Patrick Hurley. Within a matter of days, Service was informed that he was being sent back to Washington for reassignment. While passing through Chungking on his way home, he took the opportunity to invite American correspondents into his office to read the cable traffic that had passed between Stilwell and Washington during the weeks prior to the general's dismissal. Stilwell's indictments of Chiang were a bombshell, but there was no way to cable the material past the Chinese censors, and Brooks Atkinson of the *New York Times* concluded that the story was so important that he would deliver it to the States in person. Atkinson boarded a military plane and managed to get as far as Tunis, where he was bumped from his seat by a uniformed soldier. Service, who had a higher travel priority, was on the same flight and volunteered to carry Atkinson's copy back to the States in his diplomatic pouch.[21]

Atkinson's story praised Stilwell's ability as a field commander and described how Chiang had stonewalled, manipulated, and, finally, forced the ouster of Stilwell, who was only trying to do his job by pursuing the war against Japan. Much to Service's—and Atkinson's—dismay, the *Times* withheld the scoop until it received clearance from the White House. But when it finally appeared on October 30, Stilwell was hailed as a hero and Atkinson himself was the envy of his fellow China correspondents.

After a brief stay in Washington, Service spent the final weeks of 1944 at his home in northern California. Happily reunited with his family, he gave up any thought of ending his marriage, and before the furlough was ended, his wife had become pregnant with their third child. In January, he learned that John Davies was being sent to Moscow and that he would be returning to China after all since General Wedemeyer needed a Chinese-speaking aide.

In Chungking, meanwhile, the buoyantly optimistic Patrick Hurley, officially appointed American ambassador to China, set out to hack his way through the intricacies of Chinese politics. A self-educated lawyer who first came to prominence through his spirited performance as the defender of the tribal lands of the Choctaw Nation, Hurley was feisty and intelligent but completely over his head as a diplomat trying to maneuver his way through intrigue-besotted Chungking. He knew so little about China that he was under the impression that the Nationalist First Lady's name was "Madame Shek," and his interminable monologues, interspersed with irrelevant quotations from the Gettysburg Address, the Declaration of Independence, and the Bible, earned him a Chinese nickname that translated as "Big Wind."

Loud, impolitic, and ignorant of China, Hurley was nevertheless honestly committed to carrying out the policy of the U.S. government. It was not entirely his fault that he could never quite figure out what that policy was supposed to be. He had been instructed, on the one hand, to reassure Chiang and restore good relations between the Generalissimo and the American military. On the other, he was supposed to prop up the joint military effort against Japan by pushing for some sort of formal military pact—in effect, if not in name, a coalition between two mortal enemies, the KMT and the Communists. After a short visit to Yenan, where he greeted the startled Mao Tse-tung and Chou En-lai with a triumphant Indian war whoop, Hurley naively believed that he had initiated a promising dialogue.

Then, quite suddenly, the Communists showed no interest in further talks. Hurley, belatedly, learned why. In December General Wedemeyer's chief of staff, General Robert McClure, had come up with a plan for a joint U.S.-Communist campaign against Japanese occupation troops in northern China. McClure's proposal called for U.S. airborne units to be stationed in Communist territory while Red Chinese guerrillas conducted raids, built airstrips, and handled transportation and intelligence functions. Acting on his own, McClure discussed the plan with Chiang's brother-in-law, T. V. Soong, and sent a staff officer, Colonel David Barrett, and Lieutenant Willis Bird of the OSS to Yenan to sound out the Communists. Mao and Chou En-lai were delighted; they even attempted to arrange a secret trip to the United States to cement the deal.

When Hurley heard that McClure had been talking to the Communists behind his back, he was livid. He was not unalterably opposed to giving direct military aid to the Communists—during his visit to Yenan, in a moment of expansiveness, he had himself offered the Communists terms lat Colonel Barrett characterized as "the moon on a silver platter"—but he now objected that it would be foolish to do so without extracting political concessions in advance.[22] As his hopes for a pact evaporated, Hurley became convinced that McClure and Barrett were maneuvering to undercut him and that the foreign service officers attached to Wedemeyer's staff were part of a conspiracy to tilt U.S. policy in favor of the Communists.

Hurley had arrived in China with a built-in prejudice against professional diplomats, but his growing conviction that the career officers in China were mocking him was by no means empty paranoia. The younger China experts had little patience for the junketeers and amateur negotiators who continually paraded through Chungking, and wartime conditions had allowed their sense of camaraderie to flourish to the point where they scarcely bothered to conceal their contempt for the rough-hewn Hurley. Hurley's relations with his own staff soon became so strained that when the embassy offices burned down one night, no one bothered to inform him.

In February 1945, when Hurley returned to Washington for a strategy conference, a group of foreign service officers took advantage of his absence by sending a telegram to the State Department warning that there was no hope whatsoever of an agreement between the Nationalists and the Communists and that the two sides were on the brink of civil war. The telegram went on to recommend that "military necessity requires that we supply and cooperate with the Communists." The message was signed by George Atcheson, the acting chief of mission, but when Hurley saw it, he recognized at once the style of Wedemeyer's aide Service. "I'll get that son of a bitch if it's the last thing I do," he exploded.[23]

A month later, Service was in Yenan, observing the Communists' first party congress, when he received an order summoning him back to Washington at once. It had not been quite three months since his last trip home, and his position as Wedemeyer's aide had just been reconfirmed, so Service wondered if perhaps his recall presaged a major shift in American policy toward China. Something was definitely afoot, and the Communist leaders in Yenan were hopeful that the shift would be in their favor.

On arriving in Chungking, Service was surprised to find that a plane had been reserved to fly him out of the country. "I traveled by myself on an airplane from China as far as Africa," he later recalled. "Every time I stopped at a base I was taken to the V.I.P. villa. Every other time I had traveled the rule was, 'Mr. Service follows the privates.' This time a lieutenant colonel or a major met the plane with a 'Mr. Service, come this way please.' Then his sedan would take me off to the V.I.P. cottage. It was a C-54 that took me back to the States. It was on its way back for an overhaul. They had installed a special chair for me, right up behind the pilot's compartment. I sat there like a goddamn duck, in a special plane."[24]

John Service's professional duties had landed him in the middle of a fierce debate about the future of American policy in China. However heated that debate was in China, however, it was infinitely more treacherous back in the United States. When he returned to Washington, Service became enmeshed in a byzantine world in which some of his acquaintances were trying to influence America's China policy while others were anxious to learn its secrets.

The FBI Meets the Conspirators

Frank Bielaski, the OSS director of investigations at the beginning of 1945, was a former private eye. He was one of those operatives with colorful, not to mention controversial, pasts enlisted in 1941 into the newly formed OSS by Colonel "Wild Bill" Donovan to handle covert operations and intelligence gathering. With its roster of professional soldiers, eccentric professors, and even active Communists—recruited on the theory that no one was more knowledgeable about fascists or more motivated to put them out of action—the OSS quickly earned a reputation for reckless but daring amateurism. Bielaski's job as head of the Domestic Investigations Division (DID), however, had offered little scope for the action he craved. In a 1940 pamphlet, "Fifth Column Lessons for Americans," Donovan had warned that an extensive network of

Nazi saboteurs and spies was being organized in the United States and that virtually all German-Americans were potential members, either as volunteers or because, Donovan cautioned vaguely, they might be "blackmailed into the most supine submission" by the Gestapo.[1] The DID had been created specifically to deal with this threat, but the Nazi fifth column never materialized, at least not on the scale Donovan had envisioned.

Four years after joining the OSS, Bielaski was still working out of a small hotel suite on Eleventh Street in Lower Manhattan, but when Archibald Van Beuren showed up in his office with the January issue of *Amerasia*, demanding that Bielaski find out how the editors had come into possession of Kenneth Wells's report on Thailand, he at last landed an assignment worthy of his capabilities. Unfortunately, he did not have the manpower to undertake a proper investigation.

Only about thirty individuals in the government were on the distribution list for Wells's report, but Bielaski estimated that, counting secretaries and staff assistants, almost 100 people would have had access to it. "Figuring it takes about 10 persons to watch one," Bielaski reasoned that he could not possibly keep an eye on all of them. "I figured I had to have 1000 men. I never had more than twenty in my office at one time. It was out of the question to place 100 people under surveillance."[2]

Bielaski sent one agent to the New York Public Library to peruse back issues of the magazine, while another, Brendan Battle, staked out *Amerasia*'s offices at 225 Fifth Avenue, where he soon learned that the employees worked long, irregular hours. There seemed to be no time, day or night, when the OSS could count on finding the suite empty. When another operative came up with the information that *Amerasia*'s owner and publisher, Philip Jaffe, had contributed $5,000 to the Communist Party during the 1944 election campaign, Bielaski became convinced that he had stumbled onto a nest of Communist agents. Since it was unrealistic to think that he could find out who, inside the government, was leaking "Top Secret" documents by observing dozens of bureaucrats, he decided "to go right to the fountainhead of information." Assuming that the original document was still in the magazine's offices, he reasoned that by recovering it he might be able to find some clue as to how Jaffe had obtained it.[3]

What Bielaski had in mind was a surreptitious entry, or a black bag job—a form of operation with which he had plenty of experience. Bielaski's entire family was in the investigations business in one way or another. His elder brother, A. Bruce Bielaski, had been director from 1912 to 1919 of the agency that eventually became the Federal Bureau of Investigation. His sister, Ruth Shipley, as director of the passport office of the State Department had instituted a policy of denying passports to individuals considered politically suspect. Bielaski himself had specialized in security work for political organizations. In 1936 he had served as director of investigations for the Republican National Committee. Later, he became a "confidential" security adviser to two governors, a vice president, and a secretary of state. In 1940, while working for Republican governor William Vanderbilt of Rhode Island, he had placed wiretaps on the phones of several of the governor's political enemies, a service for which he received $11,000.[4]

Every evening for almost two weeks, Brendan Battle checked out the premises of 225 Fifth Avenue. Finally, on the night of March 11, he found the magazine's offices dark and called Bielaski, who hurried to the scene. With him were two more OSS men and a lock-picking specialist on loan from the ONI. Bielaski knew that what he was about to do was probably illegal, but he believed his plan was more than justified by the need to curtail wartime espionage. Nevertheless, the unusual operation gave his men a case of the jitters. "They were a little dubious about doing this thing, and I felt apprehensive about it myself," Bielaski later recalled.[5]

As it turned out, even late on a Sunday night the office building was not deserted. The arrival of five men carrying burglars' tools and cameras attracted the attention of the assistant maintenance superintendent, but Bielaski was able to persuade the man to cooperate with them "on a patriotic basis."

Seconds later, the lock on the *Amerasia* suite's door was sprung open, and Bielaski's doubts vanished. Inside were hundreds, perhaps even thousands, of pages of documents from virtually every government agency except the FBI. Most disturbing, in addition to a typed original and several copies of Wells's report on Thailand, there were five more secret OSS documents that had never been reported missing. The agents attempted to make a log, noting the routing instructions on the cover pages of the various documents, but they soon realized that the job was too big to finish in one night. At about 2:30 A.M., Bielaski concluded it was time to leave. Scooping up a few dozen of the more important-looking papers—there were so many strewn around the suite that he figured they would never be missed—he ordered his men to replace anything they might have disturbed and then leave the offices.

On their way back to Eleventh Street, the five men stopped off at an all-night diner for breakfast, where the magnitude of their discovery gradually began to sink in. Altogether, Bielaski estimated that his men had seen some 300 to 400 documents, ranging in length from 3 to about 400 pages each. Many of these documents, although marked "CLASSIFIED," were clearly of no great importance. Others, however, obviously contained highly sensitive material. Among the documents Bielaski had brought with him was a "Top Secret" report that had been routed directly from the OSS to the chief of the ONI. Another paper, on the disposition of Japanese naval units, came from a confidential weekly intelligence bulletin published by the armed forces. Another recounted gossip about the marital relations of Chiang Kai-shek and his wife.

After a quick stop at home to change his clothes, Bielaski caught a plane for Washington and took a taxi to Archibald Van Beuren's office. Van Beuren was delighted when Bielaski produced the copies of Wells's Thailand report that he had retrieved. But as Bielaski dug deeper into his briefcase, Van Beuren's face turned pale. As he later recalled, Bielaski "laid the documents on my desk one by one, and I became more and more amazed as I heard him describe the circumstances under which he had found them and saw the documents themselves." Van Beuren asked Major J. J. Donegan, the agency's chief legal counsel, to come to his office to act as a witness, and after examining the pile of documents, Donegan "nearly fainted."[6]

There would later be some confusion over precisely what documents the OSS team had seen during its midnight raid. Nevertheless, Bielaski was certainly correct in thinking that he had discovered a major penetration of government security—one perhaps never rivaled to this day, given the number of agencies involved, the classification of some of the items, and the sheer number of documents involved, to say nothing of the fact that there was a war going on.

Unfortunately for Bielaski, he was to be taken off this biggest case of his career. Van Beuren and OSS chief Donovan personally took charge of the materials Bielaski had seized, and since the majority of the papers seemed to have been routed through the State Department, they set up an appointment with Secretary of State Edward Stettinius and Assistant Secretary Julius Holmes. Because there was no way of knowing who at the State Department was the source of the leak, the four of them met secretly at Stettinius's home at ten o'clock that night.

Donovan wasted no time getting down to business. Placing the thick folder of documents on Stettinius's lap, he quickly outlined the circumstances that had led to their discovery. The top officials at the State Department had been aware for some time that they had a security problem. Now, Stettinius looked at Holmes and exclaimed, "Good God, Julius, if we can get to the bottom of this we will stop a lot of things that have been plaguing us."[7]

The next morning, Holmes consulted with Secretary of the Navy James Forrestal, whose ONI was apparently the other main source of the leaks, and Forrestal agreed that the matter should immediately be placed in the hands of the FBI. Holmes, along with Forrestal's representative, Major Matthias Correa, and two State Department security officers, Fred Lyon and Fletcher Warren, trooped over to the FBI's headquarters that afternoon to ask J. Edgar Hoover to give the investigation top priority.

Hoover designated the case "special" and assigned one of his top assistants, Myron Gurnea, to head the investigation. Like Bielaski, Gurnea quickly concluded that there were too many potential suspects at the State Department and the ONI to attack the investigation from that angle. At 6:00 P.M. the next day, March 14, he called the New York City field office of the FBI to order a twenty-four-hour surveillance of Philip Jaffe as well as wiretaps on the phone at the *Amerasia* offices and on the home phones of Jaffe, the magazine's assistant editor Kate Mitchell, and another individual whose name is blacked out in the FBI files. These taps, which at the time normally required agents to enter the premises to place a bug directly on the targeted telephone, were in place by the next evening.

The New York City agents had very little background information about the man they were now watching night and day. The FBI had maintained a desultory interest in Philip Jaffe for only about a year—the bureau even had a subscription to *Amerasia*—but Communists had not been its major concern for some years now. Indeed, its information on Jaffe was dated and fragmentary, when not actually wrong. Jaffe's FBI file identified him as a successful businessman, a personal friend of Communist leader Earl Browder, which he was, and a "key figure in the Communist Political Association," which he certainly was not.[8]

Philip Jaffe was once described by the historian Bertram D. Wolfe, a longtime acquaintance, as "a sort of super fellow-traveler of the American Communist Party."[9] Jaffe would not have disagreed with this characterization—the title he chose for his never published autobiography was "Odyssey of a Fellow Traveler"; nevertheless, the label fails to do justice to the combination of ambition, energy, and monumental insecurity that made Jaffe such a driven man. A successful entrepreneur, whose fortune was based on the sale of greeting cards printed in a nonunion shop, Jaffe longed for acceptance as a leftist intellectual. His image of himself, projected in both his published and unpublished writings, was of a maverick who refused to submit to party discipline and ridiculed the CPUSA's subservience to Moscow; in fact, he was deeply frustrated by his outsider status. Like so many others drawn into the web of espionage and "secret work," he was motivated by a bitter resentment of associates who, he believed, had failed to give his talents their due recognition.

Jaffe was born near the town of Poltava in the Ukraine in March 1895 into a poor Russian-speaking Jewish family. In 1904 his father Morris, a lumberjack, left his family in Ekaterinoslav and came to the United States. Philip attended Hebrew school and endured a 1905 pogrom before his father was able to send for him and his mother to join him in New York City.[10]

Living on the Lower East Side, the Jaffe family scraped by on Morris Jaffe's income as a plasterer. From an early age, Philip displayed entrepreneurial talent. By the time he was twelve, he was already earning more money than his father. But despite his energy, he seemed to have no clear direction to his life. He attended Brooklyn Polytechnic Institute for one year but soon decided that there was no future in electrical engineering. In 1914 he transferred to City College of New York (CCNY), where he was not only a member of the basketball and tennis teams but also a leading fraternity man. At the same time, he dabbled in the Intercollegiate Socialist Society.

Jaffe's social life proved too distracting, and he was suspended from school for low grades. He then enrolled at Columbia University but quickly dropped out. After a brief stint working for the Board of Control in the garment industry, he was taken on as a messenger by Alexander Newmark, who ran an agency that collected and filed classified ads. Newmark was also associated with the *Jewish Daily Forward* and the *Socialist Call* and was an important figure in the Socialist Party. Association with Newmark may have been decisive in cementing Jaffe's identification with the political left; it certainly had a profound influence on his personal life. Jaffe fell in love with Newmark's daughter Agnes, and the couple married in 1918.

A few months after the wedding, Agnes was diagnosed as having tuberculosis and entered a sanatorium, where she remained for three years. Philip, meanwhile, was extraordinarily busy. He enlisted in the army in October 1918 but, for unknown reasons, was honorably discharged only a month later. He then reenrolled at Columbia. While living in the dorms and attending classes, Jaffe continued to work for Newmark at night, eventually taking over the business and saving it from ruin nearly brought about by his father-in-law's alcoholism.

Some people would have worn down under this regimen, but Jaffe endured. He supported his wife in the sanatorium, visited her weekly, and completed his bachelor's degree (in 1920) at Columbia. He had just finished his master's in 1921 in English literature and was preparing to move to the University of Wisconsin to teach when Agnes suffered a relapse and had to reenter the sanatorium. The last chance for his academic career having vanished, Philip turned to business. In 1923 he also found time to become a U.S. citizen.

Looking for a business opportunity, Jaffe answered an ad in the newspaper, and with an investment of $2,000, he became a partner of stationery distributor Wallace Brown. For a time, Brown dealt with clients and Jaffe wrote the advertising copy. The partners fell out, however, after Jaffe accused Brown of milking the business's profits. He bought Brown out and diversified into selling greeting cards via direct mail or via a network of housewives who peddled the cards door-to-door. By the early 1930s, the Wallace Brown Corporation was on sound financial footing and Jaffe turned his considerable energies to politics.

Jaffe began attending classes in Marxism and contemporary politics sponsored by a tiny Communist sect that had been organized by his former CCNY friend, Jay Lovestone, who had been the leader of the CPUSA until he was expelled by Joseph Stalin in 1929. Despite his friendship with Lovestone and another member of this group, Bert Wolfe, Jaffe was soon bored by the sect's theoretical arguments, which seemed to him to be largely reactions against the Communist Party.

Another radical influence was close at hand. Harriet Levine, Jaffe's cousin, had married a young Chinese student in 1927. His name was Chi Ch'ao-ting—the same Chi who later became H. H. Kung's secretary. Chi was a man of many talents. In 1930 he played a leading role in a Broadway show, "Roar China." As a graduate student in economics at Columbia University in the 1930s, he was influenced by Karl Wittfogel, the German Communist émigré who was later to become a rabid anti-Communist. Chi's dissertation, awarded in 1936, won the Seligman Economics Prize and was published in England as *Key Economic Areas in Chinese History*. In 1929, when Jaffe first met him, Chi had just returned from a trip to Moscow, where he had worked as a translator for the Chinese delegation to the sixth Comintern congress. On resettling in New York City, he was assigned to the Chinese Bureau of the CPUSA.

For two years, Jaffe and Chi engaged in friendly arguments, Jaffe defending democratic socialism against Chi's communism. The brilliant, charismatic Chi was the better debater, and as the friendship grew, Chi gradually drew his cousin by marriage into Communist affairs, first persuading him in 1931 to join the International Labor Defense (ILD), a Communist group that focused on uncovering "capitalist injustices." Jaffe threw himself into his new work, writing for the ILD's *Labor Defender* and even producing a pamphlet entitled "The Police State in the U.S.A." Jaffe was delighted; he later explained, "I was now a published writer—something I had wanted to be since my student days."[11]

Even in the small world of Communist activists, however, there was an intellectual pecking order, and Jaffe's ranking was rather low. Although present at the inaugural meeting of the League of Professional Groups for Foster and Ford, an organization formed to support the Communist ticket in the 1932 presidential election, Jaffe was not asked to join. He speculated that he was not invited because he was already assumed to be a Communist, but several Communists were members. More likely, he was not prominent enough, and his name would not have added much luster to the list of those who did join, a group that included such luminaries as Sidney Hook, Matthew Josephson, Edmund Wilson, and John Dos Passos.

Jaffe needed his own niche, and Chi thoughtfully provided him with one, recruiting him in May 1933 to join a small group of nondescript party members in forming the American Friends of the Chinese People. Aside from Jaffe, the other founding members were working people with relatively little schooling, much less knowledge of China. Jaffe was immediately appointed executive secretary and editor of the group's paper, *China Today*.

China Today began publishing in the fall of 1933. From the beginning, it was avidly pro-Communist. Jaffe did most of the writing, but much of the material his articles were based on came from rice paper dispatches sent from the Communist underground in Shanghai to the American bureau of the CPUSA.

The editors of *China Today* adopted pseudonyms, Chi, who used the name Hansu Chan, to protect himself from the U.S. Immigration Service and Jaffe, who used the name of John W. Phillips, "for no particular reason that I remember." Two other editorial board members, Frederick Vander-

Demonstration in support of Chinese Communists mounted by the American Friends of the Chinese People in New York City in the early 1930s. (Philip Jaffe Papers, Special Collections Department, Robert W. Woodruff Library, Emory University)

bilt Field and T. A. Bisson, also disguised their involvement, listing themselves on the masthead as Frederick Spencer and Lawrence Hearn. Although the use of aliases was never very consistent—in 1950 one former employee of *China Today* told the FBI that at speeches Jaffe might be introduced to someone as Jaffe and a few moments later presented to the audience as J. W. Phillips—the ruse did succeed in confusing the authorities, particularly in the case of Chi, whose involvement with the magazine went unnoticed.[12]

Despite his work on *China Today*, Jaffe never gained the trust of the party. According to Jaffe, he was simply too independent, unwilling to parrot every slogan relayed from Moscow. In his 1975 book, *The Rise and Fall of American Communism*, Jaffe scornfully recalled an incident in which one American Communist opened a meeting in New York City with a greeting to the "Workers and Peasants of Brooklyn." "Is it any wonder then that Communist propaganda in America fell in the main on deaf ears?" he asked. Jaffe did occasionally show a spark of independence, as in 1934 when he was denounced by some party purists for calling Chiang Kai-shek a fascist—a departure from Moscow's position on Chiang at the time. But instead of defending his right to his opinions, Jaffe quickly published a clarification, arguing that the language he had used fell within existing Comintern guidelines. His reasoning was accepted for the moment, but the party reacted by assigning a reliable member, Esther Carroll, to oversee the magazine's editorial content. In 1935 Carroll became the organizational secretary of the American Friends of the Chinese People, one of about a dozen party members whose faction dominated the organization, which never had more than thirty-five members in all.[13]

Although his efforts earned him little respect, Jaffe continued to labor for party causes, including a campaign to persuade longshoremen not to load cargo for Japan and another urging blacks to oppose Marcus Garvey. *China Today* prospered, reaching a circulation of about 7,000. Although it was firmly within the Communist orbit, a handful of non-Communist fellow travelers, including Malcolm Cowley and J. B. Matthews, attended its affairs. At speeches and debates arranged by the magazine, other notables such as Rabbi Stephen Wise, Harry Ward, and Roger Baldwin appeared.

Soon after *China Today* was launched, Chi Ch'ao-ting began to disassociate himself from the magazine as he prepared the way for his apparent transformation into a supporter of the KMT and Chiang Kai-shek. His place as Jaffe's ideological mentor was soon taken over by Frederick Vanderbilt Field, a social register Communist who was a direct descendant of Commodore Cornelius Vanderbilt, once the richest man in America.

Fred Field grew up in a Fifth Avenue mansion, one block away from St. Patrick's Cathedral, and attended Harvard University, where he showed a flair for public speaking and was elected vice president of the newly formed National Student Federation. A postgraduate trip to England in 1927–28 stimulated his interest in socialism. His public announcement, soon after his return, that he was joining the Socialist Party inspired a spate of sarcastic newspaper editorials about "millionaire socialists" and prompted his uncle to disinherit him, cutting him off from the Vanderbilt fortune. But Field was still a wealthy man, having come into money from his mother's side of the family, and he used that money to support left-wing causes. By the mid-1930s, he had drifted into the orbit of the Communist Party. Field never joined a local party branch or paid dues, but he considered himself a "member at large," subject to party discipline.[14]

As part of Field's contribution to party work, he hosted a Marxist-Leninist discussion group at his elegant Manhattan townhouse. Philip and Agnes Jaffe attended these evening gatherings, which began with a formal dinner, prepared and served by an impeccably trained staff of liveried servants. Later, the guests adjourned to a sitting room, where they gathered around the fireplace to debate the fine points of Marxist doctrine.[15]

Field's chief interest, however, was the Institute of Pacific Relations (IPR), which he had joined at the invitation of its chief executive Edward Carter. Founded in 1926 to promote cooperation among the peoples and governments of the Pacific region, the IPR churned out a steady stream of publications, from pamphlets and books to its own scholarly journal, *Pacific Affairs*. It also sponsored a biannual conference that brought together scholars, businesspeople, and government figures with a common interest in Asian studies. Despite persistent rumors that Field was the IPR's chief financial backer, the institute actually received most of its support from the Rockefeller Foundation and the Carnegie Corporation. As Edward Carter later confirmed, Field—who was not quite as wealthy as many of his associates believed him to be—was not so much a financial angel as a "minor cherub," contributing perhaps $50,000 over the years.[16]

After World War II, the IPR would come under fire as a Communist front, a charge that would damage the careers of a number of scholars, journalists, and other area specialists who had been associated with it. In fact, the institute was infiltrated by Communists during the mid- and late 1930s. Fred Field, though he has always denied any such intentions, played a major role in this development, using his influence to prod the IPR into hiring both open and underground Communists for administrative positions and special projects. Among those Field promoted for institute grants was Chi Ch'ao-ting. In 1938, for example, he wrote Edward Carter: "My interest in Chi's career is so great that I feel somewhat responsible for seeing to it that he gets some sort of employment."[17]

In 1936 Field, Chi, and T. A. Bisson all used the occasion of the IPR's conference at Yosemite, California, to lobby for unofficial support of a new magazine, *Amerasia*, edited by Philip Jaffe, which would become the successor of *China Today*. Edward Carter was determined not to lend the new journal the imprimatur of IPR sponsorship, but this did not prevent Field, Chi, and Bisson from using their influence to attract a number of distinguished individuals to *Amerasia*'s editorial board, including Kenneth Colegrove, Cyrus Peake, and Robert Reischauer, all professors of Far Eastern affairs at major universities; William Stone, vice president of the Foreign Policy Association; and Owen Lattimore, editor of the IPR's official organ, *Pacific Affairs*.

Field later rationalized that the founding of *Amerasia* was part of his effort to protect the institute from becoming politicized by creating an alternative outlet for the views of some of the organization's more left-wing associates. But, in truth, it was *Amerasia*, not the IPR, that benefited from being linked unofficially to the IPR. And the replacement of the openly Communist *China Today* with the more modulated and moderate *Amerasia* coincided with the switch in Communist policy from a revolutionary line to a call for a popular front against fascism ushered in at the seventh Comintern congress held in the fall of 1935.

Cyrus Peake, who, along with other board members, would later be criticized for lending his name to a Communist front, insisted that he had no suspicion of Jaffe's Communist background at the time.[18] It is difficult to imagine that any Far East expert could have failed to notice the ideological bent of a propaganda sheet like *China Today*. On the other hand, most of those who attended the Yosemite conference where *Amerasia* was launched were only dimly aware, if at all, of Field's and Bisson's Communist connections. The new magazine thus seemed to represent a spectrum of interests, and the support of IPR members and employees gave it an aura of respectability. It also influenced IPR delegates to lend their names and reputations, as sponsors and contributors, to an enterprise that would later become notorious as a front for espionage.

Owen Lattimore, who would become a highly controversial figure in 1951, when he was accused by Senator Joseph McCarthy of being the top Soviet agent in the United States and, more plausibly, a Communist sympathizer, was perhaps a special case. While he may not have been a Communist himself, Lattimore was at the very least an opportunist. In 1938, in a letter to Carter about appointments to a special IPR research project, Lattimore complimented him for being "pretty cagey in turning over so much of the China section of the inquiry" to Chi and other pro-Communists. "They will bring out the absolutely essential radical aspects, but can be depended on to do it with the right touch," he noted, adding that it would "pay to keep behind the official Chinese Communist position—far enough not to be covered by the same label—but enough ahead of the active Chinese liberals to be noticeable." He also urged that the IPR should back the Soviet Union's "international policy in general but without using their slogans and above all without giving them or anybody else an impression of subservience." Having joined the *Amerasia* board at its founding, Lattimore continued to be a board member until 1940, despite warnings from Edward Carter that Lattimore's connection to the magazine might prove embarrassing to the institute.[19]

In April 1937, exhausted by the pressures of his business and political life and starting up *Amerasia*, Jaffe left with his wife on a four-month trip to the Far East. In Peking they joined T. A. Bisson, who was studying on a Rockefeller Foundation Fellowship. The Jaffes discovered a small colony of Westerners with whom they shared an interest in Chinese Communism, including Edgar Snow, who had just published his epic *Red Star over China*, his wife Peggy Snow (Nym Wales), Owen Lattimore, and Karl Wittfogel. Lattimore, Bisson, and Wittfogel were planning to visit Yenan, the terminus of the fabled Long March of the Chinese Communists, through the good offices of Snow. When Wittfogel decided not to make the hazardous journey, the Jaffes joined the party.

They left by train on May 17 and spent a month in Sian, where they hired Effie Hill, born in Inner Mongolia to Swedish missionaries, to drive them to Yenan. To avoid government interference, the travelers employed a ruse to leave the city. Jaffe pretended to be a rich American beset with kidney problems who was traveling to the mountains for a cure. After four days on the road, the party completed the 250-mile journey on June 21, 1937, one of the earliest groups of "blockade runners."[20]

Greeted at the gate to Yenan by Agnes Smedley, the well-known American sympathizer with the Chinese Communists, and Peggy Snow, who had arrived by a different route, the travelers were quickly overwhelmed by their admiration for their hosts. They had audiences with Mao Tse-tung, Chu Teh, and Chou En-lai, the three most important figures in the party. Their interpreter, Huang Hua, later served as foreign minister of China. Jaffe wrote soon after the trip that "we were increasingly impressed by the complete sincerity and lack of ostentation that is so typical of him [Mao] and the other leaders we saw."[21]

The visit lasted only four days, but it was an experience that moved Jaffe deeply and cemented his respect for the Chinese Communists. The trip took place just before the formation of a united front between the Reds and Chiang Kai-shek in the fight against the Japanese. The era of the popular front, albeit attenuated, had arrived in the field of Chinese affairs, and *Amerasia*, which had published its inaugural issue in March 1937, was in tune with the spirit of the times. Unlike *China Today*, which had rigidly defended the position of the Comintern, *Amerasia* was more flexible.

The Communist Party, eager to bask in the reflected glory of the New Deal, was becoming largely uncritical of Roosevelt and his policies, and Jaffe was able to attract distinguished contributors like Stanley Hornbeck, chief of the Far Eastern affairs office of the State Department, who wrote

Philip Jaffe, Peggy Snow, Owen Lattimore, Mao Tse-tung, T. A. Bisson, and Agnes Jaffe (*left to right*) in Yenan in 1937. (Philip Jaffe Papers, Special Collections Department, Robert W. Woodruff Library, Emory University)

the lead article for the inaugural issue. Scholarly analyses by State Department officials and leading academics in the field of Far Eastern affairs ran side by side with a regular column by "Asiaticus"—a German Communist whose real name was either Hans Müller or Heinz Shipper and whose somewhat mysterious activities in China were cut short by his murder in 1941.

On the practical side, Jaffe enjoyed the support of IPR officials. In those days, *Amerasia*'s headquarters were in the same midtown building as the institute's executive headquarters, and Owen Lattimore frequently recommended contributors, on occasion passing on articles that had originally been submitted to *Pacific Affairs*. Still other referrals were made by Stanley Hornbeck. *Amerasia*'s subscriptions soon topped 1,700, with about a third of the copies going to government offices. Another 300 or 400 copies of each issue were sold individually. This circulation, while small in absolute

Philip Jaffe addressing the Chinese Communist Eighth Route Army in Yenan in 1937.
(Philip Jaffe Papers, Special Collections Department, Robert W. Woodruff Library, Emory University)

numbers, was very respectable for such a specialized journal, and the subscription list included just about everyone who counted in the Far Eastern field.

After years of unrewarding labor, Jaffe had finally arrived. *Amerasia*'s success was not only a personal triumph but also a vindication of his judgment in attaching his star to the wagon of the Communist Party, which at last seemed to be moving into the mainstream of American political life. But Jaffe was not able to enjoy his triumph for long. As early as 1938, the IPR's Edward Carter had become so concerned about *Amerasia*'s pro-Communist slant that he asked Owen Lattimore to consider resigning from the editorial board. Several other board members also withdrew their names in 1940, unhappy over the journal's slavish parroting of the party line during the period of the Nazi-Soviet pact. That same year, Jaffe also had a falling out with Stanley Hornbeck, who was irate over an October 1940 article by Fred Field that fulminated against "pro-imperialist" America's policy in the Far East.[22]

Despite these predictable reactions to *Amerasia's* left-wing stance, the magazine still commanded respect, and Jaffe himself, increasingly recognized as an expert on Asian affairs, was in demand as a speaker, participating in scores of symposia and panel discussions. It was no small feat for a man who had no graduate degree in the field, no official position in academia or the government, and, in fact, only a tourist's exposure to the Far East to win acceptance as a spokesman on foreign policy issues. Suddenly, in middle age, Jaffe saw his long-deferred dream of becoming a respected scholar coming true.

But *Amerasia* was in trouble. The magazine had always operated at a deficit of about $6,000 a year, a substantial sum at the time, and during the first few years of operation, Jaffe and Fred Field had each paid half of the debt out of their own pockets. Field, however, was losing interest in the Far East. In 1940 he had become involved with the American Peace Mobilization, a Communist Party front whose chief activity was picketing the White House in opposition to the American entry into the fight against Germany. Immediately after the Soviet Union came into the war, the organization changed its name to the American People's Mobilization, broke out a new set of placards, and resumed its picketing, this time calling for all-out aid to the Allies. Field was so busy with his new activities that he had little time for *Amerasia*. By 1941, he had given up his financial support of the magazine, and Jaffe was left to carry the entire financial burden alone.

Jaffe's bank account was ample, but he resented Field's desertion as just another indication of being taken for granted by the party. One reason for his isolation, which he could never bring himself to admit, was his prickly personality and his need to run every project he became involved in as a one-man show. But now, in the era of the American-Soviet alliance, he found that his financial resources and reputation counted for little. He could hardly compete for attention with the scores of writers, artists, and entertainers who were willing to allow their names to be connected to party causes. At the height of his success, he was increasingly shunted aside by longtime party associates. It did not help that Jaffe was a difficult man for whom to work. He alienated employees and picked fights with contributors.

Editorially, *Amerasia* was also increasingly isolated. The outbreak of World War II cut off the flow of material from China—both articles by journalists such as Anna Louise Strong and Asiaticus and dispatches from Chinese sources, which had been the most interesting, if controversial, features of the magazine. Moreover, many of the American scholars who had once written for *Amerasia* had enlisted in government service and could no longer contribute to the magazine. Some of these longtime contacts were also being cultivated by mainstream journalists like Drew Pearson and so had no time to meet with Jaffe even for off-the-record briefings. By 1944, the entire editorial board had deserted the magazine, and Jaffe and Kate Mitchell, his assistant editor, were writing virtually the entire contents of the magazine.

Kate Mitchell was somehow able to work closely with Jaffe, a man others found impossibly domineering. Born in 1909, Mitchell had traveled in India after graduating from Bryn Mawr and had been deeply affected by the poverty she saw there. For three years, from 1934 to 1936, she had been the private secretary of IPR chief Edward Carter, accompanying him on several trips to the Far East. Later, under IPR auspices, she did research for her book, *The Industrialization of the Western Pacific*, before joining *Amerasia*. Mitchell lived on income from a trust fund and took no salary for her work—indeed, she contributed a substantial sum to help keep the journal going. A more fluent writer than Jaffe, whose writing talents were limited, she probably did the lion's share of the day-to-day work, but her efforts could never make up for the defection of *Amerasia*'s specialist contributors.

The pressure to come up with material to fill *Amerasia*'s pages was intense. Jaffe began making frequent trips to Washington, cultivating his narrowing circle of informants. Time permitting, the material Jaffe collected from his friends and informants would be reworked by Kate Mitchell before publication in the magazine. But on occasion, in the rush to get to press, official memoranda were inserted into the magazine with little more than a light editing job—the most likely explanation for the nearly word-for-word reprinting of Wells's report on Thailand that had focused government attention on *Amerasia*.

To round up new contacts in the capital, Jaffe came to depend on a young acquaintance named Andrew Roth, a twenty-five-year-old lieutenant attached to the ONI. Born in the Bronx, Roth entered CCNY in 1936, the same time Julius Rosenberg studied there. Although he later insisted that the dogmatism of CCNY's Communist faction "repelled" him, he was active in a radical student organization that he himself described as an "obvious front." While still enrolled at CCNY, Roth began taking evening courses in Far Eastern studies at the New School, where one of the professors was Chi Ch'ao-ting, by all accounts a dynamic and effective teacher. Through Chi, Roth met Jaffe. In 1941, while he was working toward a graduate degree in Asian studies at Columbia University, Roth received an IPR grant for his studies of the Japanese economy and also was employed briefly as a researcher for *Amerasia*. Later that same year, Roth was recruited by the U.S. Navy, which sent him to Harvard University for an intensive course in the Japanese language.[23]

As a navy officer in training, Roth promptly got into hot water by writing a letter to the *New York Times* defending the Free German Committee, an organization created in the Soviet Union to indoctrinate captured Nazi troops in the virtues of Marxism-Leninism. After investigating Roth, the ONI concluded that he was a Communist, a characterization he denied, but found no reason why he should be refused a commission. The investigative report did recommend that Roth not be assigned to the ONI; however, because Japanese-speaking officers were in short supply, Roth was posted to the ONI anyway. By 1944, he had risen to the sensitive position of ONI liaison to the State Department.

Like the overwhelming majority of Americans who had studied Asian affairs before and during the war, Roth was as intensely pro-Chinese as he was anti-Japanese. He had grown up reading the novels of Pearl Buck and later followed the articles of Agnes Smedley in the *Nation* and the *New Republic*. He was appalled by the views of Assistant Secretary of State Joseph Grew, the former ambassador to Tokyo, who was already advocating building up Japan as a U.S. ally after the war. Grew's so-called soft policy on Japan called for leaving the major institutions of traditional Japanese society largely intact, including the imperial government and the corporate cartels known as *zaibatsu*.

In his off-duty hours, Roth began writing a book eventually entitled *Dilemma in Japan*, which presented an alternative blueprint for a thorough reorganization and democratization of Japanese society after the war. Although it might be argued that the long-term aim of the program Roth advocated was to create a niche for the Communists in Japanese political life, many of the specific reforms he called for were quite sensible. But Roth's ambition to publish a book critical of U.S. policy while still serving in the navy caused repercussions. The manuscript was to be completed by mid-1945, but Roth was warned by the navy that it could not go to the publishers until it had cleared the Navy Department's censors.

Roth had another reason to be worried about the reception of his book: he had never been to Japan. Realizing that American experts on Japan, of whom he was sharply critical, would be going over his text with a fine-toothed comb, he had begun submitting chapters to various friends and acquaintances. Among those he consulted was Philip Jaffe.

In return for Jaffe's advice, Roth helped his old mentor in a number of ways—by keeping him up-to-date on Washington gossip, helping him obtain declassified papers distributed by the Office of War Information (OWI), and, on occasion, introducing him to acquaintances inside the government. In the spring of 1944, he performed the biggest favor yet by arranging for Jaffe to meet an ONI analyst named Emmanuel Sigurd Larsen, known to his friends as Jimmy.

While Philip Jaffe was consumed by his need to win acceptance as an expert on Asian affairs, Jimmy Larsen was living in happy obscurity as a civilian employee of the Navy Department, compiling biographical information about equally obscure Chinese warlords and politicians. Larsen was, in Andrew Roth's words, "a bouncy little man" who wore bow ties and who liked to brag that he was American on the outside, Chinese on the inside. In his spare time, he enjoyed nothing more than attending professional wrestling matches, and his conversation was studded with tales of his encounters with Mongolian gurus and White Russian café singers, all of which sounded like the most transparent of Walter Mitty fantasies. Larsen told his share of whoppers, but the very stories that sounded most improbable often turned out to be true.[24]

Born in San Rafael, California, Larsen had grown up in China, where his Danish-American father held a professorship at the University of Ch'eng-tu in Szechwan. By a strange coincidence, the Larsens lived for a time with Robert and Grace Service, taking refuge with them after their own home was destroyed in a flood. Larsen was only nine years old at the time and Jack Service was still an infant, too young to recall the incident when he and Larsen were reintroduced during one of Service's visits to Washington in 1944.

In 1911 the Larsen family returned to Denmark for five years, where Jimmy finished high school and then enrolled at the University of Copenhagen, graduating in 1916. After a brief trip to the United States, where he worked in the Oriental section at Marshall Field's Chicago department store, Larsen returned to China in 1916 and joined the Chinese Postal Administration.

Larsen was with the Postal Administration for twelve years, serving in a variety of cities, including Canton, Peking, and Shanghai. In 1927 he resigned after meeting a Mongolian lama who persuaded him to start a wool and skin export company in Taonan, a town in Inner Mongolia. "I was the first American pioneer in that part of Asia," he later boasted. When the political climate changed, Larsen, according to his own account, was horsewhipped in the streets by a pro-Japanese group opposed to American business interests.[25]

Next, Larsen went to work for the British-American Tobacco Corporation (BAT), managing a warehouse at the Feng-t'ai railway junction near Peking. According to his own version of his life story, he left that job when the warehouse closed. However, BAT executives interviewed by the FBI in the mid-1940s recalled that Larsen was fired for submitting expense accounts that were "anything but plausible." The executives blamed Larsen's troubles during this period on the influence of his second wife, a White Russian cabaret entertainer. She was having an affair with a German pilot who flew for the KMT air force, and soon after Larsen lost his job, she filed for a divorce.[26]

Larsen's activities during the year after leaving BAT are shrouded in mystery. He told one former colleague that he was representing an insurance company, but he later claimed that he spent five months working for Chinese military intelligence—tracking down arms smugglers, according to one version, or spying on revolutionaries, according to another. He quit, he said, when his activities were discovered by the Japanese and he received a warning that he would be run over by a truck if he did not leave the country. At any rate, Larsen returned to the United States early in 1935, where he promptly enrolled for a semester at the University of Chicago, then won a Rockefeller Fellowship to attend the summer session at Columbia University's School of Far Eastern Affairs.[27]

During these years, Larsen had been pursuing a most unusual hobby. As early as 1927, he had begun collecting data on Chinese political figures and recording the information in a card file. As a result of this hobby, after completing his courses at Columbia, Larsen soon received a grant from the American Council of Learned Societies to work at the Library of Congress writing biographical sketches of prominent figures in the Ching dynasty. A few months later, in October 1935, he was hired by the ONI.

Andrew Roth first encountered Larsen one day in the spring of 1944 when he happened to be chatting with an acquaintance who worked on the China desk at the ONI. After Roth mentioned that he had once worked for *Amerasia*, his acquaintance asked, "What is this Jaffe fellow like?" Roth answered that, among other things, Jaffe was a man obsessed with collecting obscure scraps of information, including biographical data on minor Chinese warlords. At this, Jimmy Larsen, who was working at the next desk, suddenly perked up. "I'd like to meet this guy," he told Roth.[28]

Roth agreed to make the introduction, but he remained wary of Larsen, who had about him "the smell of the comprador"—the widely detested class of Westernized Chinese and Chinese-speaking foreigners who acted as intermediaries for foreign corporations. To know Jimmy Larsen was to be exposed to his considerable repertoire of self-glorifying anecdotes—the one about the Buddhist lama who got him started in the export business was by no means the most peculiar—and some of the stories Larsen told gave Roth pause. "Larsen thought I was pro-Chinese, which I was," Roth recalled, "so he boasted to me of how he acted on behalf of the Chinese to counter racism in the Navy Department. And he told me of one specific instance when the assistant naval attaché in Chungking sent a report which was very nasty about the Chiang Kai-shek government in Chungking. He [Larsen] just took a copy of this report and showed it to the wife of the Chinese ambassador." Larsen, he concluded, "was very well dug in with the embassy . . . a Kuomintang man through and through."[29]

Despite his doubts, Roth introduced Larsen to Jaffe, and the two of them got along famously thanks to their shared obsession with biographical data on Chinese personalities.

At the end of 1944, Larsen left the ONI to take a job with the State Department. According to Roth, Larsen wanted to take his personality file with him, but the officer in command, a Colonel Bayles, objected: "Those aren't your files, they're Navy files."

"Oh no, I brought them in with me," Larsen protested.

"Yes," said the colonel, "but every day you've been adding to them from secret documents."

"Well, that's true," Larsen replied. "But there's a committee sitting on the Hill going into the causes of our being caught with our pants down at Pearl Harbor. If you don't let me take these to the State Department I think I ought to testify to the committee about how many documents were burned in this office about warnings that came in that were never passed on."[30]

Larsen himself may not have realized how potent a threat this was. The ONI's failure to predict the attack on Pearl Harbor, while highly embarrassing, had been understandable given the large volume of confusing and at times deliberately misleading traffic that crossed the analysts' desks. But when a congressional committee began looking into the matter, the navy could not even begin to defend itself without admitting that, as had been long rumored, the Japanese naval code had been cracked by the United

States as early as 1941. Although the Japanese codes had long ago been changed, this information was still considered highly sensitive, in part because there were still isolated instances when Japanese outposts in the Pacific, lacking current code books, resorted to using the old system. The navy, therefore, was stonewalling the congressional inquiry. Larsen may or may not have known about the codes, but he realized that the last thing the department needed was for a disgruntled functionary to start talking to congressmen about a cover-up.

The exercise in blackmail worked, and Jimmy Larsen was allowed to keep his card file. He installed it in his new office at the State Department, but not before he had sold a copy of the file to Philip Jaffe. "I was very wary of Larsen," Roth recalled years later, "and very surprised when he and Jaffe hit it off. They seemed to have a kind of need of each other."[31]

Through Jimmy Larsen, therefore, Jaffe began to obtain official documents that turned his thoughts toward more dangerous pursuits than merely publishing leaked government secrets. And Andrew Roth was to play a key role in the drama.

On March 14, 1945, the day the FBI took up Jaffe's case, he happened to be in Washington, where he was scheduled to meet with Roth and several other government employees. Bureau agents knew he was in town, but much to their frustration, they were unable to locate him. They would not be caught unprepared again. By the evening of March 20, 1945, as Jaffe packed his suitcase for another trip to Washington, a team of agents spent a long night at the State Department inventorying the contents of the desks of supervisors in the Office of Far Eastern Affairs in the hope of tracing any papers that later turned up in Jaffe's possession.[32]

That same evening, a group of agents made another search of the 225 Fifth Avenue offices. The agents discovered that the *Amerasia* staff's housekeeping had not improved since the OSS visit of the previous week —the "floors were dirty and strewn with small pieces of paper, pamphlets and partially written articles," the operations report noted, and the suite "was generally in an untidy condition." The agents' distaste for the dust and clutter was hardly a matter of aesthetics; it is much easier to search a neat room without leaving telltale traces of one's presence. As carefully as possible, the FBI men carried batches of documents to another room down the hall, where they photographed as many as possible, then they returned them, doing their best to cover up any signs that dusty piles of papers had been disturbed. Among the classified documents the agents photographed were several State Department reports bearing either the full name of Emmanuel Larsen or a scrawled notation, "Kindly have this returned to me, ESL."[33]

Earlier that same day, the FBI had listened in on a phone call Jaffe made to someone named Jimmy. "The bananas were good," Jaffe remarked at one point. Drawing the obvious conclusion that "bananas" was a code word for documents, the bureau investigators ordered a tap on the phone Jaffe had called. When it turned out to be listed in the name of Emmanuel Larsen, they felt sure that the investigation had struck pay dirt.[34]

Jaffe had also been calling Andrew Roth, and by this time, the bureau had not only tapped his phone but had also ordered a twenty-four-hour tail on his movements. On the night before Jaffe's return to the capital, two agents in an unmarked car sat outside Roth's apartment at 1614 North Coomb Street in Arlington. One of them must have peeked in the Roths' windows because their surveillance report noted that Roth and his wife Renée were up until midnight, working on a pile of documents. In the morning, when Roth left for work, the agents also noted, he was carrying a manila envelope about an inch thick.[35]

Philip Jaffe arrived in Washington shortly before noon, and when he checked into the Statler Hotel, Jimmy Larsen was on hand to meet him. They were joined for lunch in the Colony Room by the Roths, after which Andrew Roth and Jaffe dropped Larsen at his office, then drove "by a circuitous route" to the vicinity of the Library of Congress, where they spent a half hour sitting in their parked car examining the papers that Roth had brought with him. Later that afternoon, Jaffe met briefly with several employees from the State Department and the ONI. But the surprise of the day was the arrival at the Statler of Mark Gayn, a successful journalist whose work appeared regularly in national magazines, and his wife Sally. The couple departed after a brief visit, then Gayn returned alone to have dinner with Jaffe and Roth at a Chinese restaurant.[36]

Mark Gayn's contract with the *Chicago Sun* paid him $7,500 a year plus expenses. Another contract with *Collier's* guaranteed him a minimum of $9,000 a year for six articles—a top rate by 1945 standards—and he also published frequently in *Time*. An enthusiastic supporter of the New Deal, Gayn was thoroughly Americanized, but like Larsen, he came from an exotic background. Originally Mark Julius Ginsbourg, he was born in 1909 in Barim, a small town along the Manchurian-Mongolian border. His father was a political exile who had fled to Siberia one step ahead of the tsar's secret police; his mother was the daughter of a wealthy lumber dealer. When Mark was a young boy, the Ginsbourgs moved to Harbin, Manchuria, where he grew up in luxurious surroundings, educated by tutors and at a private academy.[37]

By the mid-1920s, however, the family's fortunes were declining. His mother studied dentistry to support the family, and they soon moved to Vladivostok, where Mark attended Soviet schools. In 1926 his father opened a sawmill in Shanghai. The rest of the family had to struggle to obtain permission to emigrate from the Soviet Union, but they finally arrived in Shanghai, just in time to witness the 1927 revolution and the massacre of Communists in the streets by cadres of the KMT, a scene of carnage that eighteen-year-old Mark never forgot.

Two years later, Mark traveled to the United States to attend Pomona College, where he changed his last name to Gayn and began to prosper. Graduating magna cum laude in 1933, he worked toward a master's degree at Columbia University's School of Journalism, then landed a choice assignment as the *Washington Post*'s Shanghai correspondent. He also reported Chinese news for Domei, the Japanese press agency, where he came to loathe the men who were gaining ascendancy in Japan.

Gayn was probably not a member of the Communist Party—Jaffe taunted him for lacking the courage to take his beliefs to their logical conclusion by joining the CPUSA—but he had a tendency to be carried away by his enthusiasms, chief among which was the Soviet Union. "In China, as in Russia," he wrote during this period, "the trend was unmistakably towards true democracy," but "in Russia alone," he had learned "the simple virtue of stubborn, uncompromising—and therefore uncomfortable—honesty."[38]

The war in the Far East had created a demand for Gayn's articles, but it had also focused attention on some of his more fatuous pro-Soviet sentiments, and by the spring of 1945, he was already encountering difficulty in getting his passport renewed for a planned sojourn in the Soviet Union. Nevertheless, he had an established reputation, and *Collier's* openly boasted in advertisements that his pieces on the Far East were based on "confidential sources."

For the moment, it was not clear to the FBI where Gayn fit in—*Collier's*, after all, was a pillar of establishment journalism. But by March 27, the FBI case supervisor, Myron Gurnea, was convinced that both Roth and Larsen were delivering secret documents to Jaffe.

During an early morning search of Larsen's State Department office, Gurnea noted, the FBI had found three documents "that can positively be identified as having been in Phil Jaffe's office last week when the examination was made there."[39]

In Roth's case, however, the evidence was less substantial. But over the next several weeks, Gurnea's team overheard a number of suggestive conversations. On the day after Jaffe's return to New York City, for example, he received a call from an obviously very nervous Roth, who warned Jaffe "to use a considerable amount of discretion on that—"

"Okay, you said that yesterday," Jaffe cut in.

"I mean not only the specific incidents, but the whole general thing," Roth insisted. "I was very slightly disturbed. I hope I don't sound needlessly cautious, but you know there's a reason for it."[40]

Immediately after this conversation, Jaffe left his apartment and headed for the headquarters of the Communist Political Association (the name of the Communist Party after 1944). He stopped next at the IPR offices. Returning home, he phoned Roth and told him that the IPR had received some Federal Communications Commission (FCC) intercepts of Japanese radio broadcasts, which he would be forwarding to him.

The bureau could not be entirely certain what all this meant, but soon Roth, a man with scarcely an unfilled hour in his appointment calendar, was attracting most of its attention. Roth seemed to know everyone in Washington and to have an inside line on which officials were willing to dispense sensitive information. Some of his discussions with Jaffe nearly burned the ears of the agents listening in.

One such discussion concerned Harry Dexter White, assistant to Secretary of the Treasury Henry Morgenthau and the chief American representative at the Bretton Woods United Nations Monetary and Financial Conference. The FBI overheard Roth confiding to Jaffe that a fellow he knew got "a lot of stuff on Far Eastern things that the other guys don't get" because once a week he saw White, who "will tell you a lot of stuff."

Jaffe was incredulous. "He goes to Harry White's office? In the Treasury building?"[41]

In a subsequent conversation, Roth and Jaffe returned to the subject of White, speculating on whether he could survive in office if Morgenthau resigned in the wake of Roosevelt's death. Roth was optimistic. White, he said, was a highly respected figure. Jaffe, however, was skeptical, since he had always thought of White as a "left winger."[42]

As a result of this discussion, Harry Dexter White was eventually interviewed by an FBI agent after the *Amerasia* arrests. He disclaimed any knowledge of leaks, and the investigation of his involvement soon reached a dead end. The bureau continued to have its suspicions, however, which were fueled six months later when a woman named Elizabeth Bentley walked into an FBI office in Connecticut and began to tell a story of serving as a courier for a Soviet spy ring whose members included Harry Dexter White.[43]

During the first two weeks of April, Roth seemed to have a lunch or coffee date almost every day, and he was constantly bustling in and out of various government offices, always with a thick manila envelope under his arm. On one occasion that particularly intrigued the FBI, Renée Roth joined her husband and Larsen for lunch and left the restaurant carrying not one but two bulging envelopes. She then boarded a train to New York City, carefully keeping her luggage in plain view on the seat beside her. The next morning, the surveillance team watching 225 Fifth Avenue saw her deliver a twelve-by-sixteen-inch manila envelope to *Amerasia's* offices.[44]

Another of Roth's lunch meetings, on April 9, was with Chi Ch'ao-ting, who was visiting the United States in connection with the UN conference in San Francisco. The FBI duly logged in the meeting, but it is not clear from the files that have been released whether any further action was taken. The FBI knew that Chi was close to Jaffe, that he had used the alias "Doonping" in the CPUSA, and that he was one of the leading Chinese Communists in the United States.[45]

Roth's lunch date for April 5, Julian Richard Friedman, also attracted scrutiny. Friedman was an assistant in the China affairs division of the State Department, where he worked under John Carter Vincent. Once again, at this meeting Roth handed over a file of papers.[46]

Gurnea's team was well aware that Roth was in the final stages of preparing the manuscript of his book on Japan. The book was a constant topic of conversation between him and Jaffe, who alternated encouragement with condescending reminders that his own projected book would sell more copies and that the stories Roth helped to place in *Amerasia*— the only pro-Communist journal that did not just serve up "the same old bologna," as Jaffe put it—would no doubt be seen by readers who would never bother to look at the finished work. Obviously, Roth was consulting Jaffe about his manuscript, but this did quite not explain Renée Roth's behavior during her trip to New York City or several recorded conversations that clearly indicated the transfer of documents. For example, on April 18, the same day he and Jaffe discussed Harry Dexter White, Roth was overheard commenting while giving Jaffe a document: "I had some job getting that thing copied off there—[I] want to get it back you know." Roth was also present that morning when Larsen delivered some papers that he said had come to his desk via the OWI. Jaffe thanked Larsen for his efforts but reminded him that he wanted more along the lines of what Larsen had given him on a previous visit—"the most sensational thing you've ever given me." He then went on to describe a report containing classified information about Chiang Kai-shek's private life, possibly the same "tea cup gossip" report filed by Jack Service from Chungking.[47]

The FBI took a special interest in Roth's lunch date with Julian Friedman because it had already established that Kenneth Wells's report on Thailand had been distributed to only thirteen people at the State Department, one of whom was Friedman's boss, John Carter Vincent. It is impossible to know just how far the bureau pursued its investigation of Friedman and Vincent because much information has been excised from the case files made public under the Freedom of Information Act. But the surveillance of Roth was definitely casting a net of suspicion over everyone he knew or even talked about.[48]

Checking out such leads consumed endless man-hours. And although a subject, once named, might never have the full trust of his superiors again, it was looking more and more unlikely that the investigation would produce any further hard evidence of wrongdoing beyond that against Larsen, Jaffe, and Roth. For these reasons, J. Edgar Hoover, despite his reputation as a dogged enemy of Communism, was reluctant to advise other agencies to retain employees who were suspects and have them watched.[49] On April 18, Hoover sent his assistant D. M. "Mickey" Ladd to discuss the Roth situation with Julius Holmes, Fred Lyon, and Matthias Correa. Ladd suggested that the wiretap conversations were a dead end; in fact, the bureau might well find that it could not even build a case against Roth himself. Despite this advice, Correa and Holmes both insisted that they wanted to maintain the surveillance at least "for the next two months or so." Even if nothing could be proven, the information gained "would be of tremendous value in any diplomatic dealings between the U.S. and Russia."[50]

Soon after this meeting, Fred Lyon confided to William Donovan that John Carter Vincent had become a suspect in the case. Donovan was about to leave for Europe at the time, and in the London airport, he happened to run into Patrick J. Hurley, who was on his way to the Teheran conference. Donovan and Hurley had time for a brief chat before Hurley boarded his connecting flight, and the OSS chief used the occasion to warn Hurley that Vincent was being investigated in connection with Soviet espionage. For Hurley, a tip from "Wild Bill" Donovan himself was as good as gospel, especially since it confirmed his own negative feelings about Vincent. Hurley leaped to the conclusion that his enemies in the diplomatic corps were not only plotting against him personally but also undermining America's China policy on direct orders from Moscow.[51]

The decision to extend the surveillance in the *Amerasia* case soon brought John Stewart Service into the web of suspicion. What initially looked like a case in which an over-eager left-wing magazine editor was scooping up government documents began to look much more ominous.

Leaks and Espionage
at the State Department

When the plane bringing Jack Service back from China landed in Washington on April 12, he discovered that he had come back to a city in mourning. The same day, Franklin Delano Roosevelt had suffered a fatal stroke at his home in Warm Springs, Georgia. Business in the capital ground to a halt as the funeral train carrying the president's remains wound its way north.

But in the offices and corridors of the federal bureaucracy, the hiatus in business did not last very long. The war in Europe was in its final stages, with new developments breaking almost daily. Moreover, the installation of a new chief executive, the first in more than twelve years, set off a scramble for jobs. At the Department of State, the transition signaled a new stage in the power struggle that had been going on since August 1943, when Stanley

Hornbeck was ousted from his post as head of Far Eastern affairs. Kicked sideways into a position as assistant secretary without portfolio, Hornbeck blamed John Carter Vincent for engineering the rebellion of his immediate subordinates on charges that Hornbeck was guilty of withholding information unfavorable to the Nationalist Chinese from his reports to the secretary of state. Under the new division chief, Joseph Ballantine, Vincent had returned to the State Department to take over the Division of Chinese Affairs, but after Roosevelt's death, the pendulum of power seemed likely to swing back once again in the direction of the conservatives, including Hornbeck.[1]

Service, meanwhile, quickly figured out that his recall had nothing to do with the high-level policy conference about the Yenan mission. On the contrary, he was unofficially in disgrace. As one of his last acts before leaving Washington for London, Patrick Hurley had arranged for Service to be removed as Wedemeyer's aide. And this was only the beginning. Indignant over the political slant of the reports he had been getting from Chungking, Hurley was determined to initiate a purge of the embassy staff.

Service was given an empty desk in the Division of Chinese Affairs, where he did his best to look busy while waiting for a new assignment. With few official duties, and his pregnant wife and two children still 3,000 miles away in California, Service had plenty of time to ponder the Hurley problem. At a critical moment in U.S.-Chinese relations, the ministry in Chungking was in the hands of a man whom many of the career officers looked on as not merely inept but also not quite in his right mind. Service later confided to *New Yorker* writer E. J. Kahn that he actually gave some thought at this time to quitting his job so that he could go public with his views on the Chinese situation. But this drastic step was soon ruled out. Instead, with encouragement from Vincent and Lauchlin Currie, Service decided to embark on a campaign of selectively leaking information. Few in Washington were aware of how chaotic the situation in Chungking had become, much less what a strong position the Reds were in. "I thought, dammit, that somebody ought to do something about getting more information out," Service told Kahn.[2]

Getting information out proved to be surprisingly easy. On April 18, just six days after his return, Service received a call from a friendly journalist who wanted to take him to lunch. Mark Gayn explained that he was preparing a series of articles for the *Saturday Evening Post* and that he wanted Service's input. Gayn had known Service's brother Robert when they were both students at Pomona College, and before the lunch was over, he had invited Service to stay at his apartment whenever he found time to visit New York City.

The next day Service accepted another invitation, this one from Andrew Roth to a party at his home. Service had met Roth when he was in Washington the previous autumn, and given that Service had recently been in Yenan, it was not surprising that Roth and his friends would be eager to talk to him. Roth, however, did make a somewhat unexpected suggestion. Philip Jaffe, who was also invited to the party, was staying at the Statler Hotel. Since Jaffe knew the way to the Roths' apartment, why didn't Service stop by the hotel so the two of them could travel out to Arlington together?[3]

At 6:00 P.M. Service knocked on the door of Jaffe's room and introduced himself. Unwittingly, he was also introducing himself to the FBI eavesdroppers installed in a nearby room.

For two men who had just met for the first time, Service and Jaffe very quickly became on the warmest of terms. Their conversation suggested a common interest in the leaking of information from the State Department to damage Chiang Kai-shek and his American supporters and an awareness that *Amerasia* tilted toward the Communists.

Service launched the conversation by bragging to Jaffe that he was responsible for the OWI's dissemination of articles from *Amerasia*. "I told the boys out in OWI in San Francisco that your thing [*Amerasia*] was the best, and I think that's what inspired them to take it out to China and broadcast it," he confided, "and they've been in hot water ever since."[4]

Within minutes of this cordial opening, the two of them fell to discussing a recent article by Mark Gayn. Service confessed that on reading the article he had been more than a little surprised to see that it was based in large part on a high-level briefing document he had prepared at the time of Vice President Wallace's mission to Chungking. He didn't especially mind that someone had been leaking his reports, but such indiscretions could be risky. As he told Jaffe, "I was rather surprised I didn't get any more violent reaction. Because anybody who had my original report could go through and pick out definitely" the similarities.

The article wasn't the least of it, Jaffe responded. A verbatim copy of Service's report had actually been passed around at an IPR conference.

"Was my name on it?" Service asked nervously.

"No, no," Jaffe assured him. But Jaffe said he was familiar with the report and had recognized the text at once. "I said, hell, that's Service's report."

Jaffe remarked that he had thought the report a superior piece of work, prompting Service to confide that, unknown to his superiors in Chungking, the Wallace briefing paper had been written with the help of his roommate, Sol Adler.

Apparently, despite Service's fears, he was not suspected of being the source of the leak. However, as Jaffe noted, Mark Gayn was still suffering from fallout over the article. His application to have his passport renewed was being held up, and as a result, he might have to cancel his plans to visit the Soviet Union. "I've been red-baited for a long time," Jaffe groused, but "there has never been an instance in which I've been red-baited as he has in this instance."[5]

The mention of Sol Adler, meanwhile, led Jaffe to confess that he was Chi Ch'ao-ting's cousin by marriage, a relationship he and Chi were trying to keep agents of the Nationalist government from discovering. Presumably, this information would have been of some interest to the U.S. State Department as well; however, Service promised not to betray Jaffe's secret. Also, he offered to let Jaffe borrow a translation he had made of some material that "was circulated among very high officials" in China but was so sensitive it could not be quoted in the pages of *Amerasia*.

But even Jaffe, who seemed quick to volunteer confidences, was not being entirely candid with Service. For one thing, he claimed that he didn't know Andrew Roth well, having only met him the previous fall. He also implied, falsely, that many pieces published in *Amerasia* were ghosted by highly placed government officials. One recent article, he claimed, had come directly "through the White House"—a suggestion, no doubt, that the source was Service's friend Lauchlin Currie. Still, the tenor of this conversation suggested that Jaffe and Service, although they had just met each other, were hardly ideological or political strangers.[6]

Service and Jaffe went on to the Roths' party, which lasted until after midnight, and when Jaffe returned to the Statler Hotel by taxi, his FBI tail noted that he was carrying a manila envelope that had not been in his possession earlier in the evening. Bright and early the next morning, Roth called to discuss how the meeting with Service had gone. Jaffe told Roth that he thought Service was "wonderful." Roth agreed, adding that it was "so refreshing to see a guy with a lot of guts."

Jaffe had arranged to meet Service again that day for lunch. He invited

Roth to join them, urging him, if possible, to show up an hour or so before Service arrived. "I have to do things before he gets here," Jaffe explained, "you know what I mean?" Roth didn't, so Jaffe elaborated, "Well, he let me read some stuff," suggesting that he needed help in copying the material and providing a clue to the FBI of what had been in the manila envelope. Roth obliged.[7]

When Service showed up for lunch, he brought other papers for Jaffe to examine. One report, he explained, consisted of notes that he had made only that morning from a paper one of his colleagues was working on—"When I was leaving, I said, hey, [name blacked out] give me a little of what you're finding out on this." Among the other documents was an article by Chi on the agrarian reform problem. About this article, Service cautioned that "the only thing is I'll have to ask you that you don't let anybody know you've seen this . . . [since Chi] would get his neck pretty badly wrung." Jaffe agreed and asked how to return the article since it would be "unwise to mail it." Service told him to return it on his next trip to Washington, or perhaps he, Service, could pick it up when he came to New York City.[8]

Although they had known each other less than twenty-four hours, Jaffe had big plans for his new contact. During lunch, he tried to coax Service into requesting a year's leave from the State Department to do a book on China with the help of Kate Mitchell, "a genius at writing." Service declined, explaining that family responsibilities would prevent him from taking a sabbatical. In that case, offered Jaffe, "anytime you fellows want to organize, want anything in the magazine issue, let me know. . . . You can say anything you like in it." He was explicit about his old connections with *China Today*, the openly Communist magazine. And, he joked, "not even Stalin could make me change it now."[9]

Service left the Statler at two o'clock in the afternoon accompanied by Roth. Three hours later, Roth returned alone, and he and Jaffe fell to speculating about Service's politics. Both men were pleased but somewhat disconcerted by Service's cooperative attitude. They had set out to win his confidence, and now he was practically pushing documents under their noses. Jaffe suggested, without much conviction, that Service might be a leftist. Roth thought not, but he was particularly impressed that both Chi and Sol Adler trusted Service and were willing to work with him. Fantasizing aloud, Jaffe brought up the possibility that Service might fit into his plans for establishing a successor to *Amerasia*, a magazine that would cover other areas of the world in addition to Asia. In the new scheme—unlikely ever to come to pass since *Amerasia* itself was in dire straits—Kate Mitchell would edit articles on India, Roth would be in charge of Japan, and Service would handle China. Of course, it was too early to know whether Service would fit in, Jaffe cautioned, since "unless he's a Communist ideologically, he would [bring] the whole thing down."[10]

Service, for his part, obviously had no reason to suspect that his private conversations with Jaffe were being recorded by the FBI. Still, a prudent man might have wondered whether it was smart to rush into a confidential relationship with a publisher who made little secret of his Communist connections.

E. J. Kahn, in *The China Hands*, makes the point that giving press briefings had been part of Service's regular duties in China, where he had frequently drawn on his personal copies of political reports to fill in background for correspondents. On leaving Chungking, Service had received permission from "the G-2 guy there" to take his personal files with him to the States, and, as Kahn puts it, "in Washington, Service saw no reason not to continue trying to be helpful to journalists." This, of course, is disingenuous. Service was doing far more than being "helpful."[11]

As a veteran of several previous run-ins with Hurley, Service certainly understood that he was playing a dangerous game. As his wiretapped conversations with Jaffe make clear, Service was well aware of the political bias of *Amerasia* and of Jaffe's Communist connections, as well as of the rapidly chilling political climate. Although the cold war had not yet begun, the ideological conflict at the State Department, fueled by Hurley's charges, had already created an atmosphere of suspicion.

Nor was Service unaware that Jaffe, Roth, and Gayn were orchestrating a campaign to get close to him. "I was being cultivated," he told the authors in a 1985 interview. Having learned from Jaffe during their first evening together that some of his memos, including the Wallace report, were already in general circulation, he must have realized that if the leaks ever became an issue, his contacts with Jaffe and Gayn would surely come under scrutiny. Overbalancing these reasons for caution were Service's sense of the urgency of his situation, his belief that he had the backing of friends who were Washington insiders, and, quite simply, his hubris. As even Kahn, a great admirer of the China Hands, acknowledged, modesty was never a characteristic of this group. Knowledge of the Chinese language and culture gave them access to a world that their elders in the foreign service could know only secondhand. A sense that Washington, like Chungking, had its own mores that a newcomer would be wise to learn was lacking.

Andrew Roth, in a later interview, recalled how, at the time, he found Service's bravado breathtaking. "He took risks, he took *enormous* risks." The difference between Service and himself, he elaborated, was that "I was a very cautious young man—a working-class kid. I had been at City College during the time of the Rapp-Coudert investigation, when the Foner brothers were sacked. I knew what could happen." Service, on the other hand, was "a most brilliant and attractive" individual, "a liberal crusader," and in Roth's view, the process of cultivation was mutual. Service, Roth observed, "wanted to use *Amerasia* as a megaphone. . . . I was *astonished* at the risks that he took."[12]

Service's sense of invulnerability was so great that he did not suspect any connection when, on the day after his first meeting with Jaffe, he was suddenly informed that a projected appointment as State Department liaison with army and navy intelligence had been canceled. That he failed to foresee trouble ahead was due in part to his confidence that his friends would be in a position to protect him. As he put it in 1985, "I was Lauchlin Currie's designated leaker."[13]

For Jaffe, Service's arrival on the scene could not have come at a more opportune moment. Shortly after his first meeting with Service, Jaffe confided to Roth that he was particularly eager to get close to Service because he needed a source inside the State Department and no longer trusted Jimmy Larsen. Certain comments Larsen had made had led Jaffe to suspect that he was negotiating to sell a copy of his personality file to another source, possibly the OSS. Roth, apparently unfazed by this possibility, agreed that Larsen was "trying to build himself up into a big shot" but warned that confronting him would probably be futile. Jaffe took the risk anyway, and Larsen flatly denied having dealings with anyone else.

Larsen was also indignant that Jaffe had enlisted Roth to help smooth things over. Over a period of several days, Jaffe and Roth had discussed the problem of the volatile moods of "Linda's father"—in other words, Larsen, who had a daughter by that name. Eventually, Roth had dinner with Thelma Larsen, who assured him that while her husband had been angry about being suspected of double-dealing, he had calmed down and all was now "hunky dory."[14]

At the same time, Roth and Jaffe were also considering Roth's plan to offer $500 to a navy officer for a set of index cards containing information about Japanese leaders. This was the first indication the FBI had that Roth was helping Jaffe by paying for information from a third party.

Before anything came of this plan, Jaffe returned to New York City, where, on April 22, he held a meeting at his home attended by Tung Pi-wu, a representative of the Communists who had been included in the Chinese delegation to the San Francisco conference. Also present were Y. Y. Hsu of the IPR, Chew Sick Hong, whom the FBI suspected of being Jaffe's source inside the OWI, and the man Jaffe referred to in his phone chats with Roth as "my big uncle, my leading uncle"—Earl Browder, the head of the Communist Political Association. Although the agents surveilling Jaffe had no way of knowing what went on during this meeting, the FBI noted that Tung's presence in his apartment provided Jaffe with an ideal opportunity to pass on classified information about American policy to the Chinese Communists.[15]

Just two days after this meeting, Jack Service arrived in New York City, where he had been invited to be the guest of honor at the IPR's monthly meeting and reception. Over the years, Asia experts of various political persuasions, including Stanley Hornbeck, had been guests at IPR functions, and it was natural that Service, who had recently been in Yenan, would be asked to appear. Jaffe and his friends, however, made it their mission to close ranks around their recent acquaintance, determined to cement their ties to this wonderful new source.

Service made the task easier by accepting Mark and Sally Gayn's invitation to spend the weekend at their apartment. The Gayns arranged a small party in Service's honor, which was attended by the Jaffes and Kate Mitchell, who asked Service for help on a book she was writing on the "New Life" movement, the KMT's attempt to revive Confucianism. While there was nothing secret about Service's attendance at the IPR function, Gayn was nevertheless oddly nervous during the visit. At one point during the weekend, while Service was out with Jaffe, someone called the Gayns' wanting to speak with Service. Gayn gave the caller Jaffe's number but told him that the phone was in Kate Mitchell's name. "I didn't give him your name," he later reported to Jaffe, "because I didn't know who the hell he was and maybe it is incriminating for a State Department guy to be seen with you."[16]

Jaffe, meanwhile, was still amazed at Service's eagerness to pass on copies of his reports. No sooner had Service returned to Washington than Jaffe was on the phone to Gayn, trying to puzzle out Service's motives. Jaffe told Gayn that he had concluded that Service was "not a leftist" as he had at first assumed. Still, he remarked, "what is valuable about him is that his stuff is just as complete . . . as we can get." Gayn agreed. Jaffe added that Service had already given them "a terrific lot" of information, including five reports "from up North" (Yenan) and "some chit chat" about the Chinese delegation to the San Francisco conference. Whatever Service had in mind, Jaffe and Gayn decided, he was obviously sincere, so there was no point wasting time trying to figure out why they were being so favored. Instead, the two of them made plans to get together to share the task of copying the documents Service had brought them.[17]

Jaffe's meeting with Tung Pi-wu, meanwhile, had put increased pressure on the FBI investigators. Not only was Jaffe collecting documents from sources inside the government, but he also had an opportunity to pass them on to the Chinese Communist representatives who happened to be in the country for the San Francisco conference. The war in Asia was at a critical phase. Plans for the invasion of the Japanese mainland and for American landings in China were in the final stages. The question of whether American troops would cooperate with the Communists or hold territory in northern China until it could be turned over to the Nationalist government was being actively debated at the State Department. Moreover, the development of the atomic bomb was still, as far as the FBI knew, at least, a closely guarded secret.

Nevertheless, nothing the agents had overheard so far demonstrated that Jaffe had any specific intent to commit espionage. Classified government documents were making their way out of Washington offices into the hands of unauthorized people, but there was no hard evidence that they had been passed along to any foreign power. All of that changed on April 30.

The break the FBI had been waiting for came the last day of April when Jaffe got a telephone call from Joseph Bernstein, a former *Amerasia* employee who was working temporarily for the American Jewish Committee. Two days later, Jaffe and Bernstein met for lunch. Their meeting was out of the range of FBI listening devices, but whatever was said sent Jaffe into a flurry of activity. First, he called John Stewart, a writer for the Communist *New Masses*, and made an appointment to see him the next day at 9:30 A.M. After meeting Stewart, then having lunch again with Bernstein, Jaffe drove to Communist leader Earl Browder's home in a quiet Yonkers neighborhood for a conference that lasted almost an hour and a half.[18]

The significance of these consultations became clear the following week when Jaffe returned to Washington. On May 7, he was met at the

Statler Hotel by Roth and Larsen. In Jaffe's room, which had been bugged before he checked in, Larsen began unpacking his latest haul of documents, including a draft of a proposed agreement between Patrick Hurley and the Chinese Communists. No doubt to the dismay of the FBI, Larsen seemed to be under the impression that Jaffe wanted at least some of the information for a book he was writing. Larsen worried that if Jaffe used the Hurley document, it would be traced to him. "The book won't come out until September," Jaffe assured him. And besides, "if anyone asks me, I'll tell them [blacked out] told me."[19]

After lunch, Roth and Jaffe returned to Jaffe's room without Larsen, and the conversation took a dramatic turn. "I shouldn't tell you this, I shouldn't tell it to anybody," Jaffe confided. "But I think I've got to tell you. You'll be the only person to know this. Not even Renée should know. A very, very funny thing happened. It's why I'm so anxious to get more contacts with the State Department. Joe Bernstein called me up."[20]

A long discussion about Bernstein and an unnamed friend Jaffe had met once at the Café Society nightclub who was "a big loudmouth," a lieutenant commander in the navy, and a former pilot followed. Jaffe stated that he and Bernstein had had a long lunch on May 2, during which Bernstein had revealed that for many years he had been an agent of the Soviet Union. He then asked for Jaffe's help. "I would like to ask you whether you are willing to give me the dope you get on Chungking out of the Far Eastern Division of the State Department," he had said, in Jaffe's retelling. Jaffe had thought for a while and answered, "I'd be willing to do anything, so long as we are both [al]right. What's your connection?" Bernstein admitted that his current contact with the Soviets was a young fellow, the former flyer, whom he did not know very well.

This made Jaffe cautious. "How do I know you're not both OSS agents?" he had asked.

Bernstein had commended Jaffe for his caution but insisted that Jaffe could check out his credentials.

Joseph Bernstein's revelation did not come as a complete surprise to Jaffe. When Bernstein had worked for *Amerasia* in 1943–44, Jaffe had been curious about his employee's mysterious comings and goings. Bernstein was frequently absent from work without an excuse, and more than once, his wife had called Jaffe at home in the middle of the night to ask him about her husband's whereabouts. The possibility that Bernstein was a Soviet spy hadn't bothered Jaffe at all then, and it didn't bother him now, but he did want to be absolutely sure that he was not being set up by the OSS.

Earl Browder, head of the Communist Political Association, addressing a rally in Madison Square Garden in September 1944. (UPI/The Bettmann Archive)

Immediately after leaving Bernstein, Jaffe told Roth, he had called his friend John Stewart, a staff writer for the *New Masses*, and set up an appointment for 9:30 the next morning. Stewart vouched for Bernstein's reliability, but this was not enough reassurance for Jaffe, who next called Earl Browder's unlisted home number. Browder did not expect to be in his office all that week because his son was ill, but when Jaffe insisted that something urgent had come up, Browder agreed to see him at his home in Yonkers.

Jaffe arrived in Yonkers, closely followed by an FBI surveillance car, but Browder lived on a quiet street where the FBI agents felt so conspicuous that they gave up any attempt to eavesdrop. Although Jaffe considered Browder a close friend, judging by his own account to Roth, this unexpected visit was not exactly welcome. When Jaffe showed up at his home, very agitated and insistent on describing Bernstein's overture, Browder did not care to hear the details. Jaffe concluded that it was because Browder wanted to remain officially ignorant about Soviet espionage in the United States.

Reluctantly, he had advised Jaffe: "As you told him yourself, you should insist on meeting this other person. Then say to him that he's got to prove his right to work with you." If Bernstein's contact was a genuine KGB man, Browder said, "he'll find a way to prove it. If he can't find a way, don't deal with him. It may be that he [Bernstein] is . . . on his own, and he just wants to put a feather in his own cap, if he can get a little something. And if it's just personal, nothing doing. Don't touch it."

So far, Jaffe had not had the chance to follow through on Browder's advice. Nevertheless, he could hardly contain his excitement at the prospect of dealing directly with a Soviet agent. Describing his great opportunity to Roth, he admitted that this, indeed, was the chance he had been hoping for all along, the real reason "why I started out to find Jimmy [Larsen] in order to get me the Russian stuff."

Roth was shocked. "Boy, you're getting yourself in deep," he warned. "I don't like it."

"I could still refuse it," Jaffe said.

"I don't like it," Roth repeated.

"I'm thinking of the future."

"I don't like it."

"I think I'm going to meet him."

"I wouldn't," Roth cut in.

But Jaffe had already made up his mind. After all, he told Roth, he did have information that the Soviets might never have seen. "For example, Jimmy, a long time ago, gave me a big dossier, thick, a hundred pages, the ONI record of all the White Russians in this country, their history, their addresses, everything." In the hands of the Soviets, such material could serve an important function. "It helps to make the kind of life we want. Why isn't that important?"

Roth countered that easier and safer ways could be used to accomplish the same ends. In a closed society, spies served a useful function, he mused. "But this country is so wide open and obvious, and [it is] so easy for dozens of newspapermen to get the information, and they proceed to state it very openly in dozens of forms, that I don't see why I shouldn't."

Jaffe expressed no surprise at Roth's observation that publishing classified information in the pages of *Amerasia* served the same purpose as espionage—that is, making information available to the Soviets—but without the risks. Nevertheless, the idea of becoming more personally involved intrigued him. "Suppose," he mused, "suppose about once a month I should have lunch with him [Bernstein] and tell him some stuff." He would not be functioning as a spy, he rationalized, but as an "intelligence agent."

"What's the difference?" Roth wondered.

The difference, Jaffe explained, was that the Soviet Union and the United States were not at war.

Roth was still wary. "How the hell can you know who the other guy is?" he asked. "What evidence would you accept?"

Most people could never be sure, Jaffe agreed, but his excellent contacts gave him an inside track. For example, an unnamed acquaintance on the staff of *Soviet Russia Today* had agreed to check out Bernstein's credentials. As he rambled on, Jaffe's imagination began to take flight. Bernstein had told him that the FEA—incidentally, the agency formerly administered by Lauchlin Currie—was "the easiest place to get into." But he thought it should also be possible to get "lots of things" from the Treasury Department. "It may last for five years," Jaffe enthused, "and then one little thing can make a big difference. . . . Jimmy's file is crappy. [But] over a period of three, four, or five years, you collect stuff. I don't care what kind, or how it is, it looks like nothing, then bang! Put it all together, and there is a pattern."

Unable to make a dent in Jaffe's visions of glory, Roth finally gave in. Contradicting the arguments he had made a few minutes earlier, he reasoned aloud that since Tass no doubt forwarded summaries of the contents of *Amerasia* to Soviet leaders anyway, Jaffe might as well go ahead and deal directly with Bernstein. Comparing Soviet agents to newspapermen covering beats, he agreed that "if the situation warrants it, whenever anything comes up that you feel is significant, you can tell Joe."[21]

Asked about this conversation in 1985, Roth claimed to have completely forgotten it.[22]

Oddly enough, this extraordinary lead—Philip Jaffe admitting on a wiretap that he was planning to cooperate with someone who said he was a Soviet spy—never surfaced during the case or in the numerous hearings that followed. One reason was that the FBI had problems figuring out just who Bernstein was. The stenographer who transcribed the surveillance recording—which was not on a tape but on a disc made with primitive portable recording equipment and was none too audible—had rendered the name of the contact man as "Bursley," and Jaffe's further comments, identifying him as a former employee and a friend of a "loudmouth" he had talked to years ago at the Café Society, did not make a positive identification much easier. Although the FBI eventually concluded that "Bursley" was really Bernstein, in late May 1945 the real identity of Jaffe's recruiter was still up in the air, despite the fact that the bureau had positively identified Bernstein, a medium-sized man with thinning brown hair who wore black tortoiseshell glasses, as the man with whom Jaffe had held several meetings during the time he was known to be meeting "Bursley."

Joseph Milton Bernstein had an interesting past, chronicled in the files of the Civil Service Commission. Born in Connecticut in 1908, he attended Yale University, where he was a brilliant student as well as a member of the John Reed Club, a Communist front group for intellectuals. After receiving his bachelor's degree, he enjoyed a brief career as an actor before returning to Yale to pursue graduate studies in the Romance languages. Later, he attended the Sorbonne and worked as a freelance journalist and translator in Europe, interrupted by a stint as a staff reporter for a newspaper in Bucharest. Exactly what he was doing in Romania remained mysterious; when he later applied for a U.S. government job, he left this portion of his life out of his biography.[23]

In 1938 Bernstein returned to the United States. He hired literary agent Maxim Lieber and assisted Julio Alvarez del Vayo, the exiled former foreign minister of Republican Spain—and a close ally of the Communists—with his writing. Bernstein also collaborated with another client of Lieber's, André Simone, in writing an eyewitness account of the fall of France, J'Accuse. Even though Simone was in New York City when Paris was captured by the Nazis, that small detail did not stop him.

Simone was better known as Otto Katz. A suave Czech Communist, he had worked closely for many years with the famous Comintern agent Willi Munzenberg. Munzenberg's specialty in the 1930s was the creation and funding of magazines, movies, books, conferences, and newspapers, seemingly independent and ostensibly staffed by liberals, progressives, and unaffiliated radicals, which invariably parroted the Soviet line.[24]

Otto was Willi Munzenberg's most trusted assistant. Yet when Munzenberg broke with Stalin in 1937, Katz became his implacable enemy. He had numerous ties with Soviet intelligence services. After spending most of World War II in Mexico, Katz returned to Prague in 1946. Following the Communist seizure of power, he became editor of Rude Pravo, a major newspaper. Arrested in 1952 on charges of being an agent of British, French, and American imperialism in the service of Zionism, he was executed after a show trial during which he publicly confessed to all the charges.[25]

The night before his execution, Katz wrote a letter to Czech Communist leader Klement Gottwald protesting his innocence but accepting his fate. He insisted that one of the charges against him, that he had "used information from the secret military service" in writing *J'Accuse*, was untrue. His sources for the book were all public: "Joseph Bernstein, member of the CP USA, helped me organize the newspaper information." Katz noted that he had asked his interrogator "to verify my statement concerning Bernstein, [but] he didn't even respond."[26]

Bernstein's career strongly suggests that he was a Comintern agent and linked to Soviet intelligence. His literary agent, Maxim Lieber, worked for the Communists; in the mid-1930s, he established a writers' syndicate as a cover for Soviet espionage. "The occasional use of this well known writer's representative," Allen Weinstein comments in *Perjury*, his study of the Hiss-Chambers case, "seemed quite normal in the more casual and free-wheeling atmosphere within which Soviet intelligence expanded operations in the United States during the '30's."[27] Both Katz and del Vayo worked and lived in that same secret world. In 1940 Bernstein had applied for a government job. Inconsistencies in his application, including his failure to mention having lived in Romania, prompted the Civil Service Commission to order a hearing. The commission's investigation revealed that Bernstein had been constantly on the move in Europe, at one point shuttling back and forth between Switzerland and Turkey. Invited to correct the statements on his application during a hearing before a civil service examiner, Bernstein gave an account of his business in Europe that was demonstrably false. The hearing officer rejected the application, commenting in his report that Bernstein was clearly lacking in "loyalty or morality." In his conversation with Roth, Jaffe reported that Bernstein had told him that he had been a Communist Party member years before but had been told to discontinue such membership.[28]

As early as November 1945, the FBI had considered it a strong possibility that Joseph Bernstein was the man who had contacted Jaffe but had no proof. The following March, an agent happened to observe Bernstein meeting in a Manhattan restaurant with a woman named Mary Jane Keeney, who had arrived in New York City earlier that day on the steamship *Mit Victory* after serving in France as a staff member of the Allied Committee on Reparations. Keeney and her husband, formerly a librarian on General Douglas MacArthur's staff in Tokyo, were already suspected of being involved in espionage, and the agent observing Bernstein was interested to note that he immediately delivered an envelope that he had received from Keeney to Alexander Trachtenberg, a Communist Party official.[29]

After the Keeney incident, the FBI applied to the attorney general for permission to tap Bernstein's home and office phones. Although the phone tap evidence could not be used in court, it convinced the bureau that Bernstein was not only a courier but the same individual who had approached Jaffe.[30]

Bernstein's approach to Jaffe was not unusual. Soviet espionage efforts in the United States had accelerated in the 1930s and 1940s. Both the KGB and the Chief Intelligence Directorate of the General Staff, or the GRU, operated their own networks to gather political, technological, and military data. Working closely and harmoniously with the Soviet intelligence agencies was a conspiratorial wing of the CPUSA called "the secret apparatus." Established in 1932 under the direction of J. Peters, a mysterious Hungarian-born American Communist leader, in 1945 the apparatus was under the direction of Rudy Baker, a Yugoslav-born party leader of many years. In a 1942 report to his Russian superiors in the Comintern, Baker boasted of his apparatus's success in helping several operatives, using their code names, and referred to his communications links with the Soviet Union through the KGB. Many of the members of Baker's network hid their Communist ties. Given Bernstein's past, it is likely—although certainly not demonstrated—that he belonged to the secret apparatus.[31]

In 1944, with the Comintern dissolved, the secret apparatus became even more enmeshed with the KGB. The FBI secretly recorded one member of the group, Steve Nelson, a veteran Comintern agent, volunteering his apparatus to the KGB's chief agent in the United States, Vasili Zubilin. The KGB was actively reevaluating groups of agents who had been organized by the Comintern. In 1944 Elizabeth Bentley was forced to hand over her ring, which included many of Lauchlin Currie's and Harry White's friends, to direct KGB supervision. Having conducted its evaluations, the KGB would naturally be anxious to fill in the gaps in its intelligence from the United States, hence Bernstein's approach to Jaffe in an effort to acquire material from the Far Eastern affairs office of the State Department that the Soviets were having difficulty obtaining.[32]

It also would not have been unusual for Earl Browder to know about Soviet espionage in the United States. Browder had engaged in clandestine operations for the Comintern in China in the 1920s. He worked as a talent spotter for Soviet intelligence in the United States. His sister worked for the KGB in Europe during the 1930s, and Earl even wrote Georgi Dimitrov, head of the Comintern, suggesting that she be released from that work lest his political enemies find out and use it to discredit the CPUSA. He also consulted often with his good friend Rudy Baker on the espionage activities of the secret apparatus.[33]

Jack Service was in a good mood when he met Jaffe in the coffee shop of the Statler Hotel on May 8, the morning after Jaffe's extraordinary conversation with Roth, unaware that his breakfast companion was preparing to put together an espionage network and that he was the prize recruit. The news had just come on the radio that the fighting in Europe was over. All Washington was celebrating, and speeches by Truman and Churchill were being broadcast over the public address system in the hotel lobby, coincidentally frustrating the efforts of FBI agents at a nearby table to listen in on Service and Jaffe's conversation.

The two men finished their meal and returned to Jaffe's room, where the hidden microphone picked up their discussion just in time to record Service's voice remarking, "What I said about the military plans is, of course, very secret. . . . That plan was made up by Wedemeyer's staff in his absence. They got orders to make some recommendations as to what we should do if we landed in Communist territory." If Americans landed in Nationalist-controlled areas, they would cooperate with representatives of Chiang's government, but "if we landed in territory where the Communists were, they, of course, would be the dominant force." Chiang, Service went on, was very unhappy about this scenario and was pressuring U.S. forces to agree to take KMT officials with them into Communist-held territory to accept the surrender of the Japanese.

Changing the subject, Jaffe mentioned that the latest news from the San Francisco conference was encouraging, and Service agreed with Jaffe that Soviet foreign minister Vyacheslav Molotov had made a good presentation. He was not so impressed with his own superior, Secretary of State Edward Stettinius. "He's running the show as a sales manager right in the camera with that toothpaste and smile of his," Service complained. "Happy as a baboon. That's the good old salesman way. . . . What an American delegation!"[34]

As far as his *bête noire*, Patrick Hurley, was concerned, Service suggested that he had gone off on a tangent, misinterpreting his orders, and Roosevelt had been unable, for political reasons, to fire him. Jaffe told Service not to worry; Drew Pearson had "all the dope on Hurley" and would be releasing it soon. Service could barely contain his glee. "You make my mouth water just to think about it."

Service was all too aware of the suspicion that devolved on anyone who had contact with Communists, American or Chinese, for whatever reasons. He mentioned that he had given a friend of his in the San Francisco office of the ONI a letter of introduction to the Chinese Communist delegation but the friend "obviously thought it too dangerous to be seen with them very much," and he wondered aloud how Chi Ch'ao-ting dared stay friendly with Jaffe. That connection, Jaffe assured him, was kept very much "in the dark."[35]

Jaffe then brought up his efforts to obtain the text of a recent speech by Mao Tse-tung. Service expressed surprise that the text of the speech would be considered confidential and invited Jaffe to come along with him to the State Department to pick up a copy. Jaffe was apparently under the impression that his five-year plan to turn himself into a master spy was off to a swimming start. Service's information must have sounded authoritative; however, in a 1985 letter to the authors, Service maintained that he had no access to military secrets and, moreover, had not revealed even the outline of the actual plan targeting landing areas in southern China.[36]

At any rate, Bernstein's appearance on the scene had already inspired Jaffe to expand his network, and he had Roth arrange a lunch date with Ted Cohen, who worked for the FEA, the second agency named by Bernstein as a possible target. Over lunch, in an effort to sound out Cohen's political views, Jaffe brought up the subject of Michael Greenberg, Lauchlin Currie's administrative assistant, who was being investigated by the Civil Service Commission. Born in England, Greenberg had been associated with the British Communist Party while a student at Cambridge University and had emigrated to the United States in the late 1930s, where he became managing editor of the IPR publication *Pacific Affairs*. Greenberg made no particular secret of his Communist connections, and his outspoken criticisms of the administration had precipitated the commission's investigation. Jaffe joked to Cohen that Greenberg would not be in hot water now if he had bothered to do any work during his three years at the FEA, which he hadn't. Still, he went on, Greenberg had influential friends, especially a certain senator—the name is blacked out in the FBI transcripts—who had threatened "to burn the Commission to a crisp" if it persisted in its investigation.[37]

Cohen was not volunteering much, and Jaffe, suddenly cautious, began complaining that the OSS was employing civilians as undercover agents. "One of them I know and two I suspect," he told Cohen. "Well, I might be an OSS agent right now. . . . I mean, this guy befriended me and then reports everything I do and say." He complained that the OSS could misconstrue even the most innocent remark and use it to suggest that "there's a ring operating." Cohen, apparently dumbfounded by this turn in the conversation, remarked that it was time for him to be getting back to work and excused himself from the room.[38]

Jaffe had only slightly better luck with Alvin Barber, another FEA employee who dropped by to see him later in the afternoon. Barber told Jaffe that he had seen "some very peculiar cables" that were being sent back and forth between the State Department and Moscow, and he predicted that U.S.-Soviet relations were about to take a turn for the worse. Jaffe, however, once again put a damper on the conversation by bringing up the subject of the OSS. Jaffe claimed to know two undercover agents personally, one at the *New York Times* and another who worked for the Henry Holt publishing house. "This Donovan thing," he groused, "is ten times worse than the Dies Committee ever was." Whatever Barber's reasons may have been for visiting Jaffe, the mention of Donovan's agency brought the meeting to a chilly conclusion.[39]

While attempting to check out Bernstein, Jaffe was also hurriedly trying to put together a package of "cigarettes," his and Larsen's code word for documents. In the three weeks after Bernstein first approached Jaffe, the FBI listened in on a series of furtive conversations concerning Jaffe's rush orders for Turkish cigarettes, Korean cigarettes, and Jewish cigarettes. The Korean "cigarettes" may have been documents concerning the Korean People's Emancipation League, an organization in which the Communist Party had considerable influence. Jaffe may have sought the Jewish "cigarettes" in response to Bernstein's request for information about certain Zionist splinter groups active in Palestine.[40]

It is difficult to imagine whom this clumsy code was intended to fool. On May 14, four days after he was observed meeting with John Thomas Find, a Chinese-language expert in the ONI, Larsen called Jaffe to report: "I have an enlargement for Andy, and I have a few other things for you. . . . Three packages of those [Turkish Helmars cigarettes] and one package of English cigarettes—so four packages will go up to you. . . . You like those cigarettes, don't you?" Jaffe then asked whether the Korean "cigarettes" were going to be expensive and complained that it was impossible to get the brands he wanted in New York City. "Here all you can get is kinds of junk. You can't get any good kind," he reiterated. Seconds later, however, Larsen simply dispensed with the subterfuge to ask how many copies of the "cigarettes" Jaffe wanted.[41]

By now, Jaffe had met with Bernstein several times, including once at the home of Mark and Sally Gayn, but, unless he was not telling Andrew Roth the whole truth—which is entirely possible—he had never actually given Bernstein any documents. During one monitored conversation with Jaffe, on May 22, Bernstein used the same "cigarette" code, telling Jaffe that he had "a package of Helmars" for him. Jaffe assured Bernstein that he was interested in receiving them, and Bernstein promised to call him in a few days to make an appointment. He then mentioned someone whose name is blacked out in the transcript, and Jaffe responded that Kate Mitchell had met that person and pronounced him "no good." The FBI speculated, not unreasonably, that Bernstein was arranging a meeting to return documents that Jaffe had given him. The individual Bernstein named may have been someone who could vouch for his reliability. On May 15, moreover, the agent who was tailing Jaffe in New York City followed him to a Chinese restaurant and sat at an adjoining table while Jaffe had lunch with an unidentified Asian man. The agent observed Jaffe handing over a thick manila envelope and was close enough to pick up snatches of conversation, including Jaffe's boast that "Jack Service is in solid."[42]

In the meantime, while trying to screw up his courage to commit espionage, Jaffe was busy feeding stories critical of America's China policy to Gayn and other journalists. On May 23, he received a call from an unidentified man who said that he had just talked to "the chief" and that approval had been given for a loan of $186 million in gold to the Nationalist government. The anonymous tipster, probably from the Treasury Department, told Jaffe that "our general feeling was that it would be a very good idea in view of the gold scandal to have an item slipped to Pearson" in the hope that he could "squash" the deal. Jaffe had already heard about the loan from "Jack" (apparently Service) and was more than willing to go along with the suggestion, but for some reason, despite leaving numerous phone messages, he was unable to get through to Drew Pearson. Instead, Jaffe decided to offer the item to Mark Gayn.[43]

Jaffe also had another tip for Gayn. He had learned the contents of a personal cable Ambassador Hurley had sent to his wife, suggesting that he would either resign or be fired that summer. The information, he told Gayn, had come "via J. S. S." Jaffe thought the story, "a big scoop," might prod Hurley into resigning immediately, but Gayn was doubtful. Hurley, Gayn observed, was just the type to respond to pressure by digging in his heels. In any case, Gayn was worried about his pending application for a passport renewal, and he thought the Hurley story was too hot for him to touch at the moment.[44]

Jaffe nevertheless continued to fret over the possibility that Service would drift out of his orbit. When Service mentioned that he was coming to New York City for another long weekend, Jaffe was distraught that Service's plans did not include either him or Mark Gayn. In a phone conversation with Gayn, Jaffe complained that he had made "three or four offers" to take Service to a certain Broadway show he had expressed an interest in seeing, but Service kept turning him down.

Unwilling to take no for an answer, Jaffe telephoned the IPR organizer and his old comrade from *China Today*, T. A. Bisson, and suggested that Bisson invite Service to his house on Long Island that Sunday. Jaffe then called Service to relay Bisson's invitation, adding that he was also welcome to attend a small party Kate Mitchell was giving on Saturday evening. Service, he suggested, could meet Mark and Sally Gayn at Mitchell's place and spend the night at their apartment. The next morning they could all drive out to Bisson's house together. And so it was arranged, once again minimizing the chance that Service would use his free time in New York City to meet other journalists and cementing Service's ties with Jaffe's ring.[45]

Although Jaffe apparently still had not received any high-level assurances that Bernstein's friend was an authentic KGB agent, he had managed to overcome his fear of entrapment, a triumph of ego over common sense. By the time he next returned to Washington on May 28, he was feeling relaxed and confident. When he called Service to make plans for their next meeting, he was amused to learn that Service was having lunch that day with someone from the OSS. "Right," Jaffe quipped, "the Office of Superfluous Secrets." With great relish, he described a newspaper item about WACs who had been assigned to test OSS security procedures and had succeeded in spiriting away thousands of documents.[46]

Ostensibly, Jaffe had come to the capital to gather background information for two articles: an *Amerasia* piece that would suggest that the KMT was trying to arrange a rapprochement with the Japanese and Gayn's forthcoming article on the gold loan. However, he also wanted to make sure that Roth approved of his arranging future contacts with Bernstein. Roth, it happened, had just learned that day that the navy had denied him permission to publish his book on Japan as long as he remained on active duty and, although this decision was hardly unforeseeable, was bitterly disappointed. Also, Roth was about to be transferred to Honolulu, halfway around the world from Jaffe and his intrigues. For whatever reasons, he was no longer hesitant. "I think it's all right for you to see him," he told Jaffe. "The more guys like that you can talk to the better. If you're careful."[47]

Jaffe himself could lose everything by pursuing his contact with Bernstein. A self-made millionaire, he was risking his financial security as well as his chance of achieving his dream of establishing himself as a respected expert on China. But, as his conversation with Roth made clear, Jaffe was resentful that his friend Earl Browder was refusing to taking him seriously. The French Communist leader Jacques Duclos had recently published an article critical of Browder and his rosy view that the end of the war would lead to a period of friendly cooperation between the United States and the Soviet Union. Jaffe agreed with many of Duclos's arguments, he told Roth. Browder was "a good Marxist but a bad Leninist" whose refusal to seek advice from others was largely responsible for his problems. "Why must he sit alone in his room? . . . If he doesn't call me in on China he must make errors, because you see, that's my life study."

Despite his claim to scholarly objectivity, Jaffe was starry-eyed about the Soviet Union. When Roth suggested that he give the story on the gold loan to I. F. Stone, then a columnist for the leftist liberal newspaper *PM*, Jaffe was horrified. Although Stone had been criticized by anti-Communist leftists like Dwight MacDonald for being soft on Stalinism, he was not pro-Soviet enough to satisfy Jaffe. Stone, Jaffe complained to Roth, lacked "that sense of defending the Soviet Union all the time. How can a real radical, or even a liberal, not have that feeling?" Even if Stone honestly thought the Soviets were wrong on a particular issue, he wasn't in a position to judge, Jaffe argued, since he himself was a victim of so much capitalist press propaganda: "I would say that the first test of a real radical is, do you trust the Soviet Union through thick and thin, regardless of what anybody says? . . . It's the workers' government, the one shining star in the whole damned world, and you got to defend that with your last drop of blood, and Izzy Stone hasn't done it all the time and there's no excuse for it."[48]

Following their conversation about Stone, Roth and Jaffe were joined by Roth's wife Renée. While the two men continued to discuss who might take over as Jaffe's contact at the State Department after Roth left Washington, Renée Roth was moving around the room. Suddenly, she interrupted the conversation to announce that she had found something that looked like a hidden microphone. Jaffe and Roth paid no attention, resuming their talk about State Department contacts and their continuing difficulties in obtaining "Jewish cigarettes."

By this time, federal agents had been inside the *Amerasia* offices on six occasions—on March 20, 26, and 27, April 23 and 24, and May 14—several of these times with the cooperation of the building superintendent. They had entered Mitchell's, Jaffe's, and Gayn's apartments in New York City (the latter two twice, for some reason) to plant phone bugs. In Washington, they had bugged Roth's and Larsen's homes and, on learning that Larsen was moving to another apartment in the same building, had received permission from the superintendent to bug the new apartment before he took possession of it. To the agents monitoring Jaffe's room at the Statler, it must have seemed incredible that despite all this activity, and despite Renée Roth's apparent discovery of the microphone, Jaffe still did not realize that he was the target of surveillance. At the end of the day, they took the case to their superiors, who began to discuss the possibility of making an immediate arrest. In the meantime, unluckily for Jack Service, the microphone remained in operation and picked up one final conversation between him and Jaffe.

Ironically, the FBI transcript of this last meeting between Service and Jaffe suggests that Service was, at long last, becoming nervous about Jaffe's solicitous manner. Jaffe kept angling to find out if the rumor that General Joseph Stilwell had returned to the Pacific was true. That information, Service said, was confidential. Jaffe laughed off the rebuff, saying that it didn't matter whether Service told him or not since he had already heard the story from Mark Gayn, who had learned it from former ambassador Clarence Gauss. Well, that, Service commented uneasily, is "how secrets get out." Jaffe then wondered aloud if any decision had been made about landing troops in China, and if so, what sites had been targeted. "I don't believe it's decided," Service said. "I can tell you in a couple of weeks when Stilwell gets back. I rather think we will."[49]

Jaffe also brought up Kate Mitchell's plans to write a book on Confucianism. Could Service get him a copy of one of his old State Department reports on the KMT's use of Confucian doctrines? Even that might be difficult, Service replied. The report was a few years old, and he no longer had a copy. He would have to retrieve one from the files of the Office of Far Eastern Affairs. "It's sort of hard for me to go messing around F.E.," Service explained, "because I'm not assigned there and don't work there. Not that there's anything confidential or secret about it." Jaffe suggested that it was odd that Service didn't have a file of his old reports. Service responded that it was not at all unusual because "it's against regulations to keep copies of your reports."[50]

Although Service may well have been trying to set some ground rules to limit Jaffe's more importunate requests, the transcript of this meeting would, in the long run, do nothing to help his case. At one point during the meeting, Service reiterated his desire to be of great help to *Amerasia* in the future and gave Jaffe his home address, so that Jaffe would not have to continue to reach him through the State Department. Shortly after Service made this remark, Andrew Roth showed up, and Service allowed himself to be drawn into a discussion of the inside story of Stilwell's recall. Jaffe, after recounting an anecdote he had heard from Mark Gayn, cautioned that the information was, of course, confidential, a remark that evoked hearty laughter all around. Service then chimed in with the story of how he had smuggled Brooks Atkinson's story on Stilwell past the military censors.

Jaffe also brought up the subject of Patrick Hurley. Drew Pearson's column, revealing that Hurley's wife had accepted the gift of a necklace from KMT officials, had finally been published; however, it had been suppressed by the Washington papers carrying Pearson's syndicated commentaries. Service assured Jaffe and Roth that the story nevertheless had an impact within the State Department. Moreover, it had riled Hurley, who had sent a cablegram to the department complaining that he was the victim of a campaign to smear his reputation through selective leaking. Amused by Hurley's reaction, Service admitted that he himself had leaked several items detrimental to Hurley that had recently found their way into the papers. Specifically, he mentioned a recently published piece predicting that Hurley was about to be recalled. "That interested me very much because as far as I know I had the idea—at least I got the idea independently and spread it around as much as I could."[51]

That evening Andrew and Renée Roth, Service, and Jaffe all attended a cookout at the home of Owen Lattimore in the Baltimore suburbs. The party was to be a send-off for the Roths, who were scheduled to leave for Hawaii in forty-eight hours. The next morning, however, Roth's orders were abruptly changed. Although his appointment as ONI liaison had been completed, he was told that he would be remaining in Washington until further notice. Unofficially, Roth was led to believe that his transfer was being held up so that he could discuss possible revisions of his manuscript with the navy review panel.[52]

While the delay in travel plans was not exactly welcome news, presumably it indicated that the navy brass were reconsidering their flat denial of permission to publish his manuscript. But according to Larsen, whose word on such matters may or may not be reliable, Roth was extremely agitated over the change in his orders. Larsen came home from work that day to find that Roth had arrived early for a planned get-together and was waiting in the Larsens' living room for his wife, who was supposed to meet him after finishing some shopping. When Renée Roth appeared and heard about the new orders, she was "dumbfounded and put out," recalled Larsen. "I tried to comfort her . . . but she brushed aside my remarks in a peeved manner that indicated anxiety and fear."[53] She sensed that something was going on; in fact, the FBI was anxious to make arrests before more damage was done to national security.

Wiretaps, Arrests, and Prosecution

Clandestine by its very nature, espionage is among the most difficult of all crimes to prosecute. Spies rarely operate in front of
witnesses or speak candidly of their motivations, even to their
confederates. If arrested, their successful prosecution may depend
on the presentation in open court of the very information that the
government wants to keep secret, thus setting up a conflict of
interest between the Department of Justice and the agencies that
are the targets of the crime. Practically speaking, it is difficult to
secure a conviction unless at least one member of the spy ring
agrees to testify against his or her fellow conspirators, yet of all
witnesses who "turn," none is more vulnerable to attacks on his or
her credibility than a confessed spy.

These factors are generally true of all spy cases, but U.S. government officials in 1945 faced certain difficulties that made the successful prosecution of espionage especially problematic. These difficulties were obvious in the *Amerasia* case and revolved around the use of information gleaned from wiretaps.

The invention of wiretapping did not lag far behind the invention of the telephone. As early as 1895, the New York City police department was using phone taps to gather evidence in criminal cases, setting an example that was no doubt promptly followed by law enforcement agencies in other parts of the country. Wiretapping did not become a public issue until 1916, when it was learned that the mayor of New York City, in connection with an investigation of Catholic charities, had authorized the police to tap the phone of a priest. Attorney General A. Mitchell Palmer became the first federal official to make extensive use of wiretapping, using intercepted phone conversations to orchestrate the roundup of suspected subversives during the Red Scare raids of 1919. A year later, when Prohibition became the law of the land, the Treasury Department also became involved in the electronic surveillance game, regularly listening in on the conversations of suspected bootleggers.

As William Fairchild and Charles Clift pointed out in a 1952 article on the growth of wiretapping, it was the targeting of bootleggers more than the mischievous potential of political surveillance that alarmed the public, since many otherwise respectable citizens had reason to fear that their phone orders for liquor would be overheard by Treasury agents. Ironically, FBI director J. Edgar Hoover was among those who lined up in the anti-wiretap camp. "While it may not be illegal," he said in 1928, "I think it is unethical, and it is not permitted under the regulations of the Attorney General." Pressure for a ban on phone tapping culminated in the passage of section 605 of the enabling act that set up the FCC in 1934, making it unlawful for any unauthorized person to "intercept and divulge" telephone communications.[1]

Section 605 set up a conflict between the federal courts and the Justice Department. The Department of Justice had come to realize what a powerful tool electronic surveillance could be and, reluctant to give it up, took the view that the antiwiretap prohibition should not apply to agencies of the federal government. In March 1940, after a series of Supreme Court decisions throwing out wiretap evidence made this interpretation untenable, Attorney General Robert H. Jackson called for federal legislation to authorize telephone surveillance in certain types of cases "under appropriate safeguard."[2]

Before Congress could act on Jackson's suggestion, Hitler's armies swept into the Low Countries and Denmark. The widening war in Europe sparked fears of Nazi sabotage against American shipping, and on May 21, 1940, President Roosevelt sent a secret memorandum to the attorney general, expressing the view that the Supreme Court had never meant its ban on wiretaps to apply "to grave matters involving the defense of the nation." The president authorized the Justice Department to use "listening devices" in its investigation of "persons suspected of subversive activities against the Government of the United States, including suspected spies."[3] The president's logic was supported to a certain degree by the confusing mélange of state laws on the subject, many of which permitted electronic surveillance under certain conditions, either by government authorities or by private citizens.

The existence of this secret presidential directive first came to light in October 1941, when attorneys representing Harry Bridges, the Australian-born head of the West Coast longshoremen's union, learned that the Justice Department had authorized taps of Bridges's phone conversations. Attorney General Jackson, meanwhile, had publicly advanced a new reading of section 605: wiretapping per se was not prohibited by this statute, which only made it a crime to "intercept and divulge" phone communications. And since the federal government was a single entity, federal agents who recorded tapped phone conversations and then reported them to their superiors could not be said to be "divulging" anything to anyone.[4]

Jackson's hairsplitting interpretation of the law convinced no one, but in 1942 the Supreme Court did take a major step backward from its previous position on section 605. In the mail fraud case of *Goldstein v. United States*, the Court ruled that information overheard on phone taps could be used against third-party defendants. Limited as this decision was, it meant that wiretapping by federal agents could potentially serve a legitimate purpose. The threat that federal employees who authorized or conducted phone surveillances might be exposing themselves to criminal penalties all but vanished. As Attorney General Jackson had already noted, this confusing situation cried out for federal legislation. Various bills were proposed, but Congress failed to take decisive action.

Hoover, meanwhile, had reason to believe that the bureau's surveillance of the *Amerasia* suspects was in line with President Roosevelt's directive and established Justice Department policy. Under the *Goldstein* precedent, Jaffe's recorded conversations could not be used directly against him, but his statements to Roth about Larsen, say, might well be admissible. In any event, since the Justice Department was on record as favoring a reinterpretation of the law, it could be expected to present the strongest possible arguments for a less restrictive interpretation of section 605. A more ideal test case than *Amerasia* could hardly be imagined.

On May 28, the day after Renée Roth apparently noticed the FBI's hidden microphone in Jaffe's hotel room, Myron Gurnea informed the State and Navy Department liaisons that the time had come to consider the immediate arrests of the suspects. Even though Jaffe had apparently not taken Renée Roth's observation seriously, his nervous talk of OSS agents in New York City suggested that he had begun to suspect that someone had been snooping around his office. Also, Roth's transfer to Pearl Harbor could not be held up indefinitely without making the lieutenant suspicious, diminishing the chances of catching him with incriminating papers in his possession.[5]

Nevertheless, from a legal standpoint, Gurnea's decision to push for arrests would seem to have been premature. Although Hoover believed Jaffe had given classified information to the Chinese delegate who had met with him and Browder at his New York City apartment, this was only a suspicion. Why not continue to monitor Jaffe's contacts with Joseph Bernstein in the hope of catching them in the act of transferring classified documents?

Several factors accounted for the bureau's haste. With the war in Asia reaching a crisis point, the government could not afford the luxury of a lengthy investigation; a period of two and a half months was already a long delay in picking up a suspected agent. Also, the Bernstein contact did not promise to be immediately productive since Jaffe had seemingly agreed with Roth that he would only give Bernstein verbal summaries, and he seemed to be taking a long time establishing Bernstein's bona fides. Lastly, the investigators would never have known about Bernstein were it not for their electronic eavesdropping, so even if Jaffe changed his mind and was caught in the act of handing over government property, any evidence seized might still be inadmissible in court under the "fruit of the poisoned tree" principle.

There may have been another reason for the FBI's haste. Bernstein's approach to Jaffe had caused a degree of confusion at bureau headquarters. The agents working on the case had never heard of this supposed KGB contact man, and Jaffe's suspicions that he was dealing with an OSS plant provoked consternation. Could Bernstein be a government agent? The bureau queried the OSS to find out if any of its operatives had approached Jaffe and apparently received a negative reply, but given the OSS's freewheeling ways, Gurnea may not have been sure that he was told the truth. Gurnea also considered the possibility that Jaffe had invented "Bursley" to impress Roth.[6]

Jaffe had also seemed reluctant to accept Bernstein's contacts as genuine. In any case, the possibility of waiting to see how Jaffe's contact with Bernstein developed was dismissed when Myron Gurnea met with Matthias Correa from the Navy Department and Julius Holmes and Fred Lyon from the State Department on May 28. They agreed with Gurnea that the best strategy would be to round up the suspects immediately before they became any more suspicious than they already were. Chances were that at least some of those arrested would be caught with classified material in their possession and would make damaging admissions.

The FBI's strategy suggests that it was operating on the assumption that papers seized from the *Amerasia* offices, a number of them initialed by Larsen, would eventually be ruled admissible in court. So far, however, none of the documents could be definitely connected with Roth. With the navy's permission, the bureau had intercepted Roth's files before they were shipped to Pearl Harbor, but an inventory of the contents had turned up nothing incriminating. Now, as the Roths proceeded with their packing despite the change in Roth's orders, Gurnea began to worry that they would use the occasion to destroy evidence.[7]

After securing the approval of the Departments of State and the Navy, Gurnea telephoned the Justice Department, and the next morning, May 29, James McInerney showed up for a briefing. McInerney had formerly been the assistant head of the Criminal Division under Tom Clark. Now, with Clark having recently been named attorney general designate by Truman, McInerney was in line to become the Justice Department's chief criminal prosecutor, and his personal involvement in the decision making at this point was indicative of the department's awareness of the sensitivity of the case. After listening to Gurnea's review of the evidence, McInerney authorized the arrest of seven suspects: Jaffe, Roth, Larsen, Mitchell, Service, and Gayn as well as Annette Blumenthal, a typist who had copied various documents for Jaffe in New York City. He assured Gurnea that in his opinion, there was sufficient evidence to indict all seven; however, he did warn that the case would be much stronger if the suspects could be arrested simultaneously at their homes or offices, maximizing the chance that incriminating documents could be seized at the same time.[8]

Only the FBI director himself, with his usual keen instinct for public relations, appeared to have any qualms. After reading Gurnea's account of another meeting with McInerney, held on June 4, Hoover dashed off a memo to his assistant and close personal friend Clyde Tolson. "I am concerned about this case. In view of its delicacy and the White House interest I want to make certain we are on sound ground. If anything goes wrong the FBI will be blamed and not McInerney. I would like you, Ladd, Gurnea and Carlson and any others you desire to go over this and be certain of our proposed actions." Tolson, in response, conceded that the legal case at this point was still "thin" because there was no evidence that any information had been transferred to foreign agents, but he pointed out that the bureau had a list of fifty persons it intended to interview once the seven suspects had been arrested and expected to seize secret government documents in the possession of several of the defendants. But most importantly, he asserted, McInerney's confidence demonstrated the attorney general's commitment to the prosecution. "Move at once," Hoover responded. "When will the arrests be made?"[9]

Hoover had grounds for concern because there were already signs that the Navy and State Departments, the agencies that had pushed for the FBI investigation in the first place, had differing ideas about how to handle the prosecution. Secretary of the Navy James Forrestal, informed that one of the suspects was a lieutenant attached to the ONI, was in favor of having Roth brought up before a court-martial, where it was almost a foregone conclusion that he could be convicted of some serious offense, even if not espionage per se. Correa carried this message back to Gurnea and McInerney, only to be warned that the Justice Department was adamantly opposed to severing Roth's case from the others. To do so, Gurnea insisted, would weaken the government's chances of proving the existence of a conspiracy.

Forrestal, when he learned of the Justice Department's position, made a personal call to Gurnea to ask if he could guarantee that Roth would be convicted. Gurnea conceded that the evidence against Roth so far was "more or less circumstantial." Nevertheless, with Micawberlike optimism, he insisted that "there was every reason to believe" that more incriminating papers would turn up when Roth's apartment was searched.[10]

Reluctantly, Forrestal agreed to let the Justice Department have its way, but he balked at the prospect of seeing a navy officer tried for conspiracy to commit espionage in a civilian court. Gurnea was forced to promise that immediately after Roth was taken into custody he would be stripped of his rank and informed of his summary transfer to the naval reserves. The press release announcing the arrests was to describe Roth as an officer "recently on active duty."[11]

Technically, the change in Roth's status would not affect the case against him. In practical terms, however, it was to make a world of difference in the way the public perceived the case—particularly since some newspapers, misreading the government statement, would characterize Roth as "*not* recently on active duty." Even as approved, the wording of the press release could be interpreted to suggest that the charges against Roth were unrelated to his duties as an intelligence officer. Indeed, Roth's attorney would later argue that by not having Roth arraigned while still in uniform, the Navy Department was signaling its belief that the charges were baseless. This was far from being the case. Forrestal simply wanted to spare the navy the embarrassment of having one of its uniformed officers on trial for espionage. Moreover, in discussing the wording of the press release with Gurnea in his office on May 30, Correa emphasized that by transferring Roth to the reserves, as opposed to ordering a dishonorable discharge, the navy was keeping open the option of a court-martial should the civil case fall apart.[12]

While Correa was meeting with Gurnea, James McInerney dropped by again to discuss the wording of the arrest warrants. The suspects were to be charged with violating section 88 of the espionage act, which made it a crime to conspire "to defraud the US in any manner or for any purpose." By prosecuting under section 88, the government would not be required to prove that any information had actually been passed on to representatives of a foreign power. However, the maximum penalty for conviction was only $10,000 and/or two years in prison—as opposed to life imprisonment or even execution.

McInerney also suggested that his superiors, Tom Clark and Assistant Attorney General James McGranery, were concerned that the case against each of the defendants be built on documents clearly related to national security, and therefore he was having second thoughts about the wisdom of arresting the journalist, Mark Gayn. Gurnea calmed McInerney's fears on the first of these points by showing him a selection of photographs the bureau had made during one of its raids on *Amerasia*'s offices. As for Gayn, Gurnea emphasized that he had been observed reading a classified State Department document while riding on a New York City bus. Moreover, both Jaffe and Service had been overheard saying that they were sharing information with Gayn.[13]

While defending the plan to arrest Gayn—even suggesting that Sally

Gayn might be indicted later—Gurnea talked McInerney into removing Annette Blumenthal's name from the list of suspects. The FBI had learned that Blumenthal had given birth a few weeks earlier, and its desire to leave her out of the case may have been inspired by Hoover's Victorian sentiments about the institution of motherhood. In any case, McInerney agreed that Blumenthal was a potential government witness and would be more likely to cooperate if she were spared the humiliation of an arrest.[14]

Having personally examined the papers already seized or photographed by the bureau and discussed the wiretap transcripts with Gurnea, McInerney was obviously well aware of how the FBI had obtained its evidence. The position of the FBI's own legal experts, based more on hope than any body of legal precedent, was that the black bag jobs on the *Amerasia* office were not in violation of the Fourth Amendment prohibition against illegal searches and seizures because their sole purpose was to locate and recover stolen government papers. The government, so the reasoning went, had the right to take extraordinary measures to recover its own property, particularly during wartime. Moreover, FBI counselors hoped that even the wiretap evidence might be allowable under certain circumstances. Even so, no one could have been unaware that the prosecutors in this case would have to negotiate a minefield of legal complications. According to a subsequent Justice Department review, the go-ahead for the arrests was given anyway because everyone at the Justice Department was looking forward to "the usual break" in the case—a decision on the part of one or more defendants to plead guilty and testify against his or her co-conspirators. As the report noted, "80% of federal law violators confess their offense after arrest."[15]

All that remained was to inform President Truman. Everyone agreed that "in view of the nature of the case," as McGranery put it, the arrests could not go forward without the president's personal approval, but no one seemed eager to undertake the task of telling Truman that a major breach of security had been discovered and was about to become public knowledge. There were also concerns about how the arrests would affect Soviet-American relations. In his diary entry for May 28, James Forrestal commented on the proposed arrests, stating that "the inevitable consequences of such action now would be to greatly embarrass the President in his current conversations with Stalin, because of the anti-Russian play-up the incident would receive out of proportion to its importance." Forrestal added that he had asked Captain James Vardaman, Truman's naval aide, to make sure the president was aware of the impending arrests; he also called Hoover to suggest that he personally brief the president on the status of the evidence. Hoover tried to pass the unwanted assignment on to Tom Clark, but in the end, it was Julius Holmes of the State Department who was stuck with the job.[16]

Truman was out of town, so Holmes was not able to see him until the morning of May 31. Once he had absorbed the bad news, Truman was decisive. Forget about the impact on the San Francisco conference, he told Holmes; this was one case he wanted to see vigorously prosecuted as an example to other government employees who might be tempted to pass government secrets to a foreign power. Truman even had a suggestion as to who should handle the prosecution. While Holmes continued his briefing, the president scribbled a note on a sheet of paper and handed it to Holmes: "Hugh Fulton for special prosecutor."[17]

Despite Truman's enthusiasm, it seemed that someone on the White House staff wanted the arrests postponed. Later that same afternoon, McInerney called Gurnea to report that Tom Clark had received orders from the president to take no action until after the San Francisco conference, which was scheduled to continue until mid-June. The long delay would be awkward for the navy, which would have to think of a way to keep Roth from becoming suspicious about why he was being detained in Washington. "O.K.," a puzzled Hoover wrote on the memo he received from Gurnea, "but I thought General Holmes this morning had indicated otherwise."[18]

Officials at the State Department did not learn of this turn of events until three days later, on June 2, when Fred Lyon called the FBI to find out why nothing had been done. Julius Holmes was so alarmed to hear that someone had countermanded the chief executive's decision that he had Undersecretary of State Joseph Grew place an "urgent" call to the president, who immediately summoned Holmes and Grew to his office. Truman, noted Holmes, was "obviously annoyed" and got on the phone to order Gurnea to "go right ahead . . . as quickly as possible."[19]

Truman also asked Holmes and Grew to find out who was responsible for issuing a direct order to Tom Clark in his name. According to FBI files, Tom Clark told Grew that the call ordering him to delay the arrests came from the president's naval aide, James Vardaman. At this point, both Holmes and the bureau decided to let the matter drop, assuming Vardaman had merely misunderstood the president's wishes. Vardaman was not asked about the incident until five years later, and when he heard the story, he was outraged, indignantly denying that he had ever placed such a call.

By that time, it was too late to ascertain exactly what had gone wrong, but there were grounds to suspect that it was either Secretary of the Navy James Forrestal or attorney general designate Tom Clark who had arranged the postponement.[20]

Once the FBI was assured that the president approved, it was ready to move. The plan was to make all six arrests simultaneously, late on the afternoon of June 6. Caught by surprise, the suspects would have no chance to destroy evidence and no way of knowing whether or not their co-conspirators had implicated them. Such perfectly timed sweeps occur regularly in fiction, but they were not an everyday practice for the FBI and there were more than a few hitches.

In New York City, two FBI agents arrived at 225 Fifth Avenue at 3:25 P.M. The arrest warrants, issued that morning in Washington, had failed to arrive, but the agents confronted Jaffe anyway, informing him that he and Kate Mitchell were under arrest and announcing their intention of searching the offices. This was in the days before the average citizen had seen thousands of arrests on television and knew the drill by heart; the bureau's prestige was at its height, and few suspects ever had the presence of mind to challenge a team of federal agents. Jaffe proved to be the exception. On learning that the agents had no warrant, he insisted on his right to leave the office, and when the agents prevented him from walking out, he launched into a nonstop harangue. The main theme of Jaffe's lecture was that the government's classification system was idiotic. Only 15 percent of the information classified was actually confidential, Jaffe complained. He kept repeating the 15 percent figure, one of the agents noted, as if once his visitors were convinced of its accuracy, they would agree that he had done nothing wrong and leave him alone.

The missing warrant was delivered about half an hour later, but Jaffe still refused to accept it as genuine, insisting that he would not submit to arrest unless the U.S. attorney personally confirmed the authenticity of the warrant. Surprisingly, he was allowed to call the Manhattan U.S. attorney's office, and at five o'clock he finally agreed to turn over the keys to his files. Jaffe's briefcase was opened first, then his desk drawers, where the agents found a State Department dispatch from Chungking entitled "Conditions in Communist Controlled Areas of Northern China" and a document from the OSS Research and Analysis Branch with a "Secret" classification. In the briefcase were eleven other documents, mostly from the State Department, of which five were classified "Secret," two "Confidential," and one "Strictly Confidential." Jaffe told the agents he couldn't remember how he had come by the papers, but in any case, even the "Secret" classification counted for little. At this point, Jaffe's attorney Martin Roob arrived. Jaffe's discourse on the evils of the classification system continued, but he answered no further questions about specific papers.[21]

While Jaffe continued to harangue the agents assigned to watch him, Kate Mitchell was being questioned in an adjoining room. At first, she claimed that the documents Jaffe had given her contained nothing more than background information. "I never asked him where he got it," she added. It was well known that officials in Washington "let you read stuff" off the record, she insisted, and Jaffe was a man who "loves facts. He loves to know his subject." Even as Mitchell was talking, an agent going through her desk reached into one of the drawers and pulled out a document plainly marked "Restricted." Another agent asked Jaffe to unlock a four-drawer file cabinet, which proved to be stuffed full of copies of papers from the State Department, the War Department, the navy, the OWI, the OSS, the FCC, and the FEA.

In the presence of an agency stenographer, the agents began the tedious progress of logging each of the papers. There were more than 500 documents in all, including some batches of papers that were logged under the heading "Miscellaneous." Many were obviously innocuous, but others bore intriguing titles. A booklet on the Japanese Army's Order of Battle, dated 1942, had Emmanuel Larsen's name on the cover. A number of other papers appeared to come from the office of Patrick Hurley, including a letter addressed to Hurley on the subject of Japanese espionage. Other reports, whose source the FBI could not immediately determine, dealt with subjects such as that covered in "Disclosure of Military Information to the Chinese." Shown some of these papers, Mitchell admitted that she knew that papers marked "Secret" and "Confidential" were for government use only. Nevertheless she insisted that she had been "extremely careful" not to quote sensitive information in the magazine.[22]

Shortly after 8:00 P.M., the agents loaded their haul of documents into the trunk of their car and drove Mitchell, Jaffe, and Martin Roob to the federal courthouse at Foley Square. In the car, Jaffe's facade of defiance seemed to break down. In the words of one of the agent's summaries, Jaffe said that "he was sorry he had retained possession of all these document and stated that now he thought he should have destroyed them sometime in the past."[23]

Mark Gayn, meanwhile, had been picked up at his home, where investigators found a file of classified documents. Gayn readily admitted that he

Mark Gayn, Philip Jaffe, and Kate Mitchell following their arrests in New York City in 1945. (UPI/The Bettmann Archive)

had violated the letter of the law, but he insisted that, in the words of an FBI summary, "he was in the same position as a government official or a person entrusted with secrets. He stated that he took good care of the documents . . . took the precaution of locking the closet." Later, in a signed statement, he added, "nor did I intend to let this information fall into hands in which it would do harm to the United States." Further, he asserted that, in the past, he had shared information that came his way with U.S. Army intelligence.[24]

By the time Jaffe had been photographed and fingerprinted at Foley Square, he had regained his composure. At about 10:00 P.M., he was allowed to meet briefly with his wife, Agnes. As Jaffe waited outside the U.S. commissioner's office for his arraignment, he was able to confer with Mitchell and Gayn. An FBI agent guarding the group overheard Jaffe complaining that the sandwiches the agents provided for his supper had been made with white bread. Trivial as the conversation may have been, it was enough for Jaffe, Gayn, and Mitchell to reassure themselves that they were presenting a solid front. Bail for each of the defendants was set at $10,000. Local bondsmen had been warned off by the FBI with the suggestion that the defendants might be likely to flee. But in the end, it made no difference. Jaffe paid for everyone.[25]

In Washington, meanwhile, the teams assigned to pick up Larsen and Service cooled their heels at the State Department, waiting to make the arrests at the appointed hour. Jack Service noticed the ill-at-ease FBI men hanging around outside his office. They were there when he left for lunch and still there when he returned, but when Service asked if there was anything he could do to help them, the visitors said vaguely that they were waiting for someone. The agent tracking Andrew Roth, meanwhile, had lost him in the crowd at Union Station. Hoover, who was following the progress of the dragnet on a minute-by-minute basis, was furious over this demonstration of incompetence. "Get facts promptly so appropriate disciplinary action can be taken," he ordered tersely.[26]

At 4:20, the hapless special agent, already targeted for demotion, ran into his quarry strolling down Jackson Place. Although, according to Larsen, Roth had been nervous and upset over the news that his transfer was being held up, he now struck the agents as almost cocky. Informed that he was under arrest, he quipped, "I knew the Navy didn't like my book but I never guessed they were going to throw it at me."[27]

As McInerney had anticipated, Roth insisted that all of the documents he had been seen delivering to Jaffe were chapters of his book or, in one instance, a draft of Ted Cohen's master's thesis. He explained that navy officers were forbidden to carry briefcases—a regulation the FBI men were apparently unaware of—and that, to avoid dirtying his uniform, he was in the habit of folding his daily paper inside a manila envelope.

Asked about his wife's trip to New York City, Roth said she had gone there to deliver sheet music. In light of what the FBI had already learned from its bugging of Jaffe's hotel room, other statements Roth made were clearly lies. For example, he denied ever being present when Larsen delivered papers to Jaffe. But the agents conducting the interrogation were unable to exploit these contradictions because they were apparently not familiar with the transcripts. In a 1985 interview with the authors, Roth recalled the agents' ineptitude as being almost laughable: "The stuff they raised in the interrogation was sort of infantile. Stuff like envelopes. And when they interrogated my wife, they asked, 'Do you know where your husband is?' as if she were a gangster's moll and I was sleeping with someone else."[28]

Roth added that during the following four days, while sitting in jail waiting for his wife and friends to raise bail, he racked his brains trying to imagine what the charges against him might be, without ever connecting his arrest to his conversation with Jaffe about espionage—a singular memory lapse.

By the time the word that Roth was in custody got through to the agents posted at the State Department, it was too late to catch Larsen and Service at work. Larsen did not get home from work until about 7:30, and a few minutes later, the agents who had been watching his apartment building knocked on his door. Realizing that the arresting officers intended to

Andrew Roth (*right*) in custody of the FBI following his arrest in Washington, D.C., in 1945. (UPI/The Bettmann Archive)

search the premises, Larsen led them to a bedroom closet and showed them a tall pile of government documents stored on one of the shelves. Among the papers the FBI took into custody were entire files on Tibet and Mongolia, background information on a number of Japanese political figures, and Larsen's own personality file.

At first, Larsen was cocky. His "gold badge" clearance from the State Department gave him the right to take papers from the office to work on at home, he told the agents. But when one of them pointed out that this couldn't account for the several hundred documents stacked in his closet, Larsen quickly crumbled, admitting that he had been exchanging information with Jaffe since March 1944. He even volunteered the information that Jaffe had been paying him and his wife an average of $75 a month for typing. Jaffe had never explicitly linked the money to the delivery of stolen documents, Larsen insisted all too candidly. "He was always very tactful that way."

Larsen rattled on that he understood "the enormous implications that can be ascribed to what I have said." Among other admissions, he said that he had shown Jaffe copies of a March 1945 report that Service had written about Yenan but that Jaffe already knew about it.[29]

While one FBI special agent was questioning Larsen, Jack Service had been brought to the office of the U.S. commissioner in handcuffs, guarded by a pair of U.S. marshals. Ironically, just a few hours earlier, while FBI agents were waiting at the State Department to take Service into custody, he had been keeping an appointment with Major Duncan Lee, a special assistant to General Donovan, who was trying to recruit Service into the OSS. Now he was shocked to learn that he was about to be charged under the espionage act. In contrast to Larsen, however, Service seemed calm, and when he learned that Philip Jaffe was also under arrest, he immediately volunteered to give a statement outlining their contacts. Service told his interrogator that he had long heard about Jaffe from mutual friends and that when he went to meet him for the first time, aware that Jaffe had been in Yenan, he took along his personal copy of a report summarizing a long conversation between himself and Mao Tse-tung. Later, he had given Jaffe more of his own reports—but only personal copies, which "did not contain any notations, comments, opinions, of any official character" pertaining to U.S. policy. Service recalled that Jaffe seemed to have a sense of "urgency" about acquiring copies of documents; he said Jaffe had offered him a job at *Amerasia* and had "suggested that I would not suffer financially." Guardedly, he admitted to having felt a "mild puzzlement" about Jaffe's motivations for their sudden friendship. As for Mark Gayn, Service had cooperated with him in the belief that Gayn was preparing a series of articles for the *Saturday Evening Post*. He was aware, however, that Gayn and Jaffe "worked closely together and shared all their information."[30]

A search of Service's office and the apartment where he was living temporarily had revealed nothing but a single scrap of outdated code. Even at this early stage of the investigation, the agents questioning Service realized they had very little hard evidence against him, but they saw him as a potentially valuable source of information. As the agents' official report put it, Service "decided that his own best interest was to look after himself and to have no scruples with regard to implicating others possibly involved. Service gave the impression during the latter part of his interview that he might wish to become a witness in the case against other subjects, particularly Jaffe, if by so doing it would be to his advantage."[31]

As in New York City, the press had been alerted to the impending arrests, and Service, Roth, and Larsen were placed together in the same waiting room, under the eyes of curious reporters, to await processing. Larsen, who happened to be next to Service, began speaking to him in Chinese. Service paled. There were reporters in the room, and the last thing he wanted was to be seen exchanging confidences in a foreign language with a codefendant. "Speak English," he snapped.[32]

Emmanuel Larsen, John Service, and Andrew Roth (*left to right*) awaiting arraignment in Washington, D.C., in 1945. (UPI/The Bettmann Archive)

Larsen was miffed. As far as he was concerned, he and Jack Service were in exactly the same situation, yet he interpreted Service's rebuff, no doubt correctly, as a signal that Service wanted to put as much distance between himself and Larsen as possible. Some hours later, Larsen called John Carter Vincent, another individual whom he thought might have been sympathetic to his plight, and received an even more stinging rejection. Informed that Larsen was calling him from the U.S. commissioner's office, Vincent had refused to even come to the phone, and the assistant who answered the call passed along Vincent's message that he "wouldn't touch Larsen with a ten foot pole."[33]

Later, as he was being transferred to his cell in the District jail, Larsen happened to run into an old acquaintance—FBI files don't say whether he was an inmate or an employee—to whom he complained bitterly that the individual in the State Department most responsible for giving out information, a man he described as "a high official and in the pay of Drew Pearson," had escaped arrest. Larsen also claimed that he knew the inside story of "the Pearl Harbor attack," a boast that suggests he may have been hoping to blackmail his way out of trouble.[34]

In Washington, too, the bail bondsmen had been warned by the FBI that the suspects were likely to try to flee the country. Jaffe, who had put up the cash bonds for Mitchell and Gayn, offered no assistance. The realization that Jaffe intended to drop them cold must have come as a severe shock to Roth and Larsen as they and Service sat in jail while their wives and friends did their best to raise bail.

Larsen was still in custody the next evening when the two FBI agents were ushered into his cell for a follow-up interview. By now, Larsen had an attorney who had warned him to stop volunteering self-incriminatory information, but in his pique at Jaffe, Larsen could not contain himself. He told the agents that he couldn't answer their questions right now but "had been giving the entire matter considerable thought and had mapped out a plan of attack." It had finally dawned on him that he had been "an unwitting tool," and once he had cleared his decision with his lawyer, the agents would be getting a phone call from him. An FBI supervisor concluded: "Maybe we can bargain with him."[35]

Two days later, Larsen was released on bond. On leaving the federal lockup, he gave a statement to the FBI thanking them for their "gentlemanly" treatment. But in a call he made from his home phone, where the FBI tap was still in place, he was less forgiving. "They break you to pieces," he told a friend. "They grill you, from 7 in the evening until 5:30 the next morning—how is that?—without dinner. They yanked me away from the dinner." What really made Larsen furious, he told this same friend, was that he was being linked to the Communists, whose influence in the State Department he had done his best to oppose, and he blamed his arrest on the FBI's need to thrust itself into the headlines in time to influence forthcoming congressional hearings that would determine the bureau's slice of the Justice Department budget.[36]

In an interview with a *New York Post* reporter, published on June 12, Larsen came up with another theory. His arrest, he said, was the result of a vendetta orchestrated by the pro-Japanese faction that had become dominant at the State Department under Joseph Grew, the former ambassador to Tokyo, who had just become acting secretary of state. "Maybe my crime is trying to mold policy that would set up China, not Japan, as the dominant power in the Far East after the war," Larsen speculated. "Maybe my mistake was lack of appreciation for the flower arrangers." Oddly enough, considering this tirade, Larsen had not yet been fired or suspended, and shortly after his release on bail, his official State Department identification badge, which entitled him to carry confidential papers, was returned to him.[37]

Emmanuel Larsen's claim that the *Amerasia* affair was essentially a political vendetta was already being echoed in the press. Initially, the newspapers had reported the arrests as a straight espionage story—even the Communist organ, the *Daily Worker*, had expressed no skepticism on that score—but within days, opinion began to split into two hostile camps. In William Randolph Hearst's *New York Journal-American*, Howard Rushmore led the chorus of praise for the FBI, lauding the arrests as "sensational proof that Communist organizers had access to highly confidential files of vital government agencies."[38]

First among the skeptics, as so often happened, was I. F. Stone, writing on behalf of the editors of the left-wing daily newspaper, *PM*. In an editorial published on June 8, Stone charged that the *Amerasia* arrests were nothing more than an effort to impose a de facto Official Secrets Act, stifling journalists opposed to the administration's policies. Like all government agencies, Stone noted, the State Department routinely leaked items to favored reporters. It was only to be expected that, in the midst of the hot debate brewing over China policy, "progressives" within the department would try to even the score. "Is the leak to be a right-wing monopoly?" Stone asked.[39]

This was a good question, and it was by no means irrelevant to the case. But it did not do justice to the government's motives. No details of what really prompted the *Amerasia* investigation had been released, and Stone based his assumptions on an unfortunate statement made by Acting Secretary of State Joseph Grew. Speaking on behalf of Edward Stettinius, whose resignation would soon become official, Grew had told the press that he wanted "to emphasize" that the *Amerasia* investigation was just "one result of a comprehensive security program which is to be continued unrelentingly in order to stop completely the illegal and disloyal conveyance of confidential information to unauthorized persons." This was not only impolitic, it was completely untrue. Far from being the first fruits of a new State Department security program, the arrest of Jaffe and the others was the result of evidence discovered accidentally and then dumped into Secretary Stettinius's lap.[40]

The press took Grew's statement as both a prediction and a threat. "War Secrets Leaks Widespread; Six Arrests May Be Only a Start," announced the *New York Herald Tribune*. "More Arrests Forecast in Spy Hunt," reported the *New York Daily Mirror*. In the meantime, Howard Rushmore, writing in the *New York Journal-American*, gleefully predicted that Grew was threatening not only to pursue leakers but also to expose additional "Red Higher Ups" in government agencies.[41]

Hours after Grew's press conference, Julius Holmes tried to reassure reporters that the case did not presage "any change in the Department's policy of making available to journalists all information possible." However, the damage had already been done. Once Grew had implied that this was only the first step in a general crackdown on the press and the use of leaks, it was difficult to tell nervous reporters otherwise.[42]

For that matter, even the defendants interpreted Grew's statement as an indication that they were the targets of a political vendetta, and it is little wonder that Jack Service, for example, was convinced that he had been set up by his conservative colleagues in the department. In fact, FBI files reveal that Grew had not known until after May 27, when the decision to move on the arrests was made, that Jack Service was under investigation. Subsequently, he had written Service a letter, saying how "inexpressibly shocked" he had been by Service's arrest.[43]

As the former ambassador to Tokyo and the leading exponent of a "soft peace" with Japan, Grew was already a controversial figure. He had been criticized regularly, and at times viciously, in the pages of *Amerasia*, and one article in particular, published in June 1944, had led to a long discussion between Grew and Jaffe over statements Grew deemed libelous. According to Grew, he dropped his complaint after Jaffe admitted that the article was unfair. Jaffe gave a different account of the outcome of the dispute, insisting that he had been told that a nephew of Grew's had later commented to a friend that "we'll get this guy Jaffe, no matter how long it takes."[44]

While stories of Grew's vindictiveness were largely exaggerated, the same could not be said of his protégé at the State Department, Eugene Dooman. Delighted by Service's arrest, Dooman told John Carter Vincent that he only hoped Service's friends would soon join him in jail— among them, Julian Friedman, who, Dooman claimed, was also guilty of leaking confidential information.[45]

As Washington insiders knew, Grew and Dooman were the primary targets of Andrew Roth's unpublished manuscript, so it is hardly surprising that they were suspected by some of taking advantage of the absence of Stettinius, who was in San Francisco attending the UN conference, to engineer the disgrace of their enemies. Though, in fact, it was Stettinius, working through Holmes, who had spurred the investigation, Grew was left behind in Washington to defend the results, and his ill-considered remarks inspired a torrent of negative commentary.

Some editorial responses to Grew's statement made I. F. Stone's reaction seem almost timid by comparison. The *New York Post*, for example, branded Grew a Japanese sympathizer. If Grew's attempt to "throttle" his critics succeeded, the *Post* predicted, then "any decent American newspaper . . . may be next on the list of Grew's State Department Gestapo."[46]

On June 9, even the moderate Republican *New York Herald Tribune* weighed in against Grew in an editorial entitled "Red Baiting." While insisting that the paper was making no judgment on the technical guilt or innocence of the accused, the editorial took the position that, unless there was more to the case than had been so far revealed, the State Department would have done better simply to fire the employees involved and beef up security procedures. As things now stood, left-wing employees at the State Department were being intimidated into "mouselike silence." This was particularly unfortunate, the editors went on, in view of the present need "to live in peace and amity in the same world with Soviet Russia."[47]

The *Herald Tribune* editorial failed to explain why simply firing Roth and Service would have been any less intimidating to government employees who shared their views. On the contrary, the charges of Redbaiting in the press made it clear that the State Department could not simply rid itself of inveterate leakers by firing them. Only a demonstration that the employees in question had actually done something illegal could protect the department from accusations of a political purge.

By the second week after the arrests, liberal radio commentators like J. Raymond Walsh, Max Lerner, Walter Winchell, and Drew Pearson had all broadcast denunciations of the *Amerasia* arrests, and the New York Newspaper Guild, meeting on June 13, condemned the prosecution as an attempt to stifle the sources necessary to "responsible journalism and intelligent public discussion." *Collier's* demonstrated its support for Mark Gayn by going ahead with the publication of his article on the American bombing of Japan, openly acknowledging that it was based on "confidential reports from various military and diplomatic sources." According to one survey, during the third week in June, 67 percent of newspapers nationwide disapproved of the arrests on a variety of grounds, claiming that the government's classification system was rigid and unreasonable, a threat to First Amendment freedoms, and that lack of action on previous violations made the system a dead letter.[48]

A few of the attacks appearing in the press stemmed from personal motives. Andrew Roth happened to be a personal friend of and occasional source for Drew Pearson's chief assistant David Karr. In retrospect, their relationship adds more fuel to suspicions about the motives and connec-

tions of the *Amerasia* defendants. David Karr was one of the more extraordinary and least well known personalities of this era.

Born in New York City in 1918, Karr, whose name was originally David
Katz, had been a reporter for the Communist *Daily Worker* before being
hired as a foreign language specialist in the OWI. In 1943 Representative
Martin Dies had uncovered Karr's Communist background, and despite a
subsequent House investigation that exonerated Karr of any wrongdoing,
he resigned from government service.

Karr's subsequent stint as Pearson's assistant was to be only a brief
episode in a colorful career. Joseph McCarthy denounced him on the
floor of the Senate in 1950 as Pearson's "KGB controller" and charged that
"Pearson's all-important job, which he did for the Party without fail, under
the direction of David Karr, was to lead the character assassination of any
man who was a threat to international communism." Karr worked for
several years as a public relations analyst in New York City, eventually
developing an expertise in using public relations techniques during hostile business takeovers. In 1959 Karr teamed up with a corporate raider to
capture the Fairbanks Whitney Corporation, a major defense contractor,
and became its CEO. Forced out by a stockholders' revolt three years later,
he became involved in a number of enterprises, including various Hollywood ventures, the Trusthouse Forte hotel chain, and Lazard Frères investment bankers, before teaming up with Armand Hammer in the early
1960s to encourage Western investment in the Soviet Union. Before the
1980 Moscow Olympics, Karr negotiated a contract giving him the marketing rights to Misha the Bear, the games' official mascot; he and Hammer
were also partners in marketing Olympic commemorative coins. Karr died
suddenly in Paris in 1979, whereupon his widow charged that he had been
assassinated by the KGB, allegedly for embezzling funds owed to the
Soviet government. A decade later, an article in the Russian press quoted
KGB documents describing Karr as a "competent source of the KGB" for
many years.[49]

In his capacity as Pearson's assistant, Karr had been instrumental in
obtaining the so-called Phillips letters, the basis of a major Pearson scoop in
mid-1944. Written by William Phillips, the American ambassador to India,
the letters expressed support for Indian independence and were critical of
British colonial policy. Although the letters were officially classified, the
Indian nationalist politician Obaidur Rahman had managed to obtain
copies from a source in the U.S. State Department, and during the summer
of 1944, he showed them around Washington, knowing that their contents

would embarrass the British government and pressure the Roosevelt administration into publicly endorsing an end to India's colonial status.

According to Andrew Roth, who told the story in an unpublished memoir, he first saw the letters at Rahman's home, where he was allowed to copy several of them by hand. Philip Jaffe happened to be in town that day, and when Roth showed up at his hotel with the letters, Jaffe wanted to make his own transcriptions immediately. Roth was hungry and the two of them were already late for a dinner engagement, so, knowing Jaffe's tendency to take hours to complete even the most simple tasks, Roth dropped his usual caution. Copies of the letters were already in the hands of Karr, and Pearson was about to break the story.[50]

"If Pearson has them, then they're already declassified," Roth told Jaffe.[51]

Thus reassured, Jaffe kept Roth's handwritten copies, which were subsequently recovered by the FBI at 225 Fifth Avenue. According to Roth, these were the only classified documents he ever gave Jaffe. Whether this is true or not, they were—with one exception—the only classified papers specifically linked to Roth by the FBI, and as such, they promised to be a key element in the legal case against him.

Drew Pearson was quick to note that Roth was being charged with espionage for releasing the very papers that he had first quoted in a published story. Not one to sit back and wait for potentially embarrassing revelations about Roth's dealings with David Karr, he went on the offensive. In his radio broadcast on June 9, Pearson predicted that the *Amerasia* case would "boomerang" against Grew and that "in the end it will be Grew and the other white-spatted gentlemen who will be forced to resign." Pearson also predicted that *Amerasia* would become "America's Dreyfus case" and, in his "Merry-Go-Round" column the following week, ascribed the arrests to a conflict between the KMT and the "so-called Chinese Communists (actually an agrarian party) in the north."[52]

Pearson's prediction that Grew's comments would boomerang proved to be a self-fulfilling prophecy. On June 16, after fifty years in government service, Joseph Grew tendered his resignation. James Byrnes was soon named by Truman to succeed Stettinius as secretary of state, and Dean Acheson, long a spokesman for the liberal faction at the State Department, became Grew's immediate replacement as undersecretary. Acheson, in turn, promoted John Carter Vincent to replace Grew's supporter Dooman as head of the Office of Far Eastern Affairs. Some years later, Grew would insist to a Senate subcommittee that his resignation had nothing to do with *Amerasia*. He was past due for retirement and was, in any case, in bad health. Nevertheless, Grew's friends in Washington felt that after half a century of loyal service he deserved a better farewell than he had received. With some justice, the conservatives noted that the liberal press, although quick to give the *Amerasia* suspects the benefit of the doubt, had been vicious in its treatment of Grew, who was not charged with anything. From day one of Acheson's and Vincent's tenure in their new positions, they were the obvious targets for the conservatives' retaliation. Senator McCarthy and his allies would later engage in shameful rhetoric, characterizing career officials at the State Department as pinkos and traitors. But it was Pearson who had first set the tone with his attacks on the "white-spatted gentlemen," Grew and Dooman.[53]

On the day before the newspaper guild vote, Frederick Woltman, a Pulitzer Prize–winning journalist whose pieces were syndicated by the Scripps-Howard newspaper chain, called a contact in the New York City field office of the FBI to warn that the *Amerasia* case was fast turning into a public relations disaster for the bureau. Another reporter, unidentified in the FBI's files, called Washington headquarters with a similar message, relaying the gist of his recent conversation with an American Civil Liberties Union official, probably Morris Ernst, who was highly distressed over the flap in the press. The American Civil Liberties Union had announced that it would not take a position on the arrests until it had more details on the charges, but pressure from the organization's members was becoming difficult to resist.[54]

J. Edgar Hoover prided himself on his mastery of the art of public relations. During the war, the bureau had largely been spared adverse criticism in the press except from a few gadflies like Pearson, making it easy for Hoover to dismiss the negative comments that did appear as the work of cranks or radicals. The director was genuinely unaware of how deeply the mainstream press resented the FBI's public information policies, and even at this point, the possibility that the bureau might have a special credibility problem with regard to the *Amerasia* case did not seem to have occurred to him. Hoover's response to the flap was to put all the blame on the State Department, which undoubtedly had mishandled the press's inquiries. In the margin of his copy of a piece that I. F. Stone had written on the case for the *Nation*, Hoover wrote, "It is too bad that the State Department is making a field day of this." He then called Assistant Attorney General McGranery to complain that off-the-record press conferences by State Department officials had led the news commentators "to believe that freedom of speech is involved." Hoover repeated this complaint a few days later in a meeting with a Scripps-Howard executive, Lee Woods, who had come to him seeking assurances that the newspaper chain would not be made to look foolish—or worse, subject itself to libel suits—by continuing to defend the government's actions. Hoover told the worried Woods that the negative criticism had come about because the FBI had been "allowing the State Department to carry the ball and they muffed it." However, there was nothing to worry about because the case against the six subjects was "airtight."[55]

Still, as Hoover well knew, the big break the FBI had been counting on had failed to materialize. Jaffe, though caught red-handed, so to speak, was in a combative mood and showed every indication that he intended to plead not guilty. The search of Roth's home had proved unproductive—either because he was tipped off by the delay of his transfer to Hawaii, as Emmanuel Larsen would later allege, or because he had been too cautious to get directly involved in the transfer of classified papers, as Roth insists. However, as might have been predicted, Roth's attorney was already saying publicly that the fact that his client was being charged as a civilian proved that the navy felt he was being prosecuted unjustly.[56]

Mark Gayn's case had been grievously mishandled, justifying James McInerney's fears that it was a mistake to target him for arrest. Although Gayn had admitted breaking the law and might have welcomed the chance to disassociate himself from Jaffe, the agents who questioned him had done nothing to follow up on this possibility. Now that Jaffe had paid Gayn's bail and was planning a joint legal strategy for all three New York City defendants, the government's determination to take a hard line was backfiring.

The bungling of the interrogations was even more apparent in the case of Emmanuel Larsen. Although Larsen's subsequent history would reveal that he was a man highly susceptible to flattery—not to mention one who took an almost masochistic delight in confession—his interrogators had somehow failed to push the right buttons. Now Larsen was out on bail and had passed the word to State Department colleagues that a Chinese friend was prepared to provide $10,000, which he intended to use to put up a vigorous defense. Also, Larsen had somehow figured out that his apartment had been illegally entered and had managed to get his building superintendent, E. R. Sager, to admit that he had allowed the FBI to tap the Larsens' phone.

Within the Justice Department, there was concern that Larsen's attorney would use this information to persuade a judge to exclude much of the evidence seized at his apartment, making it all but impossible to bring him to trial. But Sager had refused to sign a statement confirming the FBI's presence on the scene, so, for the moment, that threat was in abeyance and the Justice Department went ahead with plans to present the case to a grand jury. A week after the arrests, Attorney General Tom Clark arranged to have Robert Hitchcock, a young assistant U.S. attorney from upstate New York, come to Washington to take over the case. A few years earlier, as an assistant in the Eastern District of New York, Hitchcock had prosecuted members of the German-American Bund, and his courtroom experience in this case was said to be the major reason for the appointment.

In the basement evidence room at FBI headquarters, meanwhile, a team of agents was sifting through a mountain of papers. There were 1,722 documents in all, enough to fill fifteen file drawers.[57]

This total is somewhat misleading because almost 800 of the papers in question were not stolen documents at all—some had been seized from the State Department desks of the suspects, for example, and were being held only because they might have potential value as corroborating evidence. Hundreds of the remaining 928 documents were found to be either unclassified or of so little importance that their classification was a technicality. The presence of so many unrestricted papers did not prove Jaffe's innocence—as he himself once told Roth, the bulk of every "intelligence agent's" stock in trade was "junk"—and in any event, there was plenty of raw material for making an espionage case. According to a breakdown of the documents found in Jaffe's office submitted to Hoover on June 11, the papers examined to that date had included one "Top Secret" report, one classified as very secret, and seven OSS documents that bore warnings on their cover pages that they contained information related to national defense and that "the transmission or the revelation of [the] contents in any manner to unauthorized persons is prohibited by law."[58]

FBI investigators further estimated that 27.7 percent of the 202 documents seized at Emmanuel Larsen's apartment concerned military matters, as did 16.7 percent of those found in the *Amerasia* offices—a figure strikingly reminiscent of Jaffe's complaint that only 15 percent of all classified documents were of any importance. Among the documents seized at Jaffe's office were 1942 and 1943 military intelligence reports on the Chinese Order of Battle, an air force intelligence report on airplane and seaplane anchorages in Thailand, a confidential navy memo on counterintelligence work done by the ONI, a secret War Department memo on the disposition of the Japanese air force, military intelligence reports on supply routes to China and the Chinese air force staff, a dispatch from General Claire Chennault listing enemy aircraft destroyed and requesting replacements for his own lost craft, and "a June, 1942 listing of key airfields in China, Formosa and Korea which included descriptions of their facilities."[59]

In retrospect, one of the most damning signs of Jaffe's intentions was his card file on Chinese personalities, which included some information from Larsen. Although not seized by the FBI, the card file, far from being limited to biographical background on obscure warlords, was a who's who of secret agents in China, Russian émigrés, and other individuals likely to be of more interest to spies than to journalists. A notation on one card indicated that the subject would be "good with codes"; another observed that the subject "would be available for work in demolition." The cards even contained instructions on how the subjects should be approached. But this information, as suggestive as it was, did not bear any notations indicating that it came from government files or sources.[60]

Unfortunately, the more clearly a document relates to national security, the more likely the issuing agency is to object to using it in court. One of the more worrisome documents in the *Amerasia* haul was an OSS memo that had been recovered during the first black bag raid. The memo outlined the disposition of the Japanese fleet after the battle of Midway and was clearly based on deciphered Japanese radio transmissions.

Speculation that the ONI had broken the Japanese naval code was by now an old story and had already figured prominently in the debate over American unpreparedness before Pearl Harbor. In fact, there had already been one abortive attempt to prosecute a journalist for leaking the information. Shortly after the battle of Midway, Stanley Johnston of the *Chicago Tribune* wrote a major story revealing that advance knowledge of Japanese tactics had made the victory possible. The navy was so alarmed by Johnston's disclosure that it asked the Justice Department to prosecute Johnston for espionage. The case was put before a grand jury but fizzled when the navy's witnesses refused to explain why the information in Johnston's article would be useful to the enemy.[61]

Although by mid-1945 the role the code breakers had played at Midway was fairly well known—Walter Winchell had mentioned the rumor in several columns and Congressman Elmer J. Holland had discussed it in a speech on the floor of the House—the navy still considered code breaking

a taboo subject, and prosecutor Robert Hitchcock was informed that th
Midway memo could not be used in the grand jury proceedings or ii
court. Similar restrictions would apply to the Wells memo on Thailand—
keeping it secret had been the motive for recovering it in the first place—
and, in fact, to all the memos most likely to impress a jury with the
seriousness of Jaffe's offense. This was the familiar catch-22 of espionage
prosecutions: to convict those who steal secrets, one has to reveal the
secrets themselves. Moreover, these two items would raise the issue of
illegally seized evidence.[62]

Reduced to relying on the dregs of the evidence, Myron Gurnea's team
was working hard, trying to trace the paper trail to reveal how documents
had made their way from agency files to Jaffe. Despite the fact that everyone was putting in long hours, the investigation was floundering. In one
instance, Gurnea's agents were taken aback to discover that Elizabeth
Barker, Mark Gayn's source at the OWI, was prepared to testify that when
Gayn asked her for material, she "made an ad hoc declassification." Barker's supervisor, George Taylor, maintained that Gayn should not have
been allowed to physically remove documents from Barker's office; therefore she may have exceeded her authority. However, Barker had operated
in this manner throughout the war, and she was ready to say so in court.[63]

As of June 18, three days before Hitchcock was scheduled to present his
case to the grand jury, the FBI was still working its painstaking way
through an expanded list of sixty-two leads. But with little sophistication
and less time or resources, not to mention the sensitivity of some of the
evidence, the agents were worried. Some promising leads could not be
investigated. The FBI wanted to interview Chi Ch'ao-ting, Jaffe's cousin,
but he had left the country with his boss, KMT finance minister H. H.
Kung. The Bernstein lead was temporarily in abeyance. There was a
prima facie case of unauthorized possession of government documents
against Jaffe, Mitchell, Larsen, and Gayn, but even though several documents could be linked to all four, the paper trail would be complicated
and confusing to a jury.[64]

Just as frustrating was the thinness of the evidence against Andrew Roth.
Roth's role as a scout for Jaffe may have been no one's idea of proper
behavior for an intelligence officer, but aside from the Phillips letters, the
only classified information that could definitely be traced to him consisted
of some notes on the Japanese labor movement given to him by John
Carter Vincent's assistant, Julian Friedman. Friedman did not deny that
he and Roth had exchanged information. The notes he had given Roth

were for his book, Friedman told the bureau, and in any case, they were "mostly, if not entirely from public sources." In return, Roth had shown him a memo about a conference between Wedemeyer and Hurley that came, he said, from "a source close to the White House."[65]

Egged on by Eugene Dooman, who was convinced that Friedman was responsible for passing on insider accounts of confidential State Department meetings, the FBI invested considerable resources in trying to build a case against Friedman. But their digging pointed to nothing more serious than violations of executive branch regulations on the exchange of information—the sort of thing that went on every day in offices throughout Washington.[66]

If Andrew Roth could somehow be persuaded to testify about Joseph Bernstein, Philip Jaffe would be in very serious trouble. However, without more damaging evidence against Roth, the government would never be able to convince him to become a witness against Jaffe. Larsen had clearly given classified information to Jaffe and might be willing to cut a deal. Another defendant who might have a strong motive to testify against his codefendants was John Stewart Service. And he had friends who had no desire to see the case against him come to trial or to see him honestly answering questions about what he had been up to.

Corcoran for the Defense

As Jack Service sat in the District jail waiting for his wife and sister-in-law to raise bail, he was in shock. The spectacle of a government official being hauled off to jail was by no means as common in 1945 as it would become four decades later, and Service was "overwhelmed with disgrace and shame."[1] After his release on bail, some old acquaintances shunned him, and although his colleagues at the State Department quietly expressed sympathy, Service was bitter over their failure to warn him away from Philip Jaffe. He had made no secret around the office of his meetings with *Amerasia*'s editor, and, assuming that knowledge of the FBI investigation was more widespread than it in fact had been, he wondered why none of his superiors had taken the trouble to warn him off.

Ironically, however, Service's arrest had set the stage for the very public debate on China policy that he had been hoping to provoke. Within a few days, in the wake of the *New York Herald Tribune* editorial and other sympathetic press commentary, offers of help and advice began to trickle in. Everyone anticipated a long, hard-fought, and well-publicized trial, with Service's reports from China figuring prominently as evidence.

General Joseph Stilwell, for one, told Service he was ready and willing to be called as a defense witness. Since his recall as head of the China-Burma theater of operations, Stilwell had been under a gag order that prohibited him from giving his version of the quarrel with Chiang Kai-shek. A subpoena to testify as a defense witness for Service would give him the platform he longed for.

At first, Service was defiant. He considered resigning his government post and hiring one of several prominent civil rights attorneys who had expressed an interest in defending him—using his trial, in his words, "to raise a stink." Such talk alarmed his friends, particularly Lauchlin Currie, John Carter Vincent, and James K. Penfield, Vincent's assistant, and they hastened to assure him that such drastic measures were unnecessary and ill-advised. As Service explained in a letter to Stilwell: "A knock-down, drag-out court fight" might be a lot of fun because of the chance to get some things out into the open. But it would "pull in a great many people who now hold important jobs," and it would almost certainly finish his career in the State Department.[2]

In line with his friends' advice, Service provisionally hired a Washington attorney, the ultrarespectable Godfrey Munter, an officer of the District of Columbia Bar Association, who advised him that his best bet might be to try to overturn any forthcoming indictment on a series of technicalities. Munter pointed out that the warrant issued for Service's arrest did not specifically give the government the right to conduct a search and that the FBI had acted improperly in seizing personal papers from Service's desk at the State Department. Munter also suggested that Service could claim that the statement he gave the bureau at the time of his arrest had been obtained under duress and that, in any case, the copies of his reports that he had given to Jaffe were his personal property, not the government's.

In the meantime, although Service was not yet aware of it, Lauchlin Currie was already working on another strategy. Service later claimed that Currie felt "obligated to me because I [had been] writing letters to him from China; he was using us as leakers to speak to people like Drew

Pearson and to spread any news he wanted to spread about China, and h
felt obligated and involved when we were arrested for talking too freely."[3]

But Lauchlin Currie possibly had another motive as well. In November
1945 Elizabeth Bentley, an unassuming Vassar College graduate, told the
FBI that she had served as a courier for a Soviet espionage ring throughout
the war. Bentley named dozens of past and present government employees
from whom she received information to pass along to the Soviet Union.
Although she admitted that she had never met him, she identified Lauchlin Currie as a source of information and a "friend at court" who helped
other members of her ring. Currie's name did not surface publicly until
1948, when Bentley testified before the House Un-American Activities
Committee (HUAC). After being accused, Currie appeared before
HUAC, categorically denied the charges, and then left the United States
for Colombia, eventually becoming a citizen of that country. He did not
return to the United States for many years. If Lauchlin Currie was a Soviet
agent, a highly publicized trial that trumpeted his role in attempting to
undermine the Nationalist Chinese government or called attention to his
left-wing protégés in government would certainly not be in his interest.[4]

Currie's first move was to call Ben Cohen, the State Department's legal
counsel and a longtime friend. The two men agreed that the best course
would be to enlist the aid of the capital's premier fixer, Thomas Corcoran.

Corcoran and Cohen had been associated since 1933, when they
worked together to push New Deal legislation through Congress. Cohen,
the intellectual, detail-oriented member of the team, had been largely
responsible for drafting such key bills as the Security Exchange Act of
1934, the National Housing Act, the enabling legislation for the Tennessee
Valley Authority, and the Fair Labor Standards Act. Corcoran, by contrast,
was a mover and shaker. A blue-eyed, strapping Irishman who had gradu-
ated from Harvard Law School and clerked for Oliver Wendell Holmes,
he lived with a group of bachelor friends who shared a Georgetown mansion known as the "Little Red House," where Corcoran entertained at
parties by playing the baby grand piano. When his abundant charm failed
to bring congressmen around, "Tommy the Cork" was not above resorting
to arm-twisting. As one biographer of Roosevelt noted, "Corcoran got the
job done, but sometimes it was best not to ask how."[5]

Over time, Corcoran's activities made powerful enemies who blocked
his ambition to become solicitor general or undersecretary of the navy,
and his skill at political manipulation made him cynical. In 1940 Corcoran
left the government for private practice. Although he preferred to describe

Ben Cohen (*left*) and Thomas Corcoran testifying before a Senate committee in 1935.
(UPI/The Bettmann Archive)

himself as a "lawyer entrepreneur," the chief business of Corcoran's law firm was lobbying, and the skills he had once used to promote the legislative program of his idol, Franklin Roosevelt, were increasingly employed on behalf of the same big business clients he had once opposed during his days as the enfant terrible of New Deal Washington. Corcoran's specialty was helping corporations evade wartime quotas, price restrictions, and the very public-interest regulations he had been instrumental in bringing into being. His usual mode of operation, as one historian has noted, was the "triple play," arranging for two clients to trade favors while he received compensation for his efforts in some roundabout manner that was both tax-free and untraceable.[6]

Soon after he took office in the spring of 1945, President Truman became suspicious that Corcoran and other former Roosevelt aides were plotting against his administration, and he ordered the FBI to tap Corcoran's office phones. The tap remained in place for five years and picked up evidence of more than a few illegal deals, none of which could be prosecuted because the tap itself was illegal. Quite by accident, one of the first triple plays that the phone tap recorded was Corcoran's effort to throw a monkey wrench into the *Amerasia* prosecution.

In contrast to Corcoran, Ben Cohen had never lost faith in the aims of

the New Deal, and his reputation for financial probity was above re-
proach. Although he was wealthy, having made millions in the stock
market during the 1920s, Cohen was well known for his complete lack of
interest in material possessions. Since 1944, he had dedicated himself to
promoting the cause of the UN, which he saw as the best hope for defusing
cold war tensions, and his motive in calling Corcoran on June 10 was
probably to protect the Department of State from a scandal that could
jeopardize the chances of getting congressional approval for the UN charter and to accommodate a request from his old friend Currie.

Corcoran's reasons for getting involved were no doubt less altruistic,
though over the next several days, it became clear that his immediate goal
was to make sure that Service had no intention of turning his defense into
a political cause célèbre—or, as Corcoran put it, to make sure that Service
did not become involved with others who would be "yelling and scream-
ing about civil rights." Bright and early the next morning, June 11, Corcoran was on the phone to an unidentified Washington acquaintance,
prying him for information about Service's attorney, Godfrey Munter.
Munter, Corcoran's friend assured him, was "a high class man," in fact,
the president of the District of Columbia Bar Association.[7]

"Is he a Swedish fellow or is he a Jewish fellow?" Corcoran asked.

Corcoran was relieved to hear that Munter was Scandinavian. "Is he a
Red?" he pressed on.

No, the friend said. If anything, he was "on the conservative side."

"Well, with any kind of handling at all, he can win this one," Corcoran
said. The key was to "let the other fellows do the jumping up and down
and let him [Service] slip out."

Corcoran emphasized that he was not "the slightest interested in the
principle of the thing" but only wanted "to get my fellow and my friend
out."

In that case, his unnamed informant said cryptically, the best course
would be to "kind of watch it, and if things get to the place where you need
a little more power, chuck somebody in."

Presently, Corcoran called Lauchlin Currie directly to reassure him
about Munter. Currie told Corcoran that several well-known civil rights
attorneys had offered to represent Service, but Corcoran responded that
these men were all wrong for the case because they were identified with
"lost causes." The goal should be "to get the guy out," but these attorneys
would be interested in "making a Dreyfus case out of it."

"The Dreyfus case was wonderful for the lawyers and tough on Dreyfus," mused Corcoran. "Let someone else go up and be hanged for the wearing of the green."

"I am not going to let them push this kid around," he promised Currie. "If we have to get to the ulcer-in-the-stomach stage, I will be very much tempted to step in and sock myself without charging for it." But, Corcoran added, he felt sure the case would never be tried. His approach was going to be to "work around the edges of this thing for a day or so and see if I can liquidate the whole damn thing."

Despite his talk of stepping in to represent Service, Corcoran had a conflict that made it advisable for him to keep his involvement secret. As he reminded Currie, he could "not afford to be out front" on the matter "because of the interest of other clients that I have got in the State Department." No doubt Corcoran was referring to his position as an officer of China Defense Supplies, a private company that had been formed to channel American aid to the Chinese Nationalists. Corcoran was a director and legal counsel of the company, his former law partner was president, Roosevelt's uncle was a director, and T. V. Soong, the financier and Chiang Kai-shek's brother-in-law, was the power behind the scenes.[8]

One would think that T. V. Soong, of all people, would be rejoicing over the *Amerasia* arrests. After all, the magazine best known for its criticism of Chiang and the KMT and its support for the Communists had been exposed as a front for Soviet espionage, a charge that would inevitably cast a cloud of suspicion over the Nationalists' American critics. Corcoran, of course, was quite capable of playing one client against another. But he and his family had a substantial investment in China Defense Supplies, and it would have been most uncharacteristic of him to work against his own financial interests in order to do a favor for a friend of a friend, even at the request of an old buddy like Cohen.

Jack Service first learned of Corcoran's involvement a week or so later when Currie suggested he call Corcoran for an appointment, and he was immediately suspicious. As he wrote in a 1950 memo to his attorney: "This seemed like going into the enemy's lair." Currie told Service that while he didn't want to pressure him, he felt sure that Corcoran's advice would be given as a friend and would not be influenced in any way by his business connection with Soong. Service consulted Vincent, who agreed that Service might be well advised to stop relying on "amateurs" such as himself. Corcoran might not be able to help, but he certainly couldn't do any harm. Service, still not entirely convinced, decided to take a few days to think it over.[9]

Corcoran, however, was already carrying out his plan to "work around the edges" of the case. Attorney general designate Tom Clark was facing a potential confirmation fight, with his toughest opposition coming from Senators Burton Wheeler and Kenneth Wherry. On June 11, just hours after talking to Currie, Corcoran called Clark to assure him that, in the words of an FBI summary of the phone call, "arrangements were being completed whereby his nomination would not be opposed." The next day, Corcoran called Clark again. Senator Wheeler was in Europe, he informed Clark, and Senator Wherry was "all for him," so he had nothing to worry about. Myron Gurnea summed up these conversations bluntly in an FBI memo: "It is obvious that Corcoran is making every effort to develop Tom Clark and by inference has taken the credit for having Tom Clark's nomination approved by the Senate committee."[10]

Even though, so far, Service had not agreed to accept Corcoran's help, Corcoran was already behaving as if he were in control of Service's case. Over the next several days, he spoke to several attorneys about replacing Munter. One actually agreed to take the case but had to back out after he discovered an unspecified "ethical conflict" that would make his participation impossible.

In the meantime, while Corcoran was attempting to convince Tom Clark that he owed him a favor, Kate Mitchell and Philip Jaffe were also bringing political influence to bear on their cases. Jaffe had engaged Arthur Scheinberg, whose law partner, Emmanuel Celler, was a Brooklyn congressman well known for his progressive politics and political clout. As for Mitchell, her uncle, James McCormick Mitchell, a wealthy Republican attorney from Buffalo, had arranged for her to be represented by Lowell Wadmond, another prominent member of the New York bar. The FBI's tap on Mitchell's phone, still in place, provided the bureau with a running account of Wadmond's efforts on her behalf.

On June 20, Wadmond spoke to Arthur Scheinberg, who had just come from a conference at the Justice Department with Attorney General Clark, James McInerney, and Robert Hitchcock. According to Scheinberg, Clark had surprised everyone by suggesting that the charge of conspiracy to commit espionage might be dropped and the defendants indicted for the lesser crime of embezzlement and illegal receipt of government property —a possible concession that came as news to the FBI.

Attorney General Tom Clark. (UPI/The Bettmann Archive)

Wadmond reached Clark late that same afternoon and pleaded with him not to take any action until he had a chance to talk to him privately. Clark reminded him that all six defendants were scheduled to appear before the U.S. commissioners the following Monday for their preliminary hearings. The Justice Department was eager to dispense with the hearings since it would be required to disclose, at least in outline, the nature of the evidence against the defendants. Clark offered a deal. If Wadmond would talk the other defendants into adjourning the hearings, he would have Hitchcock go before the grand jury but "seal the indictments so that nobody will know anything about it."[11]

Although the purpose of this maneuvering was never made explicit, it would appear that Wadmond was hoping to get better treatment for his client at the expense of one or more of the other defendants, most likely Andrew Roth. Roth's attorney was particularly eager for the preliminary hearing to go ahead so that he could glean some idea of the scope of the evidence. Under Clark's plan, however, the hearings would no longer be necessary. In return, Clark would hold on to the indictments until Wadmond had a chance to meet with him personally and discuss Mitchell's situation.

Hitchcock began presenting evidence to the grand jury on the morning of June 21, just two weeks after the suspects were taken into custody. In a single day's session, the grand jurors heard testimony from 18 witnesses, 14 of them from the FBI, 2 from the State Department, and 1 from the OWI. The other witness was Philip Jaffe's typist, Annette Blumenthal.

That evening an FBI agent spoke to Hitchcock. He reported that the prosecutor was confident that all six of the defendants would be quickly indicted on charges of embezzlement of government property. The more serious charge of conspiracy to commit espionage would await the expected cooperation of at least one of the six. The records of the grand jury have never been made public, but apparently it voted indictments that Tom Clark then never bothered to file, a highly unusual, if not unethical, action.[12]

Clark's next move, six days later, was to call a meeting with the attorneys for Jaffe, Mitchell, and Gayn at the Justice Department. Also present were McInerney and Hitchcock, as well as Representative Emmanuel Celler of Brooklyn. These attorneys represented the defendants who were members of the press, as opposed to government employees, and they jointly argued that their clients had merely been pursuing sources, as any journalist would do under the circumstances. As Robert Hitchcock later recalled, the defense attorneys also stressed how embarrassing it would be for the Department of Justice if it indicted representatives of the press and then failed to make the charges stick. Hitchcock then mentioned that the grand jury's term was scheduled to expire on July 2. Instead of extending its life, Wadmond suggested, Hitchcock should start all over again, presenting the case to a new grand jury later in the summer.[13]

Normally, the purpose of such prosecutorial tactics would be to obtain plea bargains from the defendants or to arrange an agreement for one or more of them to cooperate with the grand jury. Gayn's lawyer clearly assumed this was what was going on, and he suggested that it would be possible for him to have Gayn "plead something or other to some sort of indictment." Wadmond volunteered nothing at the time, but two days later he called Tom Clark with an offer of his own: he was prepared to write a letter requesting the opportunity to produce his client, Mitchell, before the new grand jury.[14]

This was exactly the sort of break the FBI had been hoping for. Mitchell had worked closely with the documents Jaffe collected in his office; she knew the details of his comings and goings. She had also worked with Joseph Bernstein when he was on the staff at *Amerasia*. What's more, according to the transcript of one of Jaffe's conversations with Roth,

Mitchell knew about a previous attempt by a Soviet agent to recruit Jaffe. Much to Jaffe's distress, the overture had come to nothing because Mitchell, who had received the phone call from the agent while Jaffe was away on a business trip, had turned the offer down flat.

Hitchcock either had never read this transcript or was uninterested in pursuing the matter. Wadmond's claim that his client was an employee who knew little of Jaffe's private business was taken at face value. Hitchcock suddenly lost interest in using the threat of an indictment on a charge of unauthorized possession of government documents to compel Mitchell to talk. Now his main concern seemed to be to avoid disconcerting one of the defendants, and he offered to give Mitchell a preview of the questions he would ask her under oath "so that she would know just what I was going to ask her because I wouldn't want to take her to the grand jury cold. I don't think it would be fair to her."

After Hitchcock hung up, Wadmond called Kate Mitchell to tell her the good news. Although Tom Clark had specifically told the attorneys present at the meeting on June 27 that there had been no indictments as yet, Wadmond told Mitchell a different story. Wadmond explained to her that "the indictment which has been returned, but which has not yet been filed by this grand jury," would be allowed to die as the result of the deal he had worked out. More surprisingly, Wadmond suggested to Mitchell that, despite the deal, she might never have to testify at all. "I'd like to be in a position where you could, more or less, tell me that you didn't want to go before the grand jury."

Mitchell was amazed at her good fortune. How had her attorney managed to work things out so well?

Said Wadmond, "I'll let you read between the lines anything that you want to read—I remember back in college an old English professor of mine said, 'Never say the obvious.'"[15]

It would seem that there were now two unrelated strains of political pressure operating on Tom Clark. Corcoran was working behind the scenes to help Service, while two influential New Yorkers, Emmanuel Celler and James Mitchell, had combined their influence to arrange advantageous deals for Jaffe and Mitchell. A possible link between the two camps is suggested by the fact that shortly after his first conversations with Corcoran, Clark had decided to pass over the president's choice for special prosecutor—Hugh Fulton—and to put Robert Hitchcock in charge of the case.

Despite his experience in handling the Bundists' prosecution, Hitchcock, as a newcomer to the capital, was a strange choice to direct the prosecution of a major case that would inevitably involve testimony about procedures for handling confidential documents in a number of government agencies. Moreover, Hitchcock would later tell a congressional committee that he was never particularly impressed by the evidence in the case, an admission that, if true, makes his selection even stranger. On the other hand, Hitchcock had formerly been an assistant U.S. attorney in Brooklyn—Emmanuel Celler's bailiwick. Just prior to being summoned to Washington, he had been assigned to the federal prosecutor's office in Buffalo, where James Mitchell's law firm represented many clients who appeared in federal court. Also, like Corcoran, he happened to be a devout Roman Catholic active in church affairs.

Whether Hitchcock fully understood his new assignment is another matter. Despite his subsequent statements to congressional committees, he had initially delved into the case with enthusiasm. On June 21, after his first encounter with the grand jury, he had reported to the FBI that he expected to obtain embezzlement indictments against all six defendants and to pursue conspiracy charges as soon as a decision was made about the preliminary hearings. Yet one week later, even as several of the suspects were coming forward with offers to testify, Hitchcock suddenly turned pessimistic.[16]

J. Edgar Hoover was monitoring Hitchcock's mood shifts with mounting suspicion. "I don't like all this manipulation," he scrawled across the bottom of one memo that apprised him of the June 27 meeting between Tom Clark, Celler, and the various defense attorneys. Two weeks later, he was even more disgusted to learn that Hitchcock had agreed to give the defense attorneys access "to the documents that [the Department of Justice] planned to show the grand jury"—without extracting any promises of cooperation in return. "Of course give every assistance necessary," Hoover wrote, "but it looks to me as if it is hard to tell whether govt. is representing the govt. or the defendants."[17]

Like Mitchell, Jack Service had to decide whether to testify before the grand jury. On June 26, after a conference with James McInerney, Godfrey Munter reported to Service that the government basically had no case against him. His best bet, Munter advised, would be to go before the grand jury, answer all the questions it put to him, and clear the air. Although Munter never claimed to have made a deal on Service's behalf, he hinted that McInerney had no intention of pushing for an indictment.

Service was inclined to agree with Munter. But before making a final commitment, he decided that he might as well take his friends' advice and see Corcoran. The meeting, also attended by Lauchlin Currie, took place in Corcoran's office on June 29. Disconcertingly, as soon as Service was seated, Corcoran began conducting a mock cross-examination.

Why had he given papers to Jaffe and not to some other journalist?

Why had he met with him so often? Why in his hotel room and not some public place?

If he hadn't known Mark Gayn before, why had he stayed at Gayn's apartment in New York City?

The interrogation made Service realize for the first time just how easy it would be for a determined prosecutor to cast his actions in an incriminating light. This was precisely what Corcoran intended to demonstrate. But after this tension-filled preliminary, Corcoran loosened up. He wanted no payment for helping out and sought nothing in return, he told Service. He was just getting involved as a favor to "your good friend, Ben."

In fact, Service had never met Ben Cohen, and he was more than a little uneasy about Corcoran's well-known financial involvement in China Defense Supplies. But when he asked about the "Chinese connection," Corcoran responded brusquely that it would "make no difference" in how he approached the case. Nevertheless, Service was impressed with Corcoran; he was, after all, a man who could pick up the phone and dial the attorney general of the United States, a man who wanted to help get him out of his legal mess and asked for nothing in return.

Impressed that he was now in "thoroughly competent hands," Service agreed to turn over "direction of the case" to Corcoran. Godfrey Munter remained his counsel of record, quite unaware that his client was dealing with another adviser.[18]

One way or another, Corcoran soon managed to learn a good deal about the nature of the government's evidence. "I've been working on your little Chinese friend," he reported during a July 4 phone call to Ben Cohen. "Your boy friend has been all right now, but the rest of them have been pretty stinkin."[19]

"Most of these guys," Corcoran went on, "have been on the payroll at 75 dollars a month."

Cohen, incredulous, asked if Jaffe's other contacts were "really getting money."

Corcoran said they were (though actually only Larsen was taking money), but Service "just happened to be a sucker that was in the line of fire."

"Justice ought to be more careful," mused Cohen.

A new grand jury was sworn in during the last week of July, and Munter had tentatively scheduled Service for an appearance on July 30. Corcoran, however, was not satisfied. On July 24, he called Service to report: "I talked to the Attorney General yesterday and again I told him the understanding we had below about the cutting out of your name, so there wouldn't be any necessity of your going before the Grand Jury at all." Clark had promised to call back with his decision, and when he didn't respond quickly enough, Corcoran kept badgering Clark, his secretary, and Assistant Attorney General McGranery with phone calls on behalf of "my guy . . . who was just on the tag end of everything."

Service, Corcoran told McGranery, was "an awfully close friend of Ben's." And Ben, he added, was hoping that Service's case could be put on hold until after he returned from a scheduled trip to Europe. Once he was back at the State Department, Ben was sure "he would straighten this Service thing out."

Corcoran's main concern was that if Service talked to the grand jury and Jaffe and some of the other defendants were indicted for conspiracy to commit espionage, Service would eventually have to testify against them in open court. "If that guy is ever a witness in this thing," he warned McGranery in another conversation, "he is through with the State Department."

McGranery admitted that turning Service into a government witness was exactly what some people had in mind. Anyway, the general feeling was that Service deserved "a little kick in the pants."

During the course of the discussion, Corcoran apologized for twisting McGranery's arm. "I have never done this before in my life," he insisted disingenuously.

"Neither have I," McGranery responded. "It's the lousiest thing."[20]

For whatever reasons—such as Corcoran's help with Clark's confirmation problems or pressure in some other form—Clark and McGranery were persuaded to let Service off the hook. Not only would he not be subpoenaed as a government witness at the trial, but he would not have to appear before the grand jury. However, they had trouble selling Robert Hitchcock on this arrangement. Although he had agreed not to ask for Service's indictment, Hitchcock had no faith in his ability to control the grand jury. If Service didn't appear and make a good impression, he insisted, the grand jurors might insist on indicting him. Here was a novel situation: a prosecutor doing his best to prevent a grand jury from indicting a suspect and refusing to use the prospect of indictment to compel him to testify against his codefendants.

Service's testimony was postponed against Hitchcock's advice, but on July 30, the reluctant prosecutor informed the FBI that none of the six suspects would be government witnesses against any of the others. In addition, Service could be expected to escape prosecution entirely. Hitchcock volunteered that he intended to "present all sides" of Service's situation and let matters take their course. "We are not the ones who will fail to indict him," he noted lamely. "It is the grand jury that will do so."[21]

That same day, Hitchcock spoke to Service personally, assuring him that he had nothing to fear from the grand jury. Service was ready to testify, but Corcoran was adamant. "The signals have gone down that you are not to be in the thing," he told Service. But for some reason the message had failed to pass down the line to Hitchcock: "It takes a long time to permeate those instructions."[22]

Much to Corcoran's amazement and frustration, this message never did "permeate," and it fell to James McInerney to propose a compromise. Service would have to "go in there," he explained to Corcoran, but the questions he was asked would be perfunctory. The Justice Department could guarantee that there would be no indictment.

On August 2, Corcoran phoned Service to tell him the new arrangement. "This is double riveted from top to bottom," he emphasized. "I also have a deal that you are not going to be used as a [trial] witness. Just don't talk any more about anyone else than you can help." Corcoran added that he was planning to see the people at the Justice Department once more on the morning of Service's rescheduled appearance, "as I want this thing triple riveted."

Service finally went before the grand jury on August 6. On that same day, his wife gave birth to a son in California. Also, and of more interest to the world at large, the atomic bomb was dropped on Hiroshima. With the A-bomb dominating the headlines, the news that Jack Service had agreed to testify attracted little attention. Hitchcock asked few hard questions, and when the grand jury returned its bill, Service was not indicted. Officially, at least, his role in the case was finished; he had been exonerated.

What was Tommy Corcoran getting out of all of this? In 1985 Jack Service acknowledged that this was a question that had troubled him at the time. Service recalled that he went to see Corcoran in the first place only as a favor to Lauchlin Currie. "People like Currie didn't want me to appear" in court, Service explained. "I can understand that they didn't want the case broken up if I was forced to divulge all I knew." John Carter Vincent and Currie, particularly the latter, Service elaborated, had "encouraged and facilitated" his campaign of leaking anti-Hurley stories to the press. The campaign had not succeeded, and now they faced "a potential risk of embarrassment." Not only would their covert campaign to weaken Chiang Kai-shek be revealed, but their machinations against some of their own diplomatic colleagues would also be exposed. The full extent of the cozy relationship of some government officials with such Communists and Communist sympathizers as Philip Jaffe would come out. As a result, Currie might be more deeply implicated in Soviet espionage.[23]

As for Corcoran, he was, undeniably, an old friend of Ben Cohen's and may well have owed him a favor. Nevertheless, the fact remains that trading in favors was Corcoran's business, and it is highly unlikely that he would have gone to so much effort without expecting to reap some benefit in return. And despite Corcoran's assurances that his intervention had nothing to do with his friendship with T. V. Soong, Service had his doubts at the time.[24] During their subsequent conversations, Service remembered, Corcoran seemed to delight in slipping in off-the-cuff references to Soong. "T. V. is not actually a bad guy," he would say slyly. Or, again, "T. V. is not nearly the enemy you think him to be. He doesn't have it in for you." Service got the "definite impression" that Soong knew what was going on, and later, when he mentioned Corcoran's hints to either Currie or Vincent—he could not recall definitely which—he was asked: "What makes you think that Soong wants this case to go to trial?"[25]

The KMT leadership, as Service pointed out, took an active interest in maintaining a favorable press in the United States. After Stilwell's recall in November 1944, KMT spokespersons in the United States took note of the public reaction in his favor and toned down their anti-Stilwell propaganda, conceding that Stilwell was a good soldier who had merely been misled by pro-Communist advisers, particularly John Paton Davies and Jack Service. It was possible to take this position as long as Stilwell was under a gag order from Roosevelt and thus effectively neutralized. But if the *Amerasia* case came to trial, Stilwell would have had a golden opportunity to break his silence by appearing as a witness on Service's behalf. Paul Jones, who was the general's aide at the time, confirms Service's claim that this was exactly what Stilwell planned to do.[26]

More generally, the KMT, and certainly T. V. Soong personally, had an interest in protecting the sanitized image that the Generalissimo and

Madame Chiang enjoyed in the press. American magazines, from Henry Luce's *Time* on down to the widely circulated women's periodicals, regularly featured sentimentalized accounts of Madame Chiang's education at Methodist schools in the United States and her devotion to her husband. The Chiangs were supposedly an ideal couple and devout Christians who shared a highly Americanized style of living and a devotion to democratic values. A conspiracy trial would inevitably bring to light official State Department reports to the contrary.

The government's case against Mark Gayn, for example, was based on Service's classified report, the so-called "teacup gossip" memorandum, which Gayn had been observed reading on a New York City bus. This memo reported gossip about the Generalissimo's carryings on with various mistresses. Madame Chiang, it was said, had become so outraged by her husband's behavior that she threw a vase at him and, on another occasion, hurled the mistress's high-heeled shoes out a window, hitting a guard.[27]

The reality was even worse than this summary suggested, as American reporters might easily have discovered once the subject came to their attention. Chiang had a previous wife, Ch'en Chieh-ju, whom he had never divorced. After 1927, when Chiang decided to marry May-ling Soong, "Miss Ch'en," formerly known as Madame Chiang Kai-shek, lived quietly in the United States on a generous financial settlement. Despite his marriage of convenience to the well-connected Soong, Chiang had never forgotten his previous wife, and in 1942 he had her secretly brought back to China, where she gave birth to a child in the spring of 1944. The subsequent estrangement of the Generalissimo and Madame Chiang had been reported in the London press, but, somehow, the news failed to cross the Atlantic.[28]

In theory, gossip about Chiang's less than exemplary personal life need not have affected American support for his government one way or the other. But as the more recent example of the Marcoses of the Philippines demonstrates, a price must be paid for high visibility. Once a supposedly benign authoritarian leader is exposed as personally corrupt and hypocritical, the disenchantment of the American public can have devastating repercussions. Exposure of this tale of bigamy and dissension would no doubt have done more damage to U.S.-Nationalist relations than volumes of reports on the economic and political problems of the Chungking regime.

Since Corcoran and Soong are deceased, one can only speculate whether they even discussed Corcoran's intervention in the *Amerasia* affair. One principal who it was possible to interview, however, was Corcoran's former law partner, William Sterling Youngman, who was president of China Defense Supplies. Youngman was a college friend of the noted China expert, John K. Fairbank, and he recalled discussing Service's arrest with Corcoran, relaying John Fairbank's good opinion of him. Youngman insisted that it was entirely possible that Soong knew nothing about Corcoran's efforts. It would hardly have been out of character for Tommy the Cork to be working both sides of the street on any issue. Youngman, however, made the interesting remark that he and Corcoran had White House sanction for their activities and were never ideologically committed to acting as advocates for Chiang Kai-shek. As he put it, "We considered ourselves Soong men, not Chiang Kai-shek men." This remark raises the possibility that Corcoran was not acting to protect the image of the KMT in general but the specific financial interests of Soong and China Defense Supplies.[29]

The full story of Corcoran's machinations in the *Amerasia* affair may never be known. However, the outlines of the political fix are clear. Tom Clark was confirmed by the Senate without a fight. Democrat Emmanuel Celler got favorable treatment for a client, and James Mitchell's niece avoided either indictment or tough questioning before the grand jury. Neither John Carter Vincent nor Lauchlin Currie faced embarrassing questions about their possible roles in leaking anti-Chiang material to the media.

In addition to his ideological interests, Lauchlin Currie had also been the financial architect of the Chinese Lend-Lease program and for a time had been its administrator as director of the FEA. At the time of Service's arrest, Currie was back in the White House, serving as an adviser to the president on international economics, but, coincidentally or not, he submitted his resignation to Truman on June 14, just four days after Corcoran became involved with the case.

In a letter to one of the authors, Currie insisted that the timing of his resignation had nothing to do with the *Amerasia* case. He was a holdover from the Roosevelt administration, he explained, and he left the White House solely in order to give President Truman a chance to fill his job with an appointee of his own. However, the text of Currie's resignation letter makes it clear that Truman had previously asked him to stay on. Currie, however, offered his resignation, citing "urgent personal reasons" for his inability to comply with Truman's request.[30]

In his letter, Currie noted that he was friendly with John Service but "with some reserve" because he did not share Service's high opinion of

General Stilwell: "I relied more on John Carter Vincent, who, I felt, was more objective in his judgments. I have no recollection of designating Service as a 'leaker' but I think that it would have been extremely unlikely." Currie went on to say that the only help he had given Service after his arrest was to suggest that he talk to Ben Cohen. "Cohen did recommend a firm of lawyers to handle Service's case, but I forget their names. I doubt if Corcoran played any role in the case." Currie, however, was recorded by the FBI discussing the case with Corcoran. He also clearly did not send Service to Cohen since the two men never met.[31]

Currie and Corcoran did share some business interests. With World War II drawing to a close, Corcoran realized that Lend-Lease funds would come to an end, and he was busily trying to line up investments in exports and international development. To ensure his success, he was also doing his best to control appointments to the Export-Import Bank, which he had helped to establish by promoting the authorizing legislation.[32]

Currie had startlingly similar interests. Just one month after submitting his resignation as administrative assistant to Truman, Currie announced the establishment of his own company, the International World Development Corporation, whose purpose was "to make available American manufacturing methods to industries in foreign countries." Currie subsequently served as a consultant to the Peronist regime in Argentina and engaged in the import-export business.[33]

In 1948 he was appointed to a post with the International Bank for Reconstruction and Development (IBRD), like the Export-Import Bank, a major source of loans to developing countries. As the IBRD's chief of mission in Colombia and director of a team preparing a report on the Colombian economy for the World Bank, Currie had considerable influence over Colombia's ability to obtain financing to purchase imported machinery and equipment.

Although he has often discussed his role in the *Amerasia* affair, Service has never revealed his connection with Corcoran—apparently not even to his wife, who seemed startled to hear about it during Service's 1985 interview with the authors. Pressed to explain Corcoran's role, Service insisted that Corcoran had "barged into the case" uninvited and, in any event, did no more than advise him to go to the grand jury, exactly the course that he and Godfrey Munter had already agreed on.[34] In a sense, this is correct. Service would probably not have been indicted even if Corcoran had never picked up the phone in his behalf, though he might well have faced the professional embarrassment of having to testify about his dealings with

Jaffe in a public trial. Other defendants in the case also benefited from Service's elimination as a potential government witness. Jaffe, Gayn, and Roth—and perhaps Kate Mitchell as well—clearly had made a concerted effort to cultivate Service's friendship during the months of May and June 1945, and Service's testimony could have shown that the other suspects were united in a common purpose. It might also have served as an incentive for Andrew Roth to recall his conversation with Jaffe in which Jaffe admitted his true motives for orchestrating his relationship with Service.

More than 400 years ago, Niccolò Machiavelli warned that conspiracies rarely succeed, "for whoever conspires cannot act alone and cannot find companions except among those who are discontented; as soon as you have disclosed your intention to a malcontent, you give him the means of satisfying himself, for by revealing it he can hope to secure everything he wants."[35]

Given the rivalries, animosities, and widely varying motives of the six *Amerasia* defendants, it was remarkable that prosecutors were unable to break even one of these "malcontents" and persuade someone to testify, particularly since information from wiretaps, even if it was not legally admissible in court, might have had a powerful effect in persuading someone to talk. Instead of isolating the defendants and picking them off one by one, or pressuring those caught with government documents to testify against the others, the Justice Department made it relatively easy for each of them to slip out of the net.

As he prepared his case for the grand jury, Robert Hitchcock was at best going through the motions. After the arrests, FBI officials had assumed that Service, Gayn, and Mitchell would all become government witnesses. Service had indicated through his attorney that he might testify voluntarily. Mitchell and Gayn had both made self-incriminating statements at the time of their arrests. Since the bureau was tapping Corcoran's phone, Hoover and his top aides already knew about Corcoran's string pulling on behalf of Service, but they were surprised and disgusted to learn from Hitchcock on July 25 that he did not expect any of the six suspects to testify against any of the others.[36]

As it reminded Hitchcock on more than one occasion, the FBI would have been happy to see all charges against Gayn and Mitchell dropped in exchange for their testimony. Gayn's attorney, meanwhile, had actually offered to have his client plead to a reduced charge. Hitchcock, however, seemed mainly interested in making sure that nothing would happen to excite the grand jurors.

Mitchell and Gayn, along with their attorneys, had been allowed to examine all of the government's exhibits, and on August 1, an FBI agent assigned to drive the prosecutors to the courthouse overheard them discussing an agreement with Gayn's attorney that any documents Gayn was questioned about that day would not be used against him later.[37]

It would seem that Gayn had, in effect, been promised immunity. But in exchange for what?

In response to an inquiry from Hoover, Hitchcock insisted that the conversation in the taxi had been misunderstood. The only stipulation offered Gayn's attorney was that in the event that certain documents were later ruled inadmissible, his client's grand jury testimony about them would not be brought up in court. Hoover was skeptical, especially when Hitchcock's questioning of both Gayn and Mitchell turned out to be so perfunctory that it was clear that the government had no interest in pursuing a case against them or scaring them badly enough to compel them to testify for the government.[38]

Hoover was even more disturbed over rumors that Hitchcock was negotiating a deal with Philip Jaffe. On the morning of July 25, even as Hitchcock was reporting to Hoover on his failure to develop any of the defendants as witnesses, the bureau learned that Jaffe and his attorney were in Hitchcock's office going over the grand jury exhibits. Hitchcock insisted that the government was obligated to make the exhibits available to any and all of the potential witnesses who asked to see them. The FBI's legal counsel disagreed and sought a consultation with a federal judge, who gave the opinion that there was no such obligation to reveal evidence prior to the grand jury deliberations. "I can't understand the *all out* policy dept. is following in allowing *all* defendants and their attorneys in Jaffe case to examine all of Govt's evidence," Hoover complained. And on another memo, he noted that "certain aspects of this matter 'smell.' "[39]

Hoover used one last ploy to try to pressure the Justice Department. On August 4 he sent a memorandum to Attorney General Clark, hinting that the department's machinations had not gone unobserved. Hoover "wanted to advise you of rumors currently being discussed in newspaper circles in New York and Washington. The newspaper rumors allege that prosecution of this case is to be 'fixed' through the efforts of influential persons having connections with the Department of Justice. I felt that you would be interested in knowing of these rumors."[40] Hoover's bluff failed.

As it turned out, after previewing the case against him, Jaffe decided that he would rather not go before the grand jury after all. Besides Mitchell, Gayn, and Service, the only new witnesses Hitchcock called were Elizabeth Barker of the OWI and her supervisor George Taylor. Their testimony helped persuade the grand jurors that "the practice engaged in by the defendants was a common practice and that government agencies were the ones who were actually at fault in view of their laxity in caring for confidential documents."[41]

On August 10 the grand jurors completed their work. By a vote of 14 to 6 Larsen and Jaffe were indicted on a reduced charge of "conspiracy to embezzle, steal and purloin" government property. Roth was also indicted, by a vote of 13 to 7. Mitchell and Gayn were cleared, by votes of 2 to 18 and 5 to 15, respectively. The grand jurors voted unanimously to exonerate Jack Service. Since 12 votes were the minimum needed for indictment, the grand jury's reaction to the evidence did not bode well for the prosecutors' chances of getting convictions. Hitchcock reported that Jaffe and Larsen had both hinted that they would consider pleading guilty if they did not have to serve time in jail. All in all, he thought it would be in the government's interest to arrange deals with both defendants.[42]

Gurnea thought the grand jurors might have been more impressed if Hitchcock had bothered to subpoena witnesses and to avoid giving the impression that he considered the entire matter a waste of their time and his. Incredulous, he went over Hitchcock's head to McInerney. Had there been any pressure brought to bear on the Justice Department, he wondered. McInerney assured him that there had been absolutely none.[43]

Hoover's chief objection to allowing Larsen and Jaffe to plea-bargain was that Andrew Roth would be let off the hook. Based on wiretap transcriptions, Hoover was convinced that Roth was "undoubtedly the brains behind Jaffe's operations in Washington." Hoover was also set on convicting Roth because he was "more closely connected with the Communist Party" than any of the other defendants, except for Jaffe.[44]

Roth, moreover, had been attacking the government in print ever since his arrest. A series of five articles he wrote for the *New York Post* in June had begun with the challenge: "I have been accused and now it is time for me to turn accuser." Roth went on to claim that he had been framed by "a powerful conservative clique in the State Department" that sought to "crush and intimidate any liberal opposition." According to Roth, the charges against him were a crude attempt to discredit his forthcoming book engineered by Joseph Grew, whom he denounced as a "blueblood" dilettante.[45]

Roth's truculence succeeded in thoroughly irritating Jaffe, who complained to an acquaintance that Roth was silly to publish such articles while his case was pending and was being "childish" about Grew. Sally Gayn, too, was overheard on an FBI wiretap remarking that "Roth is shooting off his mouth again." Jaffe and Mark Gayn were taking the position that their activities were protected by their First Amendment rights as journalists—a defense that pointedly left the Washington defendants out in the cold—and Roth's continued insistence that he and the others had been partners in an ideological crusade threatened to spoil the image they were trying to project.[46]

Hitchcock, meanwhile, was doing his best to convince Hoover that if Larsen and Jaffe pled guilty it would still be possible to try Roth separately. Hoover was doubtful, and justifiably so since none of Hitchcock's promises had been kept so far. Always alert to the temperature of conservative opinion, Hoover warned that if this most outspoken of the defendants were not prosecuted, "it would appear that justice would not be served and that the Department might be laying itself open to considerable criticism." As a fallback position, Hoover suggested that he would be satisfied if Roth, Larsen, and Jaffe all pled guilty and received substantial fines. Even this was more than the Justice Department either could or would deliver.[47]

Much to the dismay of the FBI, Emmanuel Larsen had finally managed to convince his building superintendent, E. R. Sager, to provide an affidavit detailing the bureau's entries into the two apartments Larsen had occupied during the time he was under investigation. Larsen's attorney, Arthur Hilland, duly filed a motion to suppress the evidence arising from these warrantless searches.[48]

On the morning of September 28, James McInerney learned that Hilland had released copies of his motion to the press. He and Hitchcock realized that as soon as the story became public, Philip Jaffe would guess that his offices and home must also have been entered, so McInerney immediately called Jaffe's Washington attorney, Albert Arent, and asked him to drop by for a conference. A deal was hammered out then and there. As Hitchcock later testified to the Tydings Committee, "We did not want Mr. Arent to leave our office because we knew that once he left the office he would read in the newspapers" about Hilland's motion. In exchange for a government recommendation of a $5,000 fine, Jaffe would plead guilty the following morning, Saturday, at a specially scheduled hearing. Hitchcock further recalled that when Arent showed up at the courthouse the next morning, he greeted the prosecutors with a hostile glare and muttered, "You sons of bitches." But if Arent was really unhappy over the deal he had cut, there was no sign of it at the hearing.[49]

Nor did he have reason to be unhappy. During the course of the hearing, Hitchcock went out of his way to discredit the FBI's handling of case, going so far as to deny that there had ever been any basis for a prosecution under the espionage statute.

When it came time for the prosecutor to make his statement of facts in the case, Hitchcock deferred to Arent, who described his client as "a student of Far Eastern affairs" who had lectured at Harvard, Vassar, Dartmouth, and elsewhere. "The government does not contend that this material was used for any disloyal purpose," Arent said. He went on to describe his client's actions as "a relatively minor violation" motivated by "an excess of journalistic zeal" and "his anxiety to be accurately informed in the field of his scholarly and journalistic interest." Asked by Judge James Proctor whether he agreed with this characterization of the case, Hitchcock rose to say that it was "in substance, accurate."

Judge Proctor then suggested that the case be reviewed by a probation officer, "the usual course of such cases." Hitchcock objected that an investigation would take too much time. The government wanted the case "disposed of today." Once again he affirmed that the purloined documents had been used by Jaffe "largely [as] background material."

The only person in the courtroom not infected by the spirit of amity was Judge Proctor. Several times he interrupted Arent and Hitchcock's duet to remind them that what was being discussed was, after all, a violation of law. Now he wondered aloud whether Jaffe had not intended after all to "embarrass" the army and navy.

Hitchcock denied that anything of the kind had been in the defendant's mind. "To us it was largely to the purpose of lending credibility to the publication itself, and perhaps [to] increase its circulation and prestige."

Proctor responded by sentencing Jaffe to a fine of $2,500, half of what the government recommended. Announcing his decision, he told Jaffe, "I regret that in your zeal to carry out your work, which was evidently for a trustworthy purpose, that you were misled to do those things which of course did tend to break down the fidelity of government employees and officials in the performance of their work."[50]

The judge's statement would later be cited by several commentators on the *Amerasia* affair as a vindication of Jaffe. In the context of his previous questions, it seems possible that his remarks were tinged with sarcasm.

Jaffe was so pleased with the hearing (among other things, not one word of his connection with the CPUSA had been uttered) that on leaving the courtroom he promised Hitchcock that he would do his best to bring Larsen around to pleading guilty. The next day, October 1, Arent wrote his client, assuring him that he had passed along to Larsen and his attorney Jaffe's promise to "pay his fine and help Larsen get on his feet." Unlike Service, who had been reinstated as an active foreign service officer after the grand jury failed to indict him and was immediately reassigned, Larsen was still on unpaid leave from the State Department and would lose his job permanently if he pled guilty. In addition to covering his fine and legal expenses, Jaffe offered to compensate Larsen with an amount equal to his lost annual salary.[51]

At first, Larsen resisted. For one thing, he could not understand why Jaffe had rushed to make a separate deal instead of joining him in pressing for a discovery motion. The reason, which never seemed to dawn on Larsen, was that Jaffe, actually rather relieved that he was not being tried on a more serious charge (such as espionage), did not care to call the government's bluff on this point. Feeling bitter and betrayed, Larsen was determined to keep the case alive. As Arent reported to Jaffe, he "was embarked on a crusade."[52]

Larsen soon found an unlikely ally in Republican representative George Dondero. Dondero was already planning to sponsor a congressional inquiry into the Justice Department's handling of the case, and he persuaded Larsen that he should look to Congress for vindication. In the meantime, Dondero counseled, Larsen could increase his value as an informant by settling his legal problem. On the advice of Dondero, Larsen reluctantly negotiated a plea of nolo contendere. At his appearance before Judge Proctor on November 2, Hitchcock went so far as to state, "I have extreme doubt there were any corrupt motives on the part of Larsen." Proctor levied a $500 fine, which was paid by Philip Jaffe.[53]

For Hoover, this was the last straw. He had expected that, at the very least, Hitchcock would compel Jaffe to agree to review the seized documents so that the government could determine which of them came from Larsen and which from other sources. Now any hope of obtaining information from either of the principals had been cut off. Across the bottom of the memo informing him of the arrangement with Larsen, he wrote, "Of all the wishy washy vacillations this takes the prize."[54]

Hoover had contended all along that the FBI's actions during the investigation were lawful. This belief, based in large part on the theory that the federal government was entitled to take extraordinary measures to recover its own property, may or may not have held up in court. But Hoover was willing to take his chances, and he had assumed that the Justice Department, which had known and approved of the bureau's surveillance methods, would back him up.

According to Hitchcock's later statement to the Tydings Committee, this was never the case. As he put it, "We hoped that no defendant would ever learn of these activities." Possibly this was true and the Justice Department, swept along by the optimistic hope of obtaining confessions, had never bothered to consider the likelihood that sooner or later one or more of the suspects would figure out that his or her apartment had been searched. More likely, the department's change of heart was the result of political pressure.[55]

Andrew Roth was now the only one of the six suspects who still faced charges. During the month of December, both Jaffe and Larsen, who had submitted a job application to the War Department, gave sworn statements to the FBI minimizing Roth's involvement. Larsen said—falsely, in view of the evidence obtained from electronic surveillance—that Roth had never been present when he and Jaffe exchanged classified documents. Jaffe's interview, conducted on December 27, gave a version of events that differed with the wiretap evidence on many points. For example, he insisted that he hardly knew Earl Browder and had gone to the party chief's home only to discuss the forthcoming visit of Tung Pi-wu. Jaffe claimed that Roth had never been present when he and Larsen negotiated the transfer of the personality file, and although he had been around on six to ten occasions when Larsen delivered classified documents, he may not have realized what was going on. Angry as he was with Roth, Jaffe clearly wanted to exonerate him so that Roth would never have occasion to tell his story of Jaffe's abortive foray into espionage under oath. In this, he succeeded. On February 15, 1946, the Justice Department quietly dropped the charges against the last *Amerasia* defendant.[56]

Robert Hitchcock's agreement with the statement that Jaffe was guilty of nothing more than an "excess of journalistic zeal" was, quite naturally, interpreted by the press as an admission that the prosecution had been politically motivated from start to finish. Exactly as I. F. Stone and the *New York Herald Tribune* had contended, the case was nothing more than an attempt to punish left-wing leakers. As the *Washington Post* put it, "The government went off half-cocked in this case."[57] Ironically, there was a policy of selective leaking of information about the case, and because of it only a few conservative columnists had any idea of the number and nature of the documents that had been seized in connection with the investigation.

Mark Gayn, meanwhile, had filed a $600,000 libel suit against the *New York World Telegram*, charging that Frederick Woltman's articles had defamed him. This was exactly what Lee Woods had feared, and what Hoover had specifically promised him would never happen because the case was "airtight." Gayn's suit got bogged down in an endless succession of delays and postponements. While it was still pending, Gayn left for a reporting assignment in Japan and Korea, where he was soon accused by the army of filing a dispatch based on classified information. As a result, he lost his accreditation.[58]

Unable to cover the Korean conflict, Gayn moved on to China and then to Eastern Europe, where he reported on Tito's break with Stalin and the purge trials of various Communist officials. His experiences in this part of the world eventually soured him on the Soviet Union, and in 1949 he wrote to Jaffe that he did not dare express his true opinions in his articles because if he did he would never be allowed to visit Hungary, Poland, or Bulgaria again. Gayn begged Jaffe not to breathe a word about his change of heart, since these governments all had sources in the United States, and he specifically warned him against confiding in Johannes Steele, the left-wing radio commentator.[59]

Gayn's wife Sally died while he was abroad, and several years later he married a Hungarian woman and began a campaign to obtain a passport for her. After a long and fruitless battle to obtain an American visa, the Gayns finally settled in Canada, where he continued his career with the *Toronto Sun*. His libel suit against the *World Telegram* remained stalled in the courts until 1951, when Gayn decided to drop the complaint.[60]

Gayn was not the only defendant to go abroad. Andrew Roth also became a foreign correspondent, covering many world hot spots for the *Nation*. Army intelligence kept an eye on him, and a 1946 report from Cairo noted that he had a reputation as "a rabid Communist." Later, despite France's decision to deny him a visa for Indochina, he was able to report on the insurgency of the Communists under Ho Chi Minh. Roth was in England when his passport expired, and he was informed by the American embassy that it would be renewed only for the purpose of returning to the United States. Rather than go back home and expose himself to subpoenas from various congressional committees still looking into the aftermath of the *Amerasia* case, Roth remained in England, where he became a successful journalist and the founder of the publication *Parliamentary Profiles*.[61]

Philip Jaffe returned to his business and his magazine, which struggled on for a few more years. Kate Mitchell stayed on as *Amerasia*'s managing editor and eventually built a small house on the grounds of Jaffe's country retreat in Stamford, Connecticut. Her involvement in the case had always been peripheral, and she quickly vanished from public view. Mitchell's reasons for tying her career to Jaffe's remain somewhat mysterious. Contributors to *Amerasia* agreed that she was a talented writer, much more of an intellectual than Jaffe and largely responsible for keeping the magazine going. But Mitchell's plans to write a book on the KMT's use of Confucian symbols never came to fruition, and by the late 1940s, she was drinking heavily and her health began to break down. She died in the early 1960s.

In contrast to Jimmy Larsen, who was fired by the State Department following his plea bargain, John Stewart Service appeared to have emerged unscathed from his misadventure. After Service was cleared by the grand jury, newly appointed secretary of state James Byrnes wrote him a letter congratulating him "on this happy termination of your ordeal." Byrnes and Dean Acheson, now undersecretary of state, were sympathetic to Service's views on China policy, and he was quickly cleared for reassignment by a department Loyalty-Security Board and posted to Japan as a staff aide to General MacArthur. Even Joseph Grew wrote Service expressing his pleasure at the appointment.[62]

George Atcheson and John Emmerson, both of whom had worked with Service in China, were also assigned to occupation headquarters in Tokyo. In November, Atcheson and Service broke out a bottle from their private stock of bourbon, a rare commodity in postwar Japan, to celebrate the news that Patrick Hurley had, at last, resigned. In his resignation letter, Hurley blamed the "Hydra-headed direction" of American policy in Asia on certain career foreign service officers who used their influence to "side with the Communist armed party and at times with the imperialistic bloc against American policy," and he warned that this same group of officers was now in Tokyo. This sounded like the ramblings of a defeated man, and after hearing Hurley's disgruntled testimony a few weeks later, the Senate Foreign Relations Committee soon terminated its investigation. Service's celebration, however, was premature. The legal case may have been over, but the *Amerasia* affair was just beginning.[63]

Cover-up

Michigan congressman George Dondero was a man of many theories. He believed, for example, that modern art was being promoted by the Communists to undermine the American way of life—a proposition that would have come as news to Soviet artists laboring under the restrictions of socialist realism. Another secret weapon of the Communist movement was Drew Pearson, according to Dondero, who was advancing the cause of Communism by criticizing Dondero's hero, General MacArthur. Dondero had been watching the collapse of the *Amerasia* prosecution with mounting horror, and on October 10, less than two weeks after Jaffe's trial, he took to the floor of Congress to call for an investigation. "The case," he charged, "has all the earmarks of a whitewash."[1]

For once, Dondero's instincts were correct. However, he lacked the imagination to conceive of a cover-up involving such an unlikely cast of co-conspirators as T. V. Soong's chief American agent, a wealthy Buffalo lawyer, Lauchlin Currie, and the nation's chief prosecutors in the Department of Justice. In his speech to the House of Representatives, he cited the usual suspects—the Communists, Drew Pearson, and Undersecretary of State Dean Acheson. Dondero saw *Amerasia* as a conspiracy primarily aimed at unseating Joseph Grew in order to promote a policy that would tilt Japan's postwar political structure to the left, creating an opportunity for a Communist takeover. The congressman was correct in thinking that the Communists had some hopes along those lines, but he went on to link all who supported the restructuring of Japanese society to the Communists' aims. The *Amerasia* group had succeeded in getting rid of Grew, he noted, thanks to the help of the liberal press, and now journalists like Pearson had turned their fire on MacArthur, who was being called an appeaser for failing to insist on the removal of Emperor Hirohito.

Word that Dondero was agitating for an investigation caused consternation inside the Justice Department. On October 26, James McInerney and Justice Department attorney Lamar Caudle paid a call on the congressman in his office, where they pleaded with him that any probe of the investigative techniques used in the *Amerasia* case would inevitably compromise other ongoing investigations of Communist espionage. McInerney later complained that he had taken along more than 100 exhibits to Dondero's office, but the congressman took no interest in examining them and refused to accept his assurance that the Department of Justice had done its best to obtain convictions.

Suspecting (correctly) that Dondero was getting encouragement from the FBI, Attorney General Tom Clark sent a memo to Hoover reminding him that departmental policy prohibited direct contacts between congressmen and the bureau on any matter relating to legislation or resolutions. Hoover reacted promptly by summoning Dondero to a conference, during which he spent an hour and a half explaining to the congressman why he couldn't talk to him.[2]

Dondero's speeches make it clear that even before this meeting took place he was receiving confidential information from a source familiar with the contents of the FBI's investigative files. On November 28, six days before his talk with the director, Dondero introduced a formal resolution calling on the House Judiciary Committee to look into charges that "some influence, either within or without the Department of Justice," had been brought to bear in the case. The resolution identified specific documents seized in both the OSS and FBI raids, including the existence of one draft of an OSS memo that was not stamped with the agency of origin—all information that had never been publicly released. The resolution also mentioned the five-hour meeting between Jaffe, Browder, Chinese Communist delegate Tung Pi-wu, and others that had been held at Jaffe's apartment while the San Francisco conference was still in session. Dondero further charged that Jaffe had been in contact "directly or indirectly with known foreign Communist agents."[3]

Although Dondero's informant had apparently not mentioned any names in connection with accusations of a fix, the threat of exposure was serious enough to induce Tommy Corcoran and James McGranery to begin calling in favors in a campaign to make sure that the Dondero resolution remained bottled up in committee. With an FBI agent in his office in March 1946 while he called, McGranery persuaded Representative Eugene Cox of Georgia to agree to stop the resolution. In April, however, the issue was finally scheduled for a vote. McGranery called Corcoran to agonize over this development and complained to him that Cox "at one time gave me his word and told me he'd recommit it" but "later he told me he'd have too much trouble" preventing the resolution from passing.

"We can't do anything about it," McGranery complained. He then belittled Dondero's complaints as "a tempest in a teapot." But in the next breath, he asked Corcoran to continue to use his influence to make sure that the committee's investigation did not get out of bounds.[4]

Corcoran was unable to prevent an investigation. At the time the *Amerasia* defendants had been arrested, the United States and the Soviet Union were still allies. But by 1946, the world looked very different. The victory against fascism had quickly been followed by increasing tension among the Allies. Stalin had signaled a new turn in Soviet policy in April 1945 when the Soviet leadership sponsored the publication of an article by French Communist leader Jacques Duclos that denounced Earl Browder's policies of "class peace in the postwar era" and "peaceful coexistence" between the American and Soviet social systems. American Communists—and their compatriots in Western Europe—were put on notice that the United States and the Soviet Union were heading for confrontation and that Communist Parties would be expected to struggle vigorously against their capitalist governments.

The old allies were soon squabbling openly around the world. They disagreed over the issue of German unification and demilitarization. There were increasing tensions about the fate of Poland, growing internal conflict in France and Italy, and the threat of war in northern Iran, where Soviet troops occupied a portion of the country. In March 1946 Winston Churchill summed up the new situation in a speech at Fulton, Missouri: "From Stettin in the Baltic to Trieste in the Adriatic," the former prime minister put it, "an iron curtain has descended across the Continent."

International tensions were reflected in growing domestic hostility toward and suspicions of Communism. In September 1946 Igor Gouzenko, a code clerk in the Soviet embassy in Ottawa, asked for political asylum. Gouzenko revealed the existence of a major Soviet spy ring in Canada, but at least one of his leads pointed toward an aide to the American secretary of state, later revealed to be Alger Hiss. Security officers in the State Department asked the FBI for information on 15 to 20 people, including Hiss, who might have been involved in the *Amerasia* case.[5] The issue of Communist subversion and espionage was now on the political agenda and available for use by shrewd politicians who sensed its growing power.

Dondero's right-wing rhetoric guaranteed a partisan reception for his resolution when it finally got out of committee and was debated on the floor of the House. Democratic leaders viewed the proposal as an attack on the administration and were not reassured by Dondero's insistence that his charges were not aimed at Truman. Even some of Dondero's fellow conservatives were wary, but for different reasons. For example, John Rankin of Mississippi complained that the resolution's focus was too narrow. The recent exposure of the Gouzenko ring in Canada had convinced him that Communist agents in the United States were even now working to steal America's atomic secrets, so why not investigate the broader question of why the Justice Department had been so ineffective in unmasking American spies? Rankin pointed out that since Russia was not at war with Japan at the time the *Amerasia* documents were stolen, it was conceivable that some of them had been passed to the Japanese. Howard Smith of Virginia, on the other hand, wondered "if we have not got the wrong sow by the ear"; instead of second-guessing the Justice Department, he suggested that the probe should be targeted at the State Department.[6]

The position of Representative Eugene Cox of Georgia was more subtle. Cox had no doubt of the guilt of the *Amerasia* defendants. But, he insisted, "the astounding thing is, how could all these secret files get into the hands of those individuals in New York whose business it has been for some time to undermine the foundations of this government without someone interested in national security having detected it?" Nevertheless, Cox insisted that it was not appropriate to blame the Justice Department for the failure of the grand jury. Cox made it clear that in the event that there was an investigation, he intended to see that the committee focused not on the actions of the Justice Department and the federal court but on lax security procedures.

Only two of the House's most left-wing members, Vito Marcantonio of New York and Adolph Sabath of Illinois, expressed no dissatisfaction with the way the *Amerasia* case had been handled. Sabath, doubtless aware that Dondero had also been talking to Emmanuel Larsen, dismissed Dondero's charges about Jaffe, suggesting that these rumors came "from some disgruntled, discharged employee, or from some perverse and prejudiced meddler." Sabath also cannily suggested that reopening the case would only result in revelations embarrassing to Hoover.

Dondero responded that it was not the FBI but the ONI that was likely to be embarrassed. Why, for example, had Andrew Roth been appointed to such a sensitive post despite an earlier ONI recommendation that he not be assigned to *any* intelligence duties? Dondero was equally incensed over Hitchcock's failure to mention Jaffe's Communist connections to Judge Proctor. "How can any attorney speaking for the United States say to a court of these United States that these people intended no harm to our government?" he asked. "Had this same thing happened in certain other Governments, these people would undoubtedly have been shot, without a trial." Warming to his subject, Dondero hinted that the FBI had wanted to arrest "hundreds" of suspects but was prevented from doing so by a Communist faction in the State Department that had argued that such a dragnet operation would undermine wartime morale.

Of course this last claim had no basis in fact, and it is doubtful that even Dondero's supporters took it seriously. Yet such a claim reflects the fact that resentment of the liberal faction at the State Department played a role in the debate. Among those who spoke in favor of the resolution was Congressman Walter Judd of Minnesota, a former missionary in China who had made a fact-finding junket to Peking in 1944. In his book, *The China Hands*, E. J. Kahn recalls that Judd irritated career foreign service officials during his visit by his propensity for making off-the-cuff pronouncements while ignoring everything they were trying to tell him. One night, Kahn recounted, several career officers (not including Service) were scheduled to have dinner with the congressman but had become so irritated with him that "they stood him up; convening instead in a room just above *his* room, they sang, in what they hoped was a carrying voice, 'Poor Judd is dead.'"[7]

Now Judd, still very much alive, was more staunchly pro-Chiang and more critical of the more liberal China Hands than ever. Speaking in favor of a congressional probe of the *Amerasia* affair, he remarked that he knew some of the defendants and suspected that one, at least, was a victim of circumstances. Apparently this was not a reference to Service but to Larsen, who been making the rounds of congressional offices, telling anyone who would listen that his legal problems were the result of his being targeted as a scapegoat by the liberals in the Office of Far Eastern Affairs.

Ignoring Marcantonio's plea not to "revive a dead herring," the House eventually voted 227 to 111 in favor of an investigation, with southern Democrats joining Republicans to make up the majority.[8]

The House vote had the effect of bringing relations between J. Edgar Hoover and Attorney General Tom Clark to the boiling point. Hoover, who met again with Dondero on December 3, 1945, to discuss his inability to discuss the case with him, was incensed to learn that Caudle and McInerney were blaming the collapse of the prosecution on the FBI's use of illegal tactics to gather evidence. In a letter to Clark, Hoover protested that as far as he was concerned, the bureau's actions in the case had been within the law, and he bemoaned the failure of the Justice Department and the FBI to present a united front to Congress and the public.[9]

Clark, on his part, suspected Hoover of egging Dondero on. Conceivably, this was unfair. FBI files reveal that the bureau was conducting its own investigation into where Dondero was getting his evidence. One possibility was that the congressman had obtained a transcript of the grand jury proceedings; another, that he had a source inside the OSS. Even so, some of Dondero's information involved wiretap records available only to the FBI, and it is difficult to avoid the suspicion that the congressman was a loose cannon, aimed in Tom Clark's general direction by Hoover. If so, Hoover's purpose was not to do Clark any irreparable harm but only to remind him that the Justice Department could not afford to attempt to blame the FBI for its problems in prosecuting espionage cases or its inability or unwillingness to break one or more of the *Amerasia* defendants.[10]

Clark had apparently lost his battle to squelch Dondero's complaints of a "whitewash," but, in fact, he was in no danger. Congressman Cox's ally, Sam Hobbs of Alabama, was chosen to chair the subcommittee that would investigate Dondero's charges, and with Hobbs in charge, there was never any danger that the probe would turn in potentially embarrassing directions. A five-term congressman from Selma, Alabama, Hobbs had so far managed to attract little attention to himself, and he conducted his subcommittee as if he did not wish that situation to change.

The Hobbs Committee began its work on May 18 by voting to convene in secret session to protect the identities of its witnesses. The committee's meetings were held in Hobbs's office, and the atmosphere was, to say the least, informal. There is no indication in the transcripts that any of the witnesses were under oath, and the questioning was conducted entirely by members of Congress, not by staff counsel. Moreover, if the committee members had received any briefings from staff members, the results were certainly not apparent. Whoever prepared the transcripts of the sessions was unaware even of the correct spellings of the defendants' names—Mark Gayn, for example, was identified as Mark Jane—and the ladder of ignorance ran all the way up to Chairman Hobbs, who never did manage to sort out the identities of the six alleged conspirators or to recall correctly which of them had been indicted and convicted.

Under the lackadaisical direction of Hobbs, the subcommittee soon degenerated into a private complaint bureau for its star witness, who was none other than Emmanuel Larsen. Larsen had been reciting his story to sympathetic congressmen ever since the previous August, all the while keeping Robert Bannerman, the State Department's chief security officer, informed of the progress of his private lobbying campaign. Larsen had an application pending for a job as a researcher for a War Department bureau in Korea, and in a transparent attempt to pressure the State Department into giving him a good recommendation, he reminded Bannerman that, in Bannerman's paraphrase, "being a man of sterling character, he had refused to say anything that would in any way embarrass the State Department." Larsen's assignment to the Korean post finally came through, only to be rescinded after a newspaper article appeared drawing attention to the appointment.[11]

By the spring of 1946, Larsen was feeling sorry for himself indeed. The possibility that there might be some connection between his own actions and his present inability to find a job never seemed to occur to him. To that extent, at least, he was a textbook example of a sociopath, and like many sociopaths, Larsen could be quite convincing to those who never bothered to check out his accusations.

In his testimony to the Hobbs Committee, Larsen dropped his postarrest charge that he was being persecuted by a pro-Japanese clique in the

State Department. Now he portrayed himself as a dedicated drudge who had been lured into an association with Jaffe because he refused to cooperate with the faction composed of Service, John Paton Davies, John Emmerson, and others—"these people in the State Department who are forcing a pro-Communist policy so as to enhance their own little group at the head of which I consider Dean Acheson stands as a leader." Larsen's story was that he had begun exchanging data with Jaffe only because Jaffe seemed to have more detailed information than he did about a number of Chinese leaders. After belatedly discovering Jaffe's Communist connections, he said, he had threatened to cut off their relationship, and by the spring of 1945, "I had very little to do with him."

Then, in May, he had discovered a scheme on the part of the Acheson clique to deliver Manchuria into the hands of the Communists. After Larsen single-handedly defused this particular plot by threatening to expose it publicly, he was warned: "You will get it in the neck for this." According to Larsen, he had been in line for a post on General Wedemeyer's staff, but at the last minute, the "pro-leftist, pro-Communist" clique took its revenge and the appointment was sabotaged.

Describing himself as an "innocent victim of the left," Larsen complained that his selfless service to his country had gone unrewarded. "I have an attractive, fine young wife," yet "whereas other men go to movies and to the National Theater and go out, I sit every night until eleven and I [work on personality cards] and where does it get me?"[12]

This mélange of wild assertions and self-serving excuses was permitted to stand virtually unchallenged. Larsen praised Philip Jaffe's delicate sensibilities, stating that "he was never crude or offered anything in the way of money or anything like that," only to admit moments later that he and his wife had accepted cash payments from Jaffe, ostensibly for typing. On the one hand, he claimed to be apolitical, a scholar who had blundered into trouble because of his intense dedication to building his precious card file; on the other hand, he insinuated that he had been providing "certain little notes and evidence" to Patrick Hurley and that his relationship with Hurley was the real reason why Acheson and others were determined to destroy his career.

Larsen further suggested that Jack Service had been in touch with Jaffe even before he left China and had regularly sent him copies of his reports. This allegation—which happens to be contradicted by the FBI's surveillance transcripts—would become one of the most persistent rumors about the case, haunting Service in the years to come.[13]

The Hobbs Committee's indulgent treatment of Larsen set the tone for the remainder of its inquiry. The rest of the witnesses, all government employees, indulged in a round-robin game of shunting the blame for the *Amerasia* fiasco onto the next guy in line. Frank Bielaski, testifying under the alias Frank Brooks to protect his ongoing undercover work, expressed anger at the Justice Department for flubbing the case. James McInerney, in turn, testified that he had avoided consulting with the OSS because he did not wish to be associated with their illegal tactics.

"I do not believe I would be so squeamish in wartime," Congressman Clarence Hancock mused. It was a question of gathering admissible evidence, not squeamishness, McInerney retorted. For that matter, he suggested, whoever had supplied Dondero with information about the documents seized in the case was as guilty as the *Amerasia* defendants of breaching security.

McInerney's attempt to equate the theft of military intelligence during wartime with Dondero's behind-the-scenes sleuthing after the fact did not impress even the most ill-informed members of the committee. Nor were the congressmen inclined to buy his effort, seconded by Robert Hitchcock, to downplay the importance of the documents involved. In a particularly unconvincing performance, Hitchcock recalled that he was "not impressed" with the documents recovered from *Amerasia*'s offices, characterizing their contents as "gossip" about Chinese officials. When several members of the committee objected to this description, asking specifically about the documents mentioned in Dondero's resolution, Hitchcock claimed that he had never heard of those particular reports, or of their connection to the case, until he read about them in the *Congressional Record*—a startling admission, if true. In any event, he said, the case had been doomed by the FBI's entry into Larsen's apartment: "It was very clumsily handled. That is my candid opinion of it."

Hitchcock's remark upset the fragile peace that had been established between Hoover and Clark. Two weeks later, Assistant Attorney General McGranery was called to testify again to clear up questions raised by Hitchcock's and McInerney's testimony. This time, when he appeared in Hobbs's office, he was flanked by two FBI officials, D. M. Ladd and Myron Gurnea. They were accompanied by fifteen file boxes stuffed with some 1,700 documents seized in connection with the case. McGranery did his best to back up Hitchcock, once again belittling the importance of the papers. Asked, for example, about the report on bombing targets in Japan seized during the OSS raid, he said that the "Top Secret" stamp on the cover had probably been put there by some unauthorized person, perhaps in the hope of impressing Jaffe. This was a novel suggestion—there is no hint in the FBI's files that anyone had previously questioned the authenticity of the classifications—and it did not impress the committee. With the overstuffed boxes of documents lined up in front of them, the congressmen were finally stirred to attention.

Representative Frank Fellows cut off McGranery's speculations. "If they could take that paper, they could take any paper," he pointed out.

"I think you are right about that," McGranery admitted.

At this, D. M. Ladd chimed in, "We can show you, by the 1,700 exhibits, that they did have access to almost everything."

Myron Gurnea took advantage of this opening to give the congressmen their first real briefing on the case. He reviewed the backgrounds of the defendants and their contacts with each other, making nonsense of Larsen's claim that he had all but cut off his contacts with Jaffe by the spring of 1945. He explained that numerous documents seized in *Amerasia's* offices bore Larsen's handwriting, while others were found to bear the fingerprints of Jaffe, Larsen, and Mark Gayn. Gayn, additionally, had papers at his home that had been typed by Jaffe's typist, Annette Blumenthal. Roth was linked to the evidence by the handwritten Phillips letters and a typed document that had been produced on his own typewriter.

Gurnea emphasized that the Justice Department had expressed no qualms about the FBI's investigative methods at the time of the investigation and arrests. Its change of heart had come only after some unidentified person had ordered the arrests postponed, ostensibly so as not to create bad publicity during the San Francisco UN conference.

Gurnea obviously felt that the mysterious order delaying action on the arrests was somehow linked to the pressures that caused the Justice Department to back off from the prosecution. But since the phone call in question had allegedly been made on the president's behalf, Gurnea had handed the committee a hot potato. In defending his resolution on the floor of the House, Dondero had explicitly said that he did not hold Truman responsible for the *Amerasia* whitewash. The Hobbs Committee had neither the will nor the clout to extend its probe to the president's staff. Even if the committee had investigated the president's staff, it is doubtful if it would have discovered anything more than James Forrestal's concern that the *Amerasia* arrests might affect negotiations with the Russians.

In fact, Sam Hobbs had already taken action in at least one other instance to squelch a potentially promising lead. In May 1946, while the hearings were in progress, Hobbs received an affidavit from an unnamed State Department official charging that the department had put pressure on the Justice Department to drop criminal charges against Service. Hobbs's response was to call McGranery to ask him to look into the charges—an obvious conflict of interest.[14]

Hobbs was equally disinclined to pursue Gurnea's hint about the possibility of maneuvering on the part of someone on Truman's staff, and on July 25, he met with the FBI's Mickey Ladd to brief him on the conclusions that would appear in the committee's report and find out whether he had any objections. Reading between the lines of the FBI's memo on the meeting, it would seem that Hobbs's real purpose was to reassure himself that the bureau did not plan to discredit the committee's work by leaking its allegations to the press. In the meantime, the committee's secret sessions were quickly brought to a close, and the group finished its work by holding a public hearing on the safely generalized subject of security procedures at the State Department and the ONI.[15]

The majority report of the Hobbs Committee, released in October 1946, served only to put a new coat of whitewash on the case. The Department of Justice was completely exonerated. As for Larsen, the committee suggested that there was only "prima facie" evidence that he had broken the law. By contrast, the report lambasted the State Department and the ONI for their lax personnel procedures and handling of documents. The ONI took most of the heat for appointing Andrew Roth to a sensitive liaison post, despite its own earlier finding that he was a Communist. "The watchword and motivating principle of Government employment," the report bravely declared, "must be: None but the best."[16]

Two members of the committee, Frank Fellows and Raymond Springer, filed scathing dissents. Both Springer and Fellows were indignant over the Justice Department's attempts to minimize the importance of the documents. Fellows also took issue with the committee's conclusion that the evidence in the case had been tainted by illegal searches conducted by both the OSS and the FBI. The law on search and seizure, he argued, made a clear distinction between contraband and the government's own property, upholding the right of federal authorities to move without warrants to recover the latter. "I do not see how anybody could claim that these papers were illegally seized," he concluded.

The Hobbs Committee investigation had no immediate impact. It produced no new legislation, and the committee's proceedings were sealed, not to be made public until four years later. Because the committee made little effort to discover what the *Amerasia* case had really involved, it ensured that the issue would continue to fester. By ratifying the official conclusion—that the affair was largely a matter of excess zeal and bad judgment by several government employees and journalists—and avoiding a full and frank airing of the number of documents involved, the nature of some of them, and the questionable motives of several of the defendants, the Hobbs Committee merely provided more fuel for the fire that was sure to ignite when the American public became incensed about the Communist triumph in China.

For Emmanuel Larsen, the experience of testifying before the Hobbs Committee was a crushing disappointment. Quite irrationally, Larsen believed that he would emerge from the hearing room a hero. Instead, the record had been sealed, and once the hearings were over, Congressman Dondero dropped him flat. Worse, his appearance before the committee had cost him an appointment to another government job. As far as Larsen was concerned, there was no difference between his case and Jack Service's—hadn't both of them been giving documents to Jaffe?—yet he had been fired while Service was reinstated and posted abroad, to MacArthur's headquarters in Tokyo of all places. An even more crushing blow to his ego was his discovery that a number of State Department employees had contributed to a defense fund set up to pay Service's legal bills, while nothing of the kind had been done for him.

Based on what he had learned of the grand jury proceedings, Larsen had also convinced himself that he would not have been indicted were it not for Service's testimony. A number of official State Department copies of Service's reports had been found in the *Amerasia* offices, and Service insisted he didn't know how Jaffe got them since he had only handed over personal copies, never department ozalids—reproductions made by a primitive chemical process. In fact, these reports were the least important evidence against Larsen, but he indignantly denied (truthfully or not) that he was responsible for their having fallen into Jaffe's hands. Therefore, he concluded, Service, by also denying any knowledge of the matter, had framed him.[17]

Larsen had now been unemployed for fourteen months, and the prospect of starting a new career unrelated to his passionate interest in Chinese politics was unappealing. No longer able to afford to keep their Washington apartment, he and his wife Thelma went to St. Petersburg, Florida, where they moved in with Larsen's retired father. The elder Larsen was building a new house, and Jimmy filled his empty days by helping out at the construction site.

On August 1, 1946, two former FBI agents who identified themselves as Kirkpatrick and Higgins showed up on the Larsens' doorstep. The pair explained that they had done investigative work on the *Amerasia* case while they were still with the bureau. Now they were working for a new magazine, to be called *Plain Talk*, and they wanted Larsen to write an article on his involvement in the affair for the inaugural issue.

According to Larsen's subsequent account of the interview, he wanted no part of the offer. "Nothing doing," he told the ex-agents. "I have been punished. I have been fined, discredited. I want to be left out."[18]

Refusing to be discouraged, Kirkpatrick and Higgins returned the next day and sweetened their proposal. Among other inducements, they promised that *Plain Talk* would arrange for Larsen to have a voice test, the first step toward a new career as a radio commentator. They also offered $300 and a free trip to New York City to meet the magazine's editor and publisher. Thelma Larsen, who had been out when the ex-agents paid their first visit, was home this time, and she convinced her husband that he could not afford to turn down the offer.

Whether Larsen was really as reluctant as he later claimed is questionable. But it is true that Thelma, his third wife, was distraught over his inability to find work. Thelma considered her husband brilliant, and she was even more firmly convinced than he that he was an innocent victim of the *Amerasia* affair. At a time when vocal ex-Communists were making careers out of apostasy, perhaps it did not seem entirely unrealistic to think that a man who had pleaded no contest to charges linked to an espionage case could capitalize on his notoriety by becoming a radio personality.

At Thelma's urging, Larsen went to New York City, where he was put up in a room at the New Yorker Hotel. On his first evening in town, he had dinner with *Plain Talk*'s editor, Isaac Don Levine, and its publisher and financial backer, Alfred Kohlberg. Their conversation, or so he later claimed, put him on his guard almost at once. "I had fallen in with a group . . . who were very much against the administration," he recalled. Levine provided a rented typewriter and instructed him to write an account of his involvement with *Amerasia*, beginning with some sort of statement about his own background.

Larsen sat down in his hotel room that night and hammered out 24 single-spaced pages. His personal history filled pages 1 through 4, so it was not until page 5 that he got around to describing the State Department as he found it when he came to work there in 1944. At that time, he wrote, the department had been deeply divided, with the Office of Far Eastern Affairs split between the Grew-Dooman "strong Japan" group and the "reformers," whose "chief believer" was John Carter Vincent and which had mounted a campaign to "wilfully sabotage" Patrick Hurley's efforts to secure an agreement between the KMT and the Communists.[19]

In the scenario Larsen presented, he was the scapegoat of the case. John Service had been "the real pipeline from the State Department." And it was Service who had framed him by falsely testifying to the grand jury that Larsen was responsible for giving copies of Service's reports to Philip Jaffe.

Even those sections of the article that had some basis in fact, such as Larsen's account of the opposition to Hurley among the China experts, were hysterical in tone. The leftist clique at the State Department, wrote Larsen, professed to be dedicated to "the cause of the underprivileged Chinese, as if the latter hadn't been able to take care of himself for thousands of years in one of the greatest democracies of all mankind."

If the above sounds incoherent, particularly coming from someone who had made a lifelong study of Chinese history, Larsen, as usual, had a ready-made excuse. He had come down with a bad case of diarrhea and his concentration was undermined by the noisy revels of a party of American Legion conventioneers who occupied the other rooms on his floor. At one point, when he had given up on writing and was trying to get some sleep, he later complained, "wild women" burst into his room and flung themselves down on his bed. "I had to take one and throw her out." To top off his frustrations, Larsen got into a shouting match with Levine, who came by to read over his work and pronounced it useless.[20]

At this point, Larsen told Levine that he couldn't hang around New York City any longer. He had family business to attend to back in Florida. Levine then mentioned for the first time that Larsen's hotel expenses and incidentals were being deducted from his $300 fee. Anxious to depart before he ran up any more bills, Larsen made plans to leave on the next train south. Minutes before he was ready to catch a taxi, Levine and his managing editor, Ralph de Toledano, showed up with a typescript of the article, which they had completely rewritten, or so Larsen later claimed. Larsen was startled to see that the title had been changed from "They Called Me a Spy" to "The State Department Espionage Case." Levine and de Toledano had also padded the piece with a host of new charges, which they claimed to be able to substantiate with clippings from their own files.

Worried about missing his train, Larsen decided not to make an issue of the changes. After asking Levine to put quotation marks around the word "espionage" in the title, he hastily initialed the pages of the rewrite and left for the station.

Larsen heard no more from Levine until he received the October issue of *Plain Talk,* featuring the article under his name. The piece was entitled "The State Department Espionage Case," without the quotation marks qualifying the word "espionage." Further, the changes in the body of the article were even more extensive than he had thought. Both he and his wife were "disgusted" by its distortions and errors, Larsen insisted. "I could have cried."

This, at least, was the story as Larsen told it four years later—a story that has often been repeated as fact by writers who, while hardly sympathetic to Larsen, have found his unflattering portrait of three right-wing principals—Levine, de Toledano, and Kohlberg—irresistible.

Few American journalists were as knowledgeable about Communist espionage as Isaac Don Levine. During his long career, he befriended a host of defectors from the Soviet Union, helping them to tell their stories to the American public. In return, these individuals provided him with a wealth of information about Soviet intelligence activities, only a fraction of which could ever be published. Among Levine's sources was Walter Krivitsky, the head of Soviet intelligence in Western Europe, whose mysterious suicide in 1941 was possibly a KGB assassination. Another was Jan Valtin, whose sensational revelations in *Out of the Night* had prompted a hysterical CPUSA campaign to discredit him.[21]

In 1939 Levine had arranged for Whittaker Chambers to meet privately with Assistant Secretary of State Adolph Berle to warn him that a group of government employees, including Alger Hiss, Solomon Adler (Service's old roommate), Lauchlin Currie, and Harry Dexter White, were engaged in espionage on behalf of the Soviet Union. Much to Levine's frustration, Chambers's warning was ignored and Hiss's career continued to flourish. Thus, when talk of a Communist clique at the State Department resurfaced in connection with the *Amerasia* affair, Levine was prepared to accept it as credible. Chambers had refused to go public with his charges in 1939, but now, seven years later, the political atmosphere was ripe for a change.[22]

Levine was interested in founding a magazine dedicated to crusading against Communist influence in the United States, and in June 1946 he found a potential backer, textile magnate Alfred Kohlberg, who had made his fortune importing hand-embroidered silk from China. During the war,

Kohlberg had served as director of the American Bureau for Medical Aid to China, and he became convinced that the Communist faction within the Institute of Pacific Relations was criticizing the financial practices of the organization as part of a plot to take it over. Kohlberg himself was a longtime member of the IPR, and he launched a campaign to fight leftist influence on the foundation's board.[23]

Levine had been talking to Congressman Dondero and others about the *Amerasia* case, and Kohlberg was impressed by his grasp of the situation. When he agreed to fund Levine's magazine in June, it was understood that the first order of business would be an exposé of the affair.[24]

The inaugural issue of *Plain Talk* featuring Larsen's article was a succès de scandale. Frederick Woltman and other conservative commentators on the case had concentrated their ammunition on Philip Jaffe and Mark Gayn. The *Plain Talk* piece dramatically upped the ante, charging that the center of the conspiracy was actually inside the State Department. According to Larsen's article, the other *Amerasia* defendants were merely carrying out the plan of a secret Communist clique at the State Department whose main goal was discrediting Hurley and Grew. In support of this contention, Larsen recounted that, when he went to see Jaffe in October 1945 to ask him for financial help to pay his attorney, Jaffe had said, "Well, we suffered a lot, but anyhow, we got Grew out."[25]

There was an element of truth to this interpretation. But the article didn't stop there. It went on to name Service, Raymond Ludden, John Paton Davies, John Carter Vincent, and John Emmerson as the key members of a "pro-Soviet group" engaged in a "highly organized campaign to switch American policy in the Far East from its long-tested course to the Soviet line." With further probing, the article promised, the scandal would "assume proportions more far-reaching than those of the Pearl Harbor investigation."

Larsen would later say that he was as startled by this charge as anyone else. This and other controversial fillips had been added to the article by Levine and de Toledano—some while he was still in New York City and others later, without his permission. Even the claim that Service had lied to the grand jury had come from Levine and Kohlberg, who had told him about their supposed insider knowledge of the proceedings during their dinner together in New York City.[26]

But Isaac Don Levine's private papers tell quite a different story. All of the most controversial aspects of the piece were taken directly from Larsen's first draft. And this first draft, in turn, drew heavily on his earlier secret testimony to the Hobbs Committee. Levine's main contribution was to clean up Larsen's prose and tone down his accusations. Levine was also responsible for deleting Larsen's most sensational allegation—naming Dean Acheson as the guiding spirit of the pro-Red clique. This charge, Levine later wrote Senator Millard Tydings, "came to me as a distinct shock. I decided to omit Mr. Larsen's characterization of Acheson from the article."[27]

Moreover, as Levine's files reveal, Larsen showed no signs of disillusionment in the months immediately following his supposedly nightmarish sojourn in New York City. After parting company with Levine and de Toledano, Larsen went on to Washington, where he continued doing research to tie up the loose ends in his manuscript, and on August 8, he called Levine to report a recent phone conversation with James McInerney in which the latter admitted that the Justice Department had come under pressure from Emmanuel Celler. According to Larsen, McInerney also told him that Service had given documents to both Jaffe and Gayn, though he refused to quote a source on this.[28]

On returning to Florida, Larsen wrote Levine a friendly letter, thanking him for his hospitality in New York City and relaying the news that John Carter Vincent was up for a promotion to minister and might be sent to either Thailand or Afghanistan. "Please see what you can do to prevent such a thing from happening," he implored. "Instead of being promoted, he ought to be fired." Larsen then reiterated his conviction that both Vincent and Acheson were pro-Communist.[29]

A few weeks later, Larsen received his copy of *Plain Talk* in the mail. Far from feeling betrayed, he dashed off a letter congratulating Levine on the successful launching of the magazine. His only complaint was that *Plain Talk* was not being sold at newsstands. Larsen obviously still considered Levine a political ally, and he may well have been angling for another assignment. Several pages of the letter were devoted to the recent firing of former vice president Henry Wallace, who had been ousted from his position as secretary of commerce after he made a speech in Madison Square Garden calling for the United States to accept Soviet hegemony in Eastern Europe. Larsen hinted that he had insider information, gleaned from Andrew Roth, about Wallace's friendship with Drew Pearson's aide, David Karr. (Karr, in fact, was close to Wallace.) He also mentioned that during his 1944 visit to China, Wallace had met with a group called the Democratic League, which Larsen was prepared to prove was a front for the Communist Party.[30]

Throughout the autumn of 1946, Larsen wrote Levine regularly, sending unsolicited letters to the editor as well as suggestions to Levine and his staff for further full-length pieces. Larsen and his wife had moved back to Washington, and he typically began each letter by painting a bleak picture of his financial situation and pleading for work so that he could cover his rent and stave off the bill collectors.

In November, Larsen mentioned that he was working on a translation of Mao's speeches that would demonstrate that the Chinese Communists were "true Marxists." The statements that Mao and his allies issued for foreign consumption were intentionally deceptive, Larsen added, and "the pro-Communist writers in this country did not fall quite innocently for this deception."[31]

In December, he took up the subject of the Yalta agreement. At the Yalta conference, Roosevelt, acting on the assumption that the United States needed Soviet help to defeat Japan, had endorsed a provision that allowed the Soviets to move an army into Manchuria in exchange for a treaty under which the Soviet Union recognized the KMT as the legitimate government of China. In a letter to Levine, Larsen set forth his not entirely original view that the Yalta pact represented the triumph of the pro-Soviet cabal at the State Department. The deal, he noted, had been arranged over the protests of Nationalist leaders like T. V. Soong, who had signed the resulting Sino-Soviet treaty "with clenched fists and gnashing teeth."[32]

Some of Larsen's other article ideas anticipated the guilt-by-association tactics that would become a hallmark of Senator Joseph McCarthy. Two American officers who had been detained by Chinese Communists had reported that their captors had provided them with American books. Larsen suggested that *Plain Talk* use this information to mount an attack on the writers of the works in question, since the mere fact that their books had been "approved" by the Chinese Communists was a sign that they were suspect.[33]

It wasn't until February 1947, however, when Larsen returned to the subject of his bête noire, John Carter Vincent, that Levine expressed interest in having him write for *Plain Talk* again. Ever since his arrest, Larsen had been hinting that the FBI had failed to identify the real high-level Soviet spy ensconced at the State Department, a veiled reference to Vincent. Larsen recounted a conversation with a former aide to Patrick Hurley whom he had met in the office of Senator Styles Bridges. The aide, said Larsen, had described how Vincent had used his influence to help "guilty persons in the espionage case" evade punishment. Larsen hoped to obtain expense money from Alfred Kohlberg so that he could travel to Santa Fe, where Hurley was living, to obtain "documentary evidence" of the fix, although it stands to reason that Hurley would have publicized such evidence if he had it.[34]

Kohlberg declined to pay for the trip, but two nights later, he and Larsen met for dinner to discuss another source Larsen had lined up. Larsen told Kohlberg that he had recently learned that Syngman Rhee, the president of South Korea, had long been feuding with John Carter Vincent and had material that could be used to discredit Vincent. Nothing came of this lead.[35]

Two months later, Larsen visited Stanley Hornbeck, a former mentor who had arranged for his transfer from the ONI to the State Department in 1944. Hornbeck, at least according to Larsen, praised his *Plain Talk* article and suggested that although he could not go public on the issue, he wanted to help stop Vincent. Hornbeck may also have been the source of some additional material Larsen forwarded to Levine, purporting to show that certain anti-Nationalist information included in Jack Service's dispatches was taken directly from Communist propaganda.[36]

Hornbeck, of course, still blamed Vincent for engineering the coup that had ousted him from his position as head of the Office of Far Eastern Affairs. Larsen hated Vincent because he had defended Service but had let Larsen know in no uncertain terms that he wanted nothing to do with him. Both were determined to block Vincent's promotion to ministerial rank, which was about to be submitted to the Senate Foreign Relations Committee, and conservatives were hoping to use the occasion to denounce America's failure to commit itself to wholehearted support of the Nationalists in the Chinese civil war.

Curiously, considering that he had become the focus of such ferocious animosity, Vincent was a cautious bureaucrat, not known for taking extreme positions. Where China policy was concerned, his recommendations had always been moderate. He had never entirely supported the pro-Mao views expressed by Service and Davies in their reports from Yenan. "In the more conservative atmosphere of the State Department it seemed that they overstated their case. It seemed like they were special pleaders," he told historian Gary May many years later.[37] In the postwar era, as head of the Office of Far Eastern Affairs, Vincent had tried to steer a middle course, supporting limited aid to the KMT but doing his best to keep the

United States from making a major commitment to involvement in the Chinese civil war.

A Clemson University graduate whose hobbies included playing classical music on the flute and studying eighteenth-century English poetry, Vincent was from a Georgia farm family, not the scion of an upper-class family as was widely assumed. But to many on Capitol Hill, he and Acheson epitomized the "striped pants" intellectuals whose manners were considered condescending and lacking in candor. Vincent's very mildness encouraged his opponents to believe that he was a backstairs manipulator, and no doubt his real problem was that he was the epitome of the New Deal liberal—a group that Alfred Kohlberg denounced as "slimy traitors," even more hateful than the Communists themselves. However, persistent gossip that Vincent had been the target of an FBI investigation made even some potential supporters wary.

Patrick Hurley was already busy lobbying against Vincent on Capitol Hill and had passed on to Senator Styles Bridges the tip he had received in 1945 from William Donovan that Vincent was a Soviet spy. Larsen, who had heard the story from the source who provided him with the Syngman Rhee material, confided to Kohlberg that Hoover "had something on Vincent that would blow Vincent sky high."[38]

In fact, the FBI's investigation never had definitively established how a copy of the Wells report on Thailand, apparently routed to Vincent's desk, turned up in the *Amerasia* cache. The source of the leak is hardly likely to have been Vincent himself, since chance comments about Vincent on the FBI surveillance tapes show that Roth and Jaffe looked down on Vincent as a timid liberal who sympathized with *Amerasia's* positions but refused to go all the way by helping them out. However, Larsen would not normally have had access to the document either, so his claim to know more than he had yet told about the mystery was intriguing. If Larsen hoped to be assigned to write an article about Vincent, he was destined to be disappointed. This was a task that Alfred Kohlberg was determined to take on himself. The resulting article, entitled "The State Department's Left Hand," drew on some of Larsen's information to prop up its contention that Vincent was the head of a secret Maoist "cell" at the State Department. Although none of Kohlberg's evidence would stand up to scrutiny, reaction to the article kept Vincent's nomination bottled up in committee until July, and even then he was promoted only on the understanding that he would not be appointed to an ambassadorship in the Far East.[39]

By now it was abundantly clear to Levine that Larsen had no firsthand information about Vincent and his "clique." Even some of the more dramatic material in his *Plain Talk* piece had apparently been given to him by Congressman Dondero, who in turn was passing on what he had heard from his source close to the investigation. Levine's patience was sorely tried. He vetoed Larsen's next idea for an article that would "torpedo" Stilwell on the grounds that although the general was "a drunk" and an incompetent administrator, he was also "a top sergeant . . . [and] a brave officer, popular with his men." Levine further complained that Larsen's writing was not "newsy" enough and "too disorganized" to be publishable—as well as too "historical, too academic." He did recommend Larsen as a resource person for Freda Utley and other writers in the field, but such referrals were not always appreciated. Larsen was tired of having other people pick his brains; he wanted recognition, and with every rejection, his letters to Levine became more anguished and more strident.[40]

By 1948, Larsen had founded his own news organization, the Far Eastern Information Service, which published the right-wing *Far Eastern News Letter*. Larsen bragged that his agency had powerful backers, including Patrick Hurley and William Bullitt, the former U.S. ambassador to the Soviet Union, but for the most part it was a one-man organization, and a money-losing one at that. Although he was now, in a sense, Levine's competitor, Larsen continued to pester the editor of *Plain Talk* with proposals, usually accompanied by highly unrealistic financial demands. On one occasion, for example, Larsen suggested that he and a former Polish military attaché would coauthor a series of articles, for which he wanted several thousand dollars. Another of his schemes was for Levine to sublease space in his office in order to set up a Washington bureau of *Plain Talk* "in return for a small monthly contribution to cover my office overhead." When this suggestion was rejected, Larsen began to pursue Kohlberg, offering to make room in his office for the D.C. headquarters of Kohlberg's New York–based lobbying group, the American China Policy Association. Kohlberg rejected this suggestion outright, but Levine, whose own magazine was on the verge of bankruptcy, felt sorry enough for Larsen to send him an occasional small check out of his own funds.[41]

These acts of charity did not prevent Levine from being placed alongside Service and Vincent on Larsen's personal enemies list. Three years had passed since the appearance of Larsen's article in *Plain Talk*, and Larsen had reaped none of the rewards he had hoped for. By the end of January 1950, Larsen's correspondence with Levine had petered out, and two months later he sat down and wrote a memo to himself, venting his bitterness over the way Levine and Kohlberg had "looked upon me as a handy tool to use whenever expedient, preferring to have no other close association with me."[42]

Ironically, even as Larsen was pondering how to get revenge on mentors who had failed to promote his career, the conservative assault on Dean Acheson and his followers at the State Department was gathering steam. During the summer of 1948, Kohlberg and Levine's complaints about pro-Communist infiltration in the State Department had taken on new impetus when two self-confessed former Soviet agents appeared before HUAC to discuss their relationship with former officials in the Roosevelt and Truman administrations.

The most spectacular charges emanated from Whittaker Chambers. Repeating the story he had told privately to Adolph Berle nine years earlier, the underground Communist turned *Time* magazine editor revealed that in the mid-1930s he had received official documents from State Department official Alger Hiss, a member of the official U.S. delegation to Yalta and later an organizer of the San Francisco conference on the UN. His testimony against Hiss was the opening salvo of an ideological war. Although Chambers eventually produced damning evidence in the form of State Department memos copied on the Hiss family's personal Woodstock typewriter, leading to Hiss's conviction for perjury, many former New Dealers simply refused to consider the possibility that Chambers was telling the truth. To believe the worst about Alger Hiss seemed tantamount to accepting an indictment of the Roosevelt era as a whole. Conservatives, on the other hand, were infuriated by the reflexive defense of Hiss after Hiss's conviction made by Dean Acheson, who vowed not to turn his back on his old friend, and even by Truman, who dismissed Chambers's charges as a "red herring."

Both defenders and critics of Hiss have occasionally tried to connect his case with the *Amerasia* affair. For example, the story was circulated that Edward Stettinius had told Hiss that the documents produced by Chambers were originally among the papers seized in Jaffe's office. Hiss's attorneys did pursue such a possibility. Conservative journalists attempted to discover a connection between Hiss and Service but were unsuccessful since the two had never met.[43]

The second important witness heard by HUAC that summer cast a wider net. Elizabeth Terrill Bentley, a decidedly unglamorous Vassar College graduate whom the press insisted on calling the "blonde spy queen," had been the lover of Jacob Golos, an agent for the KGB, the chief Soviet intelligence service, until his death from a heart attack in 1943. During their affair, Bentley had made regular trips to Washington to receive documents from various members of secret party cells made up of employees from several government agencies. After Golos's death, Bentley came under increasing pressure from her KGB supervisors to turn her sources over directly to them. Disillusioned, in the fall of 1945, she walked into an FBI office in Connecticut and began telling her story. Unlike Chambers, Bentley had no documentary proof to support her allegations, but she claimed to have knowledge of over forty individuals who had been involved in espionage to one degree or another and many more who had unsavory contacts.[44]

According to Bentley, the leader of an espionage cell in the Treasury Department was one Nathan Gregory Silvermaster. Among the members or sometime contacts of the group were former assistant secretary of the treasury Harry Dexter White—also named by Chambers—Frank Coe, Solomon Adler, and Lauchlin Currie.

Bentley admitted that she had never actually met Currie. She knew his name only because she had heard of him from the Silvermasters and other members of the Treasury Department cell. On one occasion, she recalled being told, Currie had burst into the office of one of the ring members with the news that American cryptanalysts were on the verge of breaking the Soviet military code. Bentley added that, as far as she knew, Currie was "definitely not a Communist." She could only speculate on what his motives for passing information might have been, but, judging from remarks made by the Silvermasters, she surmised that Currie "certainly" knew the information he provided was going to be passed on to the Soviets.[45]

Bentley's public accusation against the economist, who had once been one of six personal assistants to the president, made front-page news. Currie, speaking from his home in Scarsdale, New York, denounced the testimony as "fantastic," adding, "To the best of my knowledge I have never known or associated in any way directly or indirectly with a Communist agent."[46]

Bentley was not the first former Soviet agent to warn the government about Currie. In his secret conversation with Adolph Berle in 1939, Whittaker Chambers had described the Canadian economist as "a fellow traveler who helped the Communists but never went the whole way."[47] By the time Bentley came forward late in 1945, Currie had already left the govern-

Lauchlin Currie appearing before the House Un-American Activities Committee in 1948 to deny Elizabeth Bentley's charges that he was a source of information for her Soviet spy ring. (UPI/The Bettmann Archive)

ment, and the FBI's investigation of him did not really go into full swing until after her HUAC testimony in 1948 had created a public furor.

Perhaps the most intriguing allegation gleaned from this belated investigation was the suggestion, made by an anonymous informant who had worked with Currie during one of his missions to Chungking, that Chi Ch'ao-ting, with Sol Adler's knowledge and acquiescence, may have deliberately promoted the collapse of the Nationalist regime's currency through a variety of ill-advised monetary policies. The pattern that emerged from the FBI's investigation was one of Currie acting as mentor to a number of younger men with Communist leanings, especially Sol Adler, Michael Greenberg, and Frank Coe. Currie's confidence in Greenberg, who was his assistant at the FEA, and in Coe, who was often selected to represent the FEA in meetings at the Treasury Department, had struck coworkers as irrational at the time because Greenberg had a reputation for laziness and Coe was well known for his drinking problem. (As one FBI source put it, Coe needed three cocktails to "warm up" for lunch.) Currie also provided a character reference for Nathan Silvermaster when he was investigated for Communist activities and—more suspiciously as far as the bureau was concerned—had sponsored the visa application of Paul Hagan, also known as Karl Josef Frank, a German national later alleged to be a Soviet agent. Another heavily censored entry in the FBI files suggests that sometime in the early 1940s Currie had made some sort of damaging admission to an individual in the Navy Department, who then reported the conversation to Secretary James Forrestal.[48]

No one who talked to the bureau seriously believed that Currie was a Communist Party member, secret or otherwise, and although one apparently knowledgeable source called him a "controlled socialist" and "the darling of the IPR," his most conspicuous public activities over the years had been as a member of a society formed to promote psychoanalysis. Overall, the FBI file suggests that Currie was hardly a controlled agent but an eccentric, rather self-aggrandizing individual who enjoyed the sensation of manipulating events from behind the scenes.

Despite the important role Currie had played in America's China policy during the war, the charges against him never captured the imagination of Kohlberg and the China Lobby. Whatever Currie may or may not have been up to, he had never been a vocal supporter of Stilwell, having concluded early on that the general had put himself in an impossible position vis-à-vis Chiang. His views, in general, were little known, and thus he did not make a tempting target for those who sought to explain why we had "lost" China to the Reds.

Moreover, in contrast to Nathan Silvermaster and Abraham George Silverman, who both took the Fifth Amendment when called before HUAC to answer Bentley's charges, Currie appeared voluntarily and answered all questions put to him. His indignant denial of Bentley's hearsay testimony and his fervent assertions of loyalty made a good impression on Congressman Richard Nixon and other committee members who took part in questioning him. Although the FBI continued to take a rather halfhearted interest in Currie for some years, the allegations against him were generally discounted by the public—as those against Hiss might have been were it not for Nixon's persistence and Hiss's own recklessness in filing a $75,000 libel suit against Whittaker Chambers.

Currie spent much of the year after Bentley made her charges in Colombia, preparing a development report on behalf of the IBRD, and in mid-1949, his mission completed, he announced that he was accepting a post as adviser to the Colombian government. He soon bought a cattle ranch outside of Bogota, and in 1953 he divorced his first wife to marry a Colombian citizen. Except for occasional business trips, he never returned to the United States and became a Colombian citizen in 1958. In 1986, at age eighty-six, he continued to dismiss assertions that he was ever involved in espionage; he died in 1993. His role in the *Amerasia* affair never became a major issue.[49]

With new spy allegations surfacing regularly, the *Amerasia* case appeared to be a dead letter by 1949. The case might have remained in obscurity had it not been for unhappiness among congressional Republicans over the State Department's tepid execution of President Truman's federal employee loyalty program. The inherent difficulties with the program, which was designed to purge Communists from the ranks of government employees, were especially acute in the case of the operation of the Loyalty-Security Board at the State Department. Foreign service officers were unlikely to report honestly on political conditions abroad when they knew that every word they wrote might later be scrutinized for evidence of pro-Communist leanings. The program was having a chilling effect on morale, to say the least. On the other hand, conservatives in Congress were frustrated by the unwillingness of high officials at the State Department to admit that the department might have a problem.

As early as 1948, a struggle was under way between the State Department and the House Appropriations Committee over the security issue. An Appropriations Committee staff investigator named Robert E. Lee reviewed several hundred State Department personnel files and concluded that the handling of 108 cases was questionable. None of these involved actual Communist Party members, although in Lee's subjective judgment, as many as fifty individuals were suspect on the ground of "loyalty." When the report was discussed by the committee in March, a State Department spokesman explained that only 51 of the 108 individuals in question were still employed by the State Department and that 22 of them were still under investigation. The department's reply satisfied the Appropriations Committee for the time being, but by early 1950, with Hiss's second perjury trial sharing the front pages with the arrest of atomic physicist Klaus Fuchs, the issue was due to be revived. And so, in the bargain, were the conservatives' unanswered questions about the "State Department espionage case" of 1945.[50]

Senator McCarthy and the Tydings Committee

In February 1950 Joseph McCarthy was an obscure first-term Republican senator of little distinction, best known for his efforts to aid Pepsi Cola end sugar rationing and for a bizarre campaign on behalf of German SS troops accused of murdering American POWs during World War II. His chances for reelection did not appear bright. The GOP was sending McCarthy on a speaking tour of the political boondocks—Wheeling, West Virginia, Reno, Nevada, and Huron, South Dakota, were among the stops on his itinerary—and McCarthy asked a Washington journalist named George Waters to help him work up a speech on the politically hot topic of Communism in government.

The speech McCarthy took with him when he left the capital was largely a rehash of anti-Communist rhetoric from recent ad-

dresses by Congressman Richard Nixon and others. But McCarthy's de
ery, before a Lincoln's Day banquet sponsored by the Ohio County ...
publican Women's Club in Wheeling, made a far bigger splash than he or
anyone else had anticipated. Warming to his theme of the assault of "God-
less Communism" on the American way of life, McCarthy denounced the
State Department as a nest of spies. The first active foreign service officer
McCarthy mentioned was John Stewart Service.

What distinguished McCarthy's speech from standard anti-Communist
oratory was his claim to have a list of "card carrying Communists" employed at the State Department. No reporter had actually had a chance to
examine the list, and as the senator's tour continued westward, the number
of names it was said to contain varied erratically—from 205, the count
dipped to 57, then rose to 81. The very wildness of the charges ignited
speculation and propelled the speaking tour onto the front pages of newspapers across the country.

McCarthy's charges, suggesting that the United States had been betrayed from within, found an audience. His Wheeling speech came just
two months after Mao Tse-tung and his Communist forces had seized
power in China. America's ally, Chiang Kai-shek, had fled to Formosa.
Five days before McCarthy's speech, Mao had signed a thirty-year mutual
aid treaty with the Soviet Union, increasing fears that the Soviet Union,
with its new, large Communist ally, was on the march. By the end of June
1950, the United States was fighting in Korea to repulse a Communist
assault on South Korea. The cold war had entered a new, more ominous
period.

Even as Americans tried to cope with a more dangerous world, they
were forced to consider whether some of their fellow citizens were working for their country's enemy. On January 21, 1950, Alger Hiss was found
guilty by a federal district court after being accused of serving as a Soviet
agent while working for the State Department. A few days later, Klaus
Fuchs, a German-born physicist, was arrested in Great Britain on charges
of giving atomic bomb secrets to the Soviet Union; he confessed two days
before McCarthy spoke in Wheeling. Fuchs soon led the FBI to Harry
Gold, a courier, who implicated David Greenglass, a technician at Los
Alamos. Before the summer of 1950 ended, Ethel and Julius Rosenberg,
Greenglass's sister and brother-in-law, were under indictment for involvement in a Soviet spy ring.

Atomic espionage, in particular, seemed to suggest an answer to the
perplexing question of how the Soviet Union, previously considered years

behind the United States in technological prowess, had so quickly breached America's atomic monopoly by exploding its own nuclear device in 1949. Atomic scientists had sold secrets. Ordinary Americans like Gold, Greenglass, and the Rosenbergs had betrayed their country for ideological principles. Just as frightening to many Americans was the possibility that government employees like Alger Hiss had betrayed their trust.

As the United States reeled under the impact of these shocks, many Americans found it plausible to believe that a "fifth column" of traitors was responsible. As historian Stephen Ambrose has noted, "McCarthy provided a simple answer to those who were frustrated as America seemed to suffer defeat after defeat in the Cold War."[1]

Back in Washington, Emmanuel Larsen was following the progress of McCarthy's tour with more than ordinary interest. As soon as he saw that McCarthy, in a speech in Reno, Nevada, had named Jack Service as one of 57 "card carrying" Communists still working at the State Department, Larsen knew that he would "sooner or later become involved" in this latest resurfacing of the *Amerasia* case.[2]

Returning from his lecture tour, McCarthy repeated his charges on the floor of the Senate in a tumultuous eight-hour speech. When enraged Democrats demanded that he either substantiate his claims or shut up, the senator refused to name his source but read what were supposedly brief excerpts of case histories, taken from State Department security files. He also hinted darkly that case numbers 1, 2, and 81 on his secret list were bombshells. These individuals were the "big three"—the secret Communists whose exposure would "break the back" of an espionage ring still operating at the State Department.[3]

Within days, the Democratic majority in the Senate had worked out an agreement with the Republicans to establish a special subcommittee of the Foreign Relations Committee, empowered to investigate McCarthy's allegations. The Tydings Committee, named for its chairman Millard Tydings, the senior Democratic senator from Maryland, scheduled its first hearings for March 8, just twenty-eight days after McCarthy's Senate speech. Although Tydings announced that the investigation would be impartial, letting "the chips fall where they may," he and the other Democratic members, Brian McMahon of Connecticut and Theodore Green of Rhode Island, clearly expected that an inquiry into the accusations would expose the wild inaccuracy of McCarthy's charges and finish him politically, perhaps even leading to censure proceedings. Of the two Republicans on the committee, Henry Cabot Lodge of Massachusetts was a moderate with a record of supporting a bipartisan foreign policy. Bourke Hickenlooper of Indiana was the only likely McCarthy ally.

As Tydings and the Democrats strongly suspected, McCarthy had been winging it all along. The secret list he claimed to be carrying in his overstuffed briefcase was nothing more than an outdated summary of State Department Loyalty-Security Board proceedings that had been given to House Appropriations Committee investigator Robert E. Lee back in 1948, its specifics garbled in McCarthy's accounts almost beyond recognition. The so-called "Lee list" was old news. Many of the cases it described involved charges of alcohol abuse, promiscuity, or, in one instance, "entertain[ing] Negroes"—complaints that had nothing to do with Communism. In other instances, the charges had long ago been investigated and disproved. Seventy-nine of the individuals involved had already left the State Department by 1946.[4]

McCarthy knew his "list" would not stand up to scrutiny, but as long as he was on the rubber chicken circuit, he had managed to push this minor detail to the back of his mind. "I've got a sockful of shit and I know how to use it," he told one Wisconsin journalist who pressed him for details.[5] With the Tydings Committee about to get under way, he needed substantiation, and fast. Fortunately for him, anti-Communist activists were soon beating a path to his office door. The volunteers were a mixed lot, ranging from the Pulitzer Prize–winning journalist Frederick Woltman on down to the sleaziest of would-be informers.

Several of McCarthy's volunteer informants had followed the *Amerasia* affair closely. Alfred Kohlberg was feeding the senator documents on the IPR. Another source, attorney Robert Morris, who was eventually taken on as minority counsel to the Tydings Committee, had been a lawyer for the Rapp-Coudert investigation of Communist teachers at the City College of New York and later served on the naval intelligence committee that recommended against appointing Andrew Roth to the ONI. McCarthy—who at the time of his return from his cross-country trip knew so little about American Communism that he could not even identify Earl Browder— was also being coached by conservative senators and representatives, including George Dondero.[6]

It isn't clear who first steered McCarthy in the direction of Emmanuel Larsen—Dondero, Morris, and Kohlberg are all possibilities—but on March 18, 1950, Larsen was delighted to receive a call inviting him to a private conference that afternoon at five o'clock in the senator's cramped office in the basement of the old Senate office building.[7]

first, the meeting went well. McCarthy, Larsen later recalled, was ᵊmely pleasant." He badly needed a witness who could substantiate his accusation against Service, the only active State Department official on his list who was remotely close to the policy-making level, and Larsen was all too happy to oblige. Larsen began briefing the senator and his aide, Don Surine, on the complexities of the case. Soon, however, he found that he was having trouble holding McCarthy's attention. The meeting was repeatedly interrupted by phone calls, a problem the senator finally solved by shouting to his secretary to make excuses for him: "Tell them I have to go to China or I'm having a baby," he ordered. Larsen then tried to explain that discrediting Service would not be easy; his reporting from China had been "realistic," so it might be embarrassing if the full texts of his dispatches were read into the record. Such a warning, an uncharacteristic moderation from Larsen, only made McCarthy restless. He wanted rhetorical ammunition, not a lecture.[8]

As Larsen put it, the senator "gave me to understand rather clearly that I was to testify for him in the manner he wanted." After hinting that he might attack Larsen, too, unless he testified "correctly," McCarthy left the room. As soon as his boss was gone, Don Surine threatened, "You are equally guilty with the others," but, he added, switching to a cajoling tone, "if you string along with us, then it will go easy for you."

McCarthy and Surine's improvised good cop/bad cop routine may have worked on others, but it was the wrong approach to take with Jimmy Larsen. A bit of an amateur blackmailer himself, Larsen understood instinctively that McCarthy needed him more than he needed McCarthy. Larsen had learned from experience to be cynical about the promises of those who wanted his testimony, and in any case, his fondest wish was to somehow work his way back into the good graces of the State Department, a favor it was not in the senator's power to bestow.

Larsen also had a problem that anyone unfamiliar with the still-secret evidence in the *Amerasia* case could not fully appreciate. He—not Service—had been identified by the FBI as Philip Jaffe's most important source. He had been paid by Jaffe. If he admitted that the purpose of the *Amerasia* conspiracy was espionage, then he would be implicating himself as one of the key figures in a spy ring. It was one thing to talk about an undiscovered State Department conspiracy involving Vincent, Acheson, and others, as he had in his testimony to the Hobbs Committee and in *Plain Talk*, and quite another to point the finger back at himself for filching documents. Larsen saw the pitfall in front of him and exasperated

Surine by repeatedly objecting to the latter's use of the word "espionage" in connection with *Amerasia*.

Surine angrily pointed out that this was not what Larsen had said in his *Plain Talk* article. "Are you defending *Amerasia*?" he demanded.

"No, Mr. Surine. I am defending myself," Larsen retorted.[9]

Two days later, a nervous Larsen went to the State Department to see John Peurifoy, the deputy undersecretary of state for administration. A year earlier, when he was in the process of applying for yet another government position, Larsen had asked one of his contacts in Congress to phone Peurifoy and find out whether there was anything in his personnel file besides the *Amerasia* affair that might be held against him. Peurifoy had looked over the records and sent word that there was not, a favor that Larsen interpreted as evidence that Peurifoy was, if not on his side, at least not an enemy. Now Larsen told Peurifoy that McCarthy had threatened to include him on his enemies list because he was refusing to testify before the Tydings Committee against Jack Service.

Peurifoy listened to Larsen's complaints and promised to refer the matter to the legal division of the State Department. This must have made Larsen fear that he had not gone far enough. Later that same afternoon, he paid a second call on Peurifoy, bringing with him a written memorandum summarizing his contacts with McCarthy. The memo hinted that McCarthy had not only pressured him to name Service as a Communist but had wanted him to accuse *Peurifoy*—"the first person to give me a lift when I asked for State Department clearance last year," as Larsen put it.

Larsen left this insurance policy with the State Department's legal division, then went home and waited to see whether anyone would have the nerve to subpoena him.[10]

McCarthy, meanwhile, was floundering. On March 14, four days before his meeting with Larsen, McCarthy had gone over the case against Service with the committee. As David Oshinsky has written, Service's case was "vital to McCarthy's indictment of the China hands." But the senator's knowledge of Service's career was vague at best. He erroneously identified Service as a close "friend and associate of Frederick Vanderbilt Field" and reported, again incorrectly, that "a number of members of the grand jury, but not the required twelve," had voted to indict Service for espionage. The only reason Service had been arrested, McCarthy claimed, was that Joseph Grew had insisted on it, despite the fact that the FBI had discovered that Service "was in communication from China with Jaffe"—another canard, this one drawn from Larsen's *Plain Talk* article.[11]

With Larsen refusing to testify against Service, McCarthy's case had reached a dead end. In the meantime, the subjects from the Lee list that the senator produced during the opening days of the Tydings hearings were, comparatively speaking, small fish. One was Harvard astronomer Harlow Shapley, whose only work for the State Department consisted of serving on the National Commission to the United Nations Educational, Scientific, and Cultural Organization. Another, a highly respected former New York municipal judge who had worked briefly at the State Department, had in fact been part of the anti-Communist faction of the American Labor Party. With nothing new to report on John Service, McCarthy was in need of a big name, and on March 22, he held a press conference to announce that he was about to go after the "top Russian espionage agent" in the United States, the man who was "Alger Hiss's boss."

This proved to be Owen Lattimore, the expert on Mongolian history and politics who had edited the IPR's official journal until 1941. In a sense, Lattimore was a brilliant choice. As editor of *Pacific Affairs*, he had compiled a rather shoddy record for following the twists and turns of the Communist line; a reliable defender of Stalin, he had actually said of the Moscow purge trials in 1938, "They sound like democracy to me." Lattimore, however, had worked most of his life in the private sector. Like many academics with expertise in Asian affairs, he had volunteered for government service during the war, briefly serving as Roosevelt's adviser to Chiang Kai-shek and later as an administrator in the OWI. His postwar work for the State Department consisted of chairing a two-day panel discussion and submitting one memorandum; he was hardly one of the State Department's "top advisors on Far Eastern Affairs," as McCarthy claimed.[12]

Lattimore happened to be in Afghanistan on a UN mission when McCarthy first began mentioning his name. Alerted by his wife, he rushed back to the United States, arriving in time to be present, conspicuously taking notes on a steno pad, as McCarthy's star witness, Louis Budenz, a former managing editor of the *Daily Worker*, was sworn in.

In 1945, Bishop Fulton J. Sheen, whose television sermons would soon become a long-running feature on network television, had persuaded Budenz to renounce Marxism and return to his Catholic roots. Deserting the Communist Party for the faculty of Fordham University, Budenz began cooperating in federal prosecutions of party leaders, appearing as one of the chief government witnesses in the Smith Act trial of 1948. Testifying before the Tydings Committee, Budenz recalled being told by party official Jack Stachel that Philip Jaffe, Frederick Vanderbilt Field, and Lattimore were all part of a ring set up to infiltrate the IPR. Budenz claimed to have seen letters on onionskin paper, presumably from Moscow, that identified Lattimore by the code name "X." Further, he added for good measure, John Stewart Service had been known in party circles as "Lattimore's pupil."[13]

Budenz also obligingly linked Lattimore to the fixing of the *Amerasia* case. When Philip Jaffe was first arrested, he said, the reaction at party headquarters had been consternation. There was even talk of denouncing him as a pro-Japanese, pro-Nazi infiltrator. Instead, the party decided to remain silent, and Budenz later heard from Stachel that Lattimore had "been of service" in getting the charges against the *Amerasia* defendants reduced. When Jaffe's legal problems were finally resolved, Budenz went on, the Jaffes had thrown a party at their apartment, where the guests drank toasts to the coming victory of Communism in China and the defeat of American imperialism.

In a letter to Senator Tydings, Budenz elaborated on this account, recalling that he had overheard William Weiner, the party's chief financial officer, remarking that he had been responsible for "the specific financial arrangements for the settlement of the case satisfactorily." Budenz claimed that he knew of other occasions in the past when Weiner had paid witnesses not to testify in court cases of interest to the party.[14]

Budenz's testimony was shocking. It was not, however, particularly believable. Since the *Amerasia* case had never come to trial, and did not depend on outside witnesses at the grand jury stage, it isn't clear just whom the Communist Party would have paid off. Budenz, moreover, had been talking to the FBI and local law enforcement agencies for five years without ever mentioning the Jaffe-Field-Lattimore espionage ring, which he now claimed was so important. He had even written a magazine article on the *Amerasia* case for *Collier's* in 1949, giving a version of the case quite different from the one he presented to the senators. In the *Collier's* article, it was Alger Hiss, not Lattimore, who was asked by the party to fix the case.[15]

Budenz was not a fraud. He had, indeed, been a party insider, and for all we know, he may actually have attended a victory celebration at the Jaffes' apartment and heard the very rumors he passed on in his testimony. But Budenz, who had testified effectively at the Smith Act trial in New York City, was uncharacteristically hesitant and vague during his appearance before the Tydings panel. Budenz's nervousness was noted by several reporters present at the time, who wondered whether he had been pressured into appearing. And, in fact, minority counsel Robert Morris had spent several days at Budenz's home in suburban New York City, coaching him on his testimony and even hiding in another room of the house when the majority counsel, Edward Morgan, happened to show up to deliver a subpoena.[16]

In spite of this thorough preparation, Budenz backed down under stern questioning by Morgan and Senator Theodore Green. He admitted that even if his information about Lattimore's relationship to the party was correct, Lattimore's role at the IPR would have been to influence other writers and scholars, not to conduct espionage.

Even McCarthy's allies realized that Budenz had gone too far. The anti-Communist journalist Freda Utley, called to rebut Lattimore's own lengthy, and rather selective, description of his published writings, was cut off by Tydings after a few minutes. Even so, the testimony Utley did manage to give did nothing to support McCarthy's claim that Lattimore was a spy. Lattimore, she said flatly, was a propagandist whose "great talents" would have been wasted in espionage.

Democrats on the committee, meanwhile, fought back by seeing to it that a subpoena was issued to Earl Browder, long since expelled from the Communist Party, who denounced Budenz as a "professional perjurer." Browder's objectivity on the subject of apostate Communist leaders was somewhat suspect, of course, and he rounded out his testimony by denying that Philip Jaffe was a Communist and characterizing Lattimore as an individual who held anti-Communist views "of a profound character." Unfortunately, since Browder had consistently taken the position that he had no knowledge whatsoever of Soviet intelligence operations, he was forced to concede that even if Lattimore were a spy, he would not be in a position to know about his activities. The senators unfortunately did not have access to the wiretapped conversations indicating that Browder knew quite well that Philip Jaffe had been attempting to develop an espionage network.[17]

Out of all this, only one undisputed fact emerged linking Owen Lattimore to the *Amerasia* affair. Two days before the arrests, the Roths, Jack Service, and a woman named Rose Yardoumian who was employed at the Washington office of the IPR had attended a cookout at Lattimore's home in Towson, Maryland. While the other guests ate hamburgers cooked on the grill in the Lattimores' backyard, Roth and Lattimore spent a good part of the evening huddled together over a pile of papers. Lattimore insisted, under oath, that the papers in question were pages from Roth's manuscript, and he was able to produce a witness who had been at the party to back up his story. By all odds, he was telling the simple truth, but for the senators who had heard five years of gossip and speculation about *Amerasia*, the account of the party—with its hint of a closer relationship between Service and his cosuspect than many outsiders had assumed—was tantalizing.[18]

Lattimore had already been given an opportunity to testify on his own behalf on April 6. On that occasion, he spoke uninterrupted for an hour and forty-five minutes, reading a 10,000-word statement prepared in collaboration with his attorney Abe Fortas that attacked McCarthy as "tool" of Alfred Kohlberg and the "dupe" of fanatic right-wingers. On May 2 and 3, he once again appeared in a public session of the Tydings Committee, introducing into evidence letters of support from 170 experts in Asian affairs and ripping into McCarthy and Budenz. Lattimore was impressive on the attack, and he was undoubtedly right in charging that his real sin in McCarthy's eyes was his stand in favor of recognizing Red China and withdrawing U.S. troops from Korea. Testifying under the harsh glare of the klieg lights, the professorial Lattimore, with his thick glasses and well-tailored clothes, was the picture of composure. The spectator seats in the Senate caucus room were filled with supporters who rewarded his performance with enthusiastic applause.

Lattimore's appearance was great theater; however, as historian David Oshinsky has pointed out, some of his statements to the committee were, at best, insincere. Lattimore claimed, for example, to be unaware that a number of individuals connected with the *Amerasia* magazine were either Communists or very close to the party. He described Frederick Field as "a rather liberal young man," with whom he had rarely discussed politics. And, asked about Chi Ch'ao-ting, who had recently been designated as the Communist Chinese government's future ambassador to the UN, Lattimore said he doubted that Chi was actually a Communist.[19]

For anti-Communist moderates, there was a certain irony in watching Lattimore, the defender of the Moscow show trials, indignantly presenting himself as a champion of free speech and being cheered for it. During the last four years, Americans had seen Eastern Europe fall into the Soviet orbit. Fighting in Korea would break out even as the Tydings Committee was continuing its deliberations. Midterm elections were coming up in the fall, and the mood of the voters was deeply conservative. If the alternative to sanctioning McCarthy's loudmouthed irresponsibility was to be lionizing Lattimore and endorsing his version of history, then a lot of senators had a problem.

Moreover, as unconvincing as Budenz's story was in retrospect, the impression it made at the time was by no means entirely unfavorable. Following in the wake of the Chambers and Bentley revelations, Budenz's claims about Lattimore were not to be dismissed out of hand. At the very least, it was as easy to believe that Owen Lattimore was a Soviet agent as it was to believe that Frederick Vanderbilt Field was a liberal and Chi Ch'ao-ting a non-Communist. *Time* magazine, previously a critic of McCarthy, noted that while Budenz had not proven his case, Lattimore had not proven his either.

The Scripps-Howard newspapers, meanwhile, were running a major series on the *Amerasia* case by Frederick Woltman. Since the Hobbs Committee proceedings had never been made public, Woltman's account, pointing out that the editor of *Amerasia* had collected hundreds of documents, came as a revelation to many readers. Echoing the charges of Kohlberg's China Lobby, Woltman reasoned that were it not for the Justice Department's "whitewash" of the case and the resulting ouster of Joseph Grew, "probably China would not have been handed to the Soviets on a silver platter."[20]

Other discomfiting hints of malfeasance were surfacing. A few weeks earlier, on March 27, the local Scripps-Howard outlet, the *Washington Daily News*, had reported that Robert Hitchcock, the chief Justice Department prosecutor in the case, left government service in December 1945 to join the Buffalo law firm of Kenefick, Cooke, Mitchell, Bass, and Letchworth. The Mitchell of this partnership was, of course, Kate Mitchell's uncle, who been active in negotiating the dismissal of the charges against her. The *New York Daily News* further noted that in early 1945 Hitchcock had been brought to Washington from Buffalo by Attorney General Tom Clark specifically to handle the *Amerasia* prosecution.

Robert Hitchcock was duly invited to Washington to explain this odd chain of coincidences. Testifying before an executive session of the committee, Hitchcock said that the Kenefick partner who originally approached him about a job was unaware of his background. When he warned that he was a Democrat and a Catholic and had been the *Amerasia* prosecutor, Hitchcock said, he was assured that none of these factors would he held against him. Hitchcock professed to find it insulting that he was even being asked about a connection between his law partnership and his handling of the *Amerasia* case. Far from benefiting from a conflict of interest, he complained, "nothing in my life has hurt me more than this case."[21]

Under normal circumstances, or what passes for normal in Washington, this testimony would have spawned a major scandal; considering Attorney General Clark's reputation for favoring an active policy of bringing prosecutions against Communist Party leaders, there had always been something puzzling about his lack of enthusiasm for the *Amerasia* case. Was it possible that he had suborned the bribing of a U.S. attorney? That Clark had been elevated to the Supreme Court in 1949 only magnified the potential political damage.

In a bizarre turn of events, McCarthy and his allies had been handed a stick of political dynamite. But curiously enough, they were almost as reluctant to use it as the Democrats. Don Surine, the ex-FBI man whose files were overflowing with anti-Communist research, was hardly interested in pursuing allegations of malfeasance within the Justice Department. Alfred Kohlberg was completely focused on linking *Amerasia* to a Maoist conspiracy in the State Department. As for McCarthy himself, he appears to have been disinclined to pursue a fellow Republican, James Mitchell, or, for that matter, Tom Clark, one of the most vocal proponents of jailing Communists in the early years of the Truman administration. Isaac Don Levine was an exception. As early as August 1946, in a memo on the *Amerasia* case that he prepared for Alfred Kohlberg, Levine had recognized that Hitchcock's appointment might be part of a larger picture—"it is believed in some quarters that it was certainly more than a coincidence," he wrote.[22]

Nevertheless, blinded by their own ideological rigidity, the conservative critics of the *Amerasia* affair wound up dismissing Hitchcock's role as a side issue. Instead of concentrating their fire on the Justice Department, McCarthy and his supporters in the Senate pushed for the release of the State Department's loyalty investigation files. Truman, who had so far backed up the State Department's refusal to release the raw files, was forced to back down, at least part way. The files of seventy-one individuals implicated by McCarthy's charges were deposited in a White House office, where members of the Tydings Committee, but not their staffs, would be allowed to peruse them. From the Democrats' point of view, this was an inspired compromise. Neither Bourke Hickenlooper nor Henry Cabot Lodge, the two Republicans on the committee, were diligent researchers, to say the least. And one could be sure that none of the three Democrats would be likely to spend many hours searching the raw files for evidence that the Truman administration had employed Communist agents in responsible positions.

Even so, Tydings could not resist the pressure to undertake a full-scale investigation of the *Amerasia* affair. The probe, launched on May 4, with an appearance by Frank Bielaski, would eventually consume six weeks of the committee's time, but once again the conditions for digging up the truth were less than auspicious. Even less than McCarthy, Tydings, Green, and McMahon had no interest in uncovering Justice Department malfeasance. Citing security considerations, Tydings ordered that most of the testimony on the *Amerasia* case be conducted in executive session.

McCarthy, meanwhile, was still pinning his hopes for making political capital out of the case on Emmanuel Larsen. On his behalf, Congressman George Dondero invited Larsen to his office early in May to urge him once again to testify. Dondero was perhaps not the ideal intermediary since Larsen blamed him for leaking the story published by the Hearst press that had cost him his chance to land a War Department job in Korea back in 1946. Even so, Larsen was willing to reconsider his opinion of McCarthy. The senator was faring better than expected, and Larsen was always eager to side with a winner—a goal that, in any event, he seldom realized.

Dondero wrapped up their discussion by suggesting to Larsen that he might be able to incorporate into his testimony some information about Owen Lattimore that had recently come to the attention of Republican senator Kenneth Wherry of Nebraska. The two of them trooped over to Wherry's office, where the senator briefed Larsen on allegations that Lattimore, though married, was actually a homosexual. Covering up his embarrassment at even broaching the subject, Wherry joked awkwardly that he was the Senate's "expert on homosexualism in the State Department."[23]

Wherry's veiled hints that Larsen might be able to tell the Tydings Committee something about Lattimore's sexual proclivities threw Larsen into a panic. Although presumably he had given Dondero the impression that he might have something to say about Lattimore—otherwise, why the trip to see Wherry?—he now insisted that he did not know Lattimore, had never met him, and in any event wanted no part of the Tydings Committee.

Wherry's friend Senator Homer Ferguson called Larsen a few days later in an obvious attempt to undo the damage. Assuring Larsen that there was no reason to suppose that he would incriminate himself by appearing before the committee, he suggested that no doubt it was naïveté that had led Larsen to get involved with Jaffe. Larsen warily admitted that he had been "indiscreet," but he was still not ready to finger Lattimore.

Despite his nose for intrigue, Emmanuel Larsen was unable to find a safe haven from the crosscurrents of the *Amerasia* affair. His contacts with McCarthy and Wherry only reconfirmed his disillusionment with the right-wing mentors who had promised so much and delivered so little. His best bet, he now concluded, was to sit tight and avoid becoming too closely identified with either side in the debate. Although two U.S. senators were now, in his words, "disgusted" with his vacillations, he once again refused to get involved.

On May 4, in what can best be described as an atmosphere of minimally controlled hysteria, the Tydings Committee turned its attention to a review of the *Amerasia* case. The Democratic majority of the Senate was in disarray. Intimidated by public opinion polls, which showed a plurality of Americans supporting McCarthy, Tydings had resorted to a defensive strategy of trying to dispose of McCarthy's allegations one by one, and with as little fuss as possible.

The decision to hold closed sessions during the *Amerasia* testimony quickly backfired. Although McCarthy was not a member of the committee, he had the benefit of insider reports from minority counsel Robert Morris and others and was soon dominating the news coverage of the hearings, leaking selected items from the testimony in support of his contention that Tydings was presiding over yet another whitewash of the case. As far as the media were concerned, Tydings found himself in the galling position of providing McCarthy with better and certainly fresher material than he could have gleaned from his own sources.

While the committee was still hearing from its first *Amerasia* witness, Frank Bielaski, for example, McCarthy passed on two tidbits to a reporter from the *Washington Evening Star*. First, so many documents were involved in the *Amerasia* affair that fifteen reports seized by the OSS from the magazine's headquarters were never missed. Second, that "six months before the atomic bomb was dropped on Hiroshima, the people who operated *Amerasia*, with the assistance of State Department personnel, were collecting and transmitting to the Soviet Union the secrets of the atomic bomb." Both charges were widely discounted by McCarthy's critics. In fact, McCarthy's first charge was apparently true. The second was doubtful at best. Testifying just a few months after exiled German scientist Klaus Fuchs had admitted turning over atomic secrets to the Soviet Union, Bielaski had told the Senate panel that four years earlier, a member of the Hobbs Committee queried him about the possibility that some of the documents he saw in Jaffe's offices were related to the Manhattan Project. At the time, Bielaski had testified that he probably wouldn't have noticed if they were: "I had never heard of it. . . . It would not have meant anything to me if I had." But since then, he had "racked my memory" in an effort to recall if he might have seen evidence that Jaffe knew about the atomic bomb's development. And sure enough, he had remembered that one of the reports he saw the night of the break-in was entitled "A Bombing Plan for Japan," or something of the sort. Bielaski told the Tydings Committee that this report was included among the group found in the envelope with writer John Hersey's name on it. Admittedly, though, he hadn't actually read the report and could not say whether the title referred to "a bombing plan" or the A-bomb specifically.[24]

Following McCarthy's leak to the newspapers, Frank Bielaski appeared on the May 21 edition of the radio interview show, *Meet the Press*. This time, in repeating his story, he did not mention Hersey by name, saying only that the return address on the envelope was that of a well-known writer "of greater fame . . . than anyone who has been mentioned" who "is involved in this case up to his ears." He strongly intimated that Jaffe had advance knowledge of the plan to use the atomic bomb against Japan.[25]

Had Bielaski actually seen a report on the A-bomb? Possibly. However, as Senator McMahon noted at the time, it is not clear that the term A-bomb was even in use in early 1945. Moreover it seems likely that John Hersey's book *Hiroshima*, published in 1946 and, of course, not even conceived of until months after the OSS raid, suggested the connection in Bielaski's mind.

Hoover, for one, was mystified by Bielaski's suggestion that the case involved a famous author. "Do we know who this refers to?" he wrote on a newspaper clipping describing the *Meet the Press* interview. After checking into the records, the FBI sent an agent to talk to Hersey, who explained that he had once worked with Mark Gayn at *Time* magazine and had met Kate Mitchell at several cocktail parties. Although Hersey couldn't explain why an envelope with his return address would have been found in the *Amerasia* offices, there could have been any number of perfectly innocent reasons. Hoover's assistant Mickey Ladd reviewed the log of *Amerasia* documents seized by the OSS and reported to the chief that none of them related to the Manhattan Project. Both the FBI and Congress dismissed the "atom secrets" charges as just another McCarthy red herring.[26]

Inside the Senate hearing room, meanwhile, the leading Justice Department witness, James McInerney, was once again blaming the FBI for bungling the Jaffe investigation. Some of McInerney's statements were obviously conflicting. Summarizing the evidence, he described Emmanuel Larsen as the "main abstractor of documents" but later justified reducing Larsen's charges in exchange for a plea of nolo contendere by saying that "we took the position that Larsen was a nonentity."[27]

Only Senator Henry Cabot Lodge showed any genuine interest in probing these contradictions. The forty-seven-year-old patrician from Massachusetts, a grandson of the Henry Cabot Lodge who had been a close friend of Teddy Roosevelt's and one of two Republicans on the committee, was repelled by McCarthy's style, and during the early sessions of the committee, he gave observers the impression that although he was present in body, he was not present in spirit. But when the subject turned to the *Amerasia* affair, he came alive, doggedly asking all of the obvious questions that no one else seemed interested in pursuing.

One such exchange was touched off when McInerney insisted that none of the documents seized by the government related to national defense. The *Amerasia* papers "were of innocuous, very innocuous character," he said; it was "nothing short of silly" that they had been classified at all.[28]

Lodge objected that several reports on military topics, dealing, for instance, with the disposition of the Pacific fleet, had been mentioned in published accounts of the case. McInerney reluctantly conceded that "perhaps 1%" of the documents had military significance. If that were so, Lodge wondered aloud, why had Jaffe decided to plead guilty?

McInerney seemed momentarily caught off guard. "I think now that Jaffe may have been an espionage agent," he said, "which information we did not have at the time." McInerney then explained that he had changed his mind about Jaffe on the basis of reports from another investigation, unrelated to the *Amerasia* case. This extraordinary admission did not arouse the curiosity of the Democratic members of the committee. McInerney, of course, was not being strictly truthful in giving the impression that there had been no reason, in the spring of 1945, to assume that Jaffe was in contact with foreign agents. As for new information that may have turned up later connecting Jaffe to espionage, he did not elaborate and no one pressed him on the subject.

Senator Lodge, meanwhile, had fastened onto McInerney's assertion that the FBI's use of electronic surveillance and illegal searches had tainted the entire investigation, making the case impossible to prosecute. Surely during wartime, Lodge insisted, there must have been some way to recover the documents and still proceed to trial: "It must stand to reason that there is some obligation for the security of the troops, the security of the men at sea, and the security of all the men in uniform; and it is just going to be hard to convince an awful lot of people that this great store of information that was of great military value—at least supposed to be, some-body thought it was—and here these people had it, and they got off with a slap on the wrist. It must have seemed to a great many people that where there is a will there is a way."[29]

Lodge's comments must have gladdened the heart of Hoover, who had been saying essentially the same thing for years. At about this time, Hoover learned that Congressman Sam Hobbs, in preparing for a *Meet the Press* appearance, had been warned by Peyton Ford of the Justice Department not to mention that the FBI had entered Emmanuel Larsen's apartment to plant an eavesdropping device. This prompted assistant FBI director L. B. Nichols to remind Ford that the FBI still believed that the Justice Depart-ment should have been prepared to contest Larsen's motion to suppress the eavesdropping evidence on the grounds that it was permitted under Roosevelt's wartime security directive. If the evidence had been tainted from the beginning, Nichols asked, then why had the Justice Department okayed the arrests? Hoover was delighted. "At last, for the *first* time to my knowledge, we are fighting back," he wrote Nichols.[30]

Hoover's ire did not prevent the Justice Department witnesses before the Tydings Committee from continuing to malign the FBI. Most zeal-ously, however, they defended their own actions as stemming from legal necessity. The legal case had been tainted from the very beginning by the OSS raid on *Amerasia*'s offices. It was a weak case. Following McInerney to the witness chair, Robert Hitchcock defended his presentation before Judge Proctor at the time of Jaffe's guilty plea. Hitchcock said that he had not mentioned Jaffe's Communist contacts, including his meetings with Browder or with Tung Pi-wu, because he believed that information about Jaffe's political beliefs would have been inadmissible. Elaborating, Hitch-cock joked that "it would have been admissible for one purpose, to show that he was a no good louse, which I do not believe anybody will deny, but it would not have been any more admissible than to try to put in evidence that Jaffe had a past criminal record if that had been a fact." Hitchcock did not mention that Judge Proctor had specifically asked for a probation report before sentencing, a request the prosecutor successfully deflected.

In any event, the significance of Jaffe's meeting with Tung Pi-wu was not that Jaffe had Communist sympathies, or even that he was a "louse," but that the meeting gave him the opportunity to pass the Communist diplomat classified information.[31]

Defending Hitchcock on this point, Senator McMahon observed lamely that mentioning Jaffe's Communist connections might have actually worked in his favor since the Soviets were America's ally at the time. Aside from being untrue, the remark was so far beside the point that it is no wonder that Lodge, a fence-sitter by nature, had become thoroughly exasperated. Lodge had the reputation of being none too bright, but he persisted in thinking the hearings were about what they claimed to be about.

The testimony of both McInerney and Hitchcock was riddled with unchallenged misstatements of fact and canny evasions. Hitchcock said, for example, that Mark Gayn had never received any classified documents, which was untrue. Both men denied that the government had any evidence that Jaffe was collecting materials for the purpose of transmitting them to a foreign power, an evasion they presumably justified on the grounds that the wiretap records did not amount to legally admissible evidence. As McInerney explained it, he had never thought beyond the likelihood that the defendants would confess, "which would obviate the need for a trial, and obviate the need for presenting or tendering this evidence"—"I was guilty of overzealousness in prosecution." Senator Tydings summed up the prosecution's point of view with no irony: "You detected nobody stealing documents. You detected nobody passing documents. You detected nobody in possession of documents."

In the meantime, on May 22, the same day he was interviewed on *Meet the Press*, Sam Hobbs moved to insert the entire transcript of his 1946 subcommittee investigation into the *Congressional Record*. Hobbs's resolution prompted a rancorous exchange on the floor of the House, which began with Congressman Dondero objecting that the transcript "was a serious repudiation of one of the greatest law enforcement agencies in the world." Dondero then brought up a statement made by McCarthy two months earlier in which he had quoted a Hoover memorandum calling the *Amerasia* case "100% airtight." Dondero wondered how an investigation that was supposedly "airtight" had developed so many holes. Representative Eugene Cox then mused aloud that it might be a mistake to make the Hobbs deliberations public "because it [*Amerasia*] is a nasty mess that the more you stir it the worse it smells." Nevertheless, he planned to vote in favor of printing the transcript. Hobbs, speaking in favor of his own motion, insisted that the FBI was a "wonderful organization" despite the fact that it had arrested six people on the basis of insufficient evidence. Hobbs's backhanded compliment made front-page news, much to Hoover's discomfiture. Worse, when the Hobbs Committee transcript was published, Hoover realized for the first time that it, too, explicitly blamed the FBI for mishandling the case.[32]

Hoover's quoted comment that the *Amerasia* case was "100% airtight" also caught the attention of Jack Service. When McCarthy began making headlines in February, Service was at home in Berkeley, California, packing for a new assignment in India. Two years earlier, at the age of thirty-nine, he had become a class 2 foreign service officer, the youngest in his grade. After the embarrassment of the *Amerasia* affair, his career at last seemed firmly back on track. Then came the fall of the Nationalist Chinese government in 1949 and the flight of Chiang Kai-shek and his supporters to Taiwan. That same August, the State Department issued a White Paper, "United States Relations with China," which incorporated a number of political reports written by Service during his assignment as Stilwell's aide. The publication of the White Paper once again made Service a target of the China Lobby, just as he was about to receive an appointment as U.S. consul general in Calcutta, a position that required senatorial confirmation. Informed that Congressman Walter Judd intended to oppose the nomination, the State Department had downgraded the appointment, first to an assistant consulship, then to a post as a mere counselor at the New Delhi embassy.

Service had been investigated and cleared three times by the State Department's Loyalty-Security Board, and when he realized that McCarthy had fastened onto the Lee list, he suspected that he might become a focus of the battle brewing in the Senate. However, on orders from the State Department, he and his family set sail for India by freighter on March 14, even as McCarthy was going over his case with the committee. On the freighter's fourth day at sea, Service received a wireless message from Washington, ordering him to leave the ship at Yokohama and return home. The family's household goods, including their furniture and car, were all in the freighter's cargo hold, so Caroline Service had little choice but to go on to New Delhi with the children and hope Jack would join them soon. As it turned out, the family would not be reunited until the next year.[33]

Back in Washington, Service was told that the department's Loyalty-Security Board would be reopening his case. Realizing that a subpoena to testify before the Tydings Committee might soon follow, he retained a lawyer and began making the rounds of congressional offices, hoping to find a sympathetic ear. Since few would see him, he began sending out letters; those congressmen who happened to be Masons even received photographs of Service in full Masonic regalia.

Service was following McCarthy's press conferences carefully, and like Congressman Dondero, he wondered about the source of Hoover's "100% airtight" remark. On April 12, he wrote a letter to the FBI director, asking him whether he had been accurately quoted. Service noted that the statement "would carry great weight, and that an improper attribution to you of any such an expression would necessarily be highly damaging to me."[34]

In fact, the quote was accurate. It came from an FBI memorandum summarizing Hoover's meeting with Scripps-Howard executive Lee Woods that had been leaked to McCarthy by someone at FBI headquarters. Since this would have been embarrassing to admit and might have even violated Justice Department regulations against commenting on issues pending before Congress, the director dictated a terse reply, saying simply, "I have never made any public statements about the *Amerasia* case." Service took this to mean that the quote was inaccurate, yet McCarthy continued to use it, repeating it in a speech he made in late April.[35]

On May 1, John Peurifoy of the State Department wrote to Assistant Attorney General Peyton Ford, asking him to look into McCarthy's use of the quote. Ford prepared a response that said flatly, "You are advised that Mr. Hoover did not make the statement which was attributed to him." Ford routinely sent a draft of his reply to Hoover, who refused to approve it. Again, Hoover did not care to acknowledge the truth, so he fudged a bit. "In the event that I had been asked at the time the arrests were made whether I thought we had an airtight case," he wrote, "I would have stated that I thought we had. Further, if I were asked today, I would have to so state." Ford somehow failed to get the point. His original reply went out to Peurifoy unchanged, and on May 20, the State Department released the letter to the press.[36]

Hoover was livid, and his mood did not improve when he called Ford's office to demand an explanation and was told that Ford "was tied up and couldn't talk." Later that day, Ford tried to explain to Nichols that the letter to Peurifoy had been mailed "accidentally"—an excuse few at the bureau found believable. "It is about time our [skirmishing] . . . with Ford and McInerney stopped," Hoover wrote Nichols later that day. "Bureau interests *should* come first."[37]

FBI director J. Edgar Hoover testifying before the House Un-American Activities Committee in 1947. (UPI/The Bettmann Archive)

Hoover took the unusual step of filing an official protest with Attorney General J. Howard McGrath over the issue. In addition to the matter of the letter, he summarized his complaints against the way Justice Department witnesses called by the Tydings Committee were trying to make the FBI the scapegoat of the affair. The FBI's chance to tell its side of the story was fast approaching; Mickey Ladd and L. B. Nichols were busy preparing their statements, and Senator Tydings had obligingly sent the bureau a list of eleven questions the committee would ask the FBI spokesmen when they testified in closed session. A draft of Ladd's and Nichols's intended replies was completed and duly forwarded to Peyton Ford, who read the text with consternation and alarm.

In an effort to counter McInerney's description of the *Amerasia* papers as "silly" and "innocuous," Ladd and Nichols proposed to give the Tydings Committee a partial list of the documents taken in connection with the case. They also intended to emphasize that the Justice Department—and, for that matter, James McInerney personally—was well aware that the FBI had entered the *Amerasia* offices and the suspects' homes without a warrant. Ford was shocked. To release this information, he wrote Hoover, would cause trouble for McInerney, exposing him to "censure from Bar Associations."[38]

Days of acrimonious discussions followed. Ford pleaded that Tydings was a difficult man to work with; he was defending the administration as best he could and now the FBI seemed determined to sabotage his work. Once the hearings were over, he promised, he would go to the committee counsel and get them to revise the record to remove some of the more unflattering references to the bureau.

On the basis of this promise, Hoover reluctantly approved a considerably softened version of the Ladd-Nichols draft testimony. In a phone call to Ford, however, he stressed that there was one subject that must not be allowed to come up: the FBI's file on Tommy Corcoran. The file contained "bad conversations . . . that in themselves you can interpret one way or another," he warned. Ford pledged cooperation, agreeing that "Justice didn't want this whole case to blow up again."[39]

On the morning of May 31, Nichols and Ladd appeared outside the Senate hearing room, where they were met by Peyton Ford. While they were waiting to be called, majority counsel Edward Morgan, a former FBI agent, happened to pass by. Recognizing Nichols, he stopped to warn him that he would be asked one question that was not on Tydings's prepared list: Did the FBI have any information about a cover-up or fix in the case?[40]

Nichols was stunned. After some hesitation, he told Ford that such a question could be answered in two ways. He could simply say that this was a matter best taken up with the Justice Department. Or he could give "a full and complete disclosure of such information as we have." Ford wondered just what that might be, and Nichols responded with a concise rundown of the Corcoran-Clark-McGranery maneuvering that had taken place back in 1945.

Although he had been warned that the Corcoran file was damaging, Ford apparently had not realized just how bad matters were. "We could never admit this," he gasped. The FBI didn't want to admit it, Nichols told him. "But if we were ever forced into a position, the only thing we could do would be to tell the truth and point out how we were ordered to do this."

Ford hastily assured him that he would not allow matters to go that far. When the subject came up, Nichols should defer to McInerney, who would give an account of his pretrial conversations with the defendants' attorneys. But the Corcoran tap must not be discussed. The Justice Department "would stand behind the Bureau thoroughly and completely. . . . [Nichols and Ladd] would not be pushed on this answer," said Ford.

Inside the hearing room, things did not go entirely according to plan. Asked about a fix, Nichols said simply that no one had ever approached the FBI. Tydings next asked if Nichols had any knowledge that anyone else in the government had been approached. "That is a difficult question for me to answer," Nichols replied. What was that supposed to mean, another member of the committee asked. It meant, said Nichols, that no evidence of a fix had ever been "given" to the FBI.[41]

At this point, McInerney interrupted to say that rumors of improper influence had been traced to a State Department spokesman, but on investigation they had proved to be groundless. Contrary to Ford's earlier promise to Nichols, McInerney volunteered nothing about his own contacts with defense lawyers.

This exchange marked the beginning of a difficult day. Committee transcripts show that Ladd and Nichols's testimony was continually interrupted by objections on the part of Ford and McInerney and by numerous off-the-record conversations. In the confusion, Tydings again departed from the previously agreed on script. Following up a question about the FBI's search of Jaffe's home and office, he asked, "Did you enter these places surreptitiously and by stealth?" Nichols and Ladd responded by describing the break-ins. Though admitting that Jaffe's home and office had been entered, Ladd claimed that the FBI had never broken into Larsen's apartment—only technically accurate, since a telephone bug was placed on the premises of the Larsens' second apartment a few days before the Larsens moved in—and he defended the FBI's position that Larsen's motion for dismissal would never have held up in court.

Nichols also departed from the program in his testimony about Service. In response to a query about whether any State Department officials had actually been seen transferring documents, Nichols noted that Service, during a conversation with Jaffe in his hotel room on May 8, 1945, had warned, "What I said about the military plans is, of course, very secret." In offering this snippet of conversation, he had disclosed for the first time that Jaffe's hotel room was bugged.

Possibly, Nichols let this information slip accidentally, as most accounts of the Tydings hearings assume, but since he was able to quote accurately from the transcript, the disclosure may well have been deliberate. After seething in silence for five years over the Justice Department's contention that the *Amerasia* case was not about espionage, Hoover and his aides were ready to strike back.

Within forty-eight hours of the Ladd-Nichols testimony, the texts of some of the more sensitive *Amerasia* documents found their way into the hands of certain Republican senators and conservative journalists. Republican senator William Knowland was particularly incensed by a confidential telegram from Secretary of State Cordell Hull to Ambassador Clarence Gauss that summarized without comment an *Amerasia* article that advocated setting up a Japanese Communist politician, Okano, as a sort of "Japanese Tito" after the war. Other leaked documents, pinpointing the location of the American fleet and troop dispositions in Malaysia, gave the lie to McInerney's testimony that no military intelligence had been stolen; one, for example, consisted of handwritten notes describing a State Department briefing in which Joseph Grew had described the activities of twenty-five U.S. submarines operating in the Tsushima Strait.[42]

Hoover and Ford, meanwhile, were soon wrangling over Ford's promise to have the transcript of the Ladd-Nichols testimony edited to remove anything detrimental to the FBI. Hoover, who continued to insist that the FBI's tactics had been legal under wartime conditions, wanted to strike Tydings's suggestion that searches of the suspects' homes had been accomplished "surreptitiously and by stealth." Ford, on his part, was equally determined to excise the reference to Service's conversation with Jaffe, arguing that it would only "enrage the liberals."[43]

"I wash my hands of the entire matter," Hoover wrote on a memo informing him of Ford's demand. "Let Nichols and Ladd deal directly with Ford, Morgan, Tydings, etc. I want nothing more to do with it." But in the end, it was the FBI that prevailed. When Senator Tydings refused to approve the alterations in the record, Edward Morgan took it upon himself to delete the words "surreptitiously and by stealth" from the transcript. The Service quote, however, was allowed to stand.[44]

Spurred on by continuing leaks to the press, and by Senator Knowland, who was calling for a full-scale Senate investigation into the events leading up to Patrick Hurley's resignation, the Tydings Committee reluctantly continued its probe of the *Amerasia* affair, issuing subpoenas to Service, Larsen, and Jaffe. Contributing to the committee's discomfort, on May 24 newspaper headlines announced the arrest of Harry Gold, Klaus Fuchs's courier, for atomic espionage. Within one month, Gold would lead the FBI to David Greenglass, one of his contacts at Los Alamos, who, in turn, would implicate his sister and brother-in-law, Ethel and Julius Rosenberg. Concern about Soviet espionage was at a fever pitch.

Emmanuel Sigurd Larsen had gone through several ideological transformations in his lifetime, but the man who answered the Senate's subpoena on June 5, 1950, was in yet another incarnation: Emmanuel Larsen, self-described liberal. Larsen took the witness chair and repudiated his notorious *Plain Talk* article in toto. "I wrote what Mr. Don Levine asked me to write," he said.[45]

By way of an example, Larsen insisted that he had not even mentioned General Stilwell in the first draft of his manuscript. Levine, however, had shown him a copy of a letter from Stilwell to his wife, allegedly revealing the general's pro-Communist sympathies, and at Levine's insistence, Larsen said, he had reluctantly agreed to the insertion of a statement that Stilwell was a Communist sympathizer. Similarly, he claimed that Levine and Ralph de Toledano had inserted without his consent the material suggesting that a proleftist clique existed in the Office of Far Eastern Affairs. They were also responsible, he said, for planting the idea in his mind that Jack Service had lied about him to the grand jury.

As for his earlier remarks before the Hobbs Committee, remarks that contradicted the testimony he was now giving, Larsen suggested that the record was inaccurate. "I didn't see anybody transcribe anything at these meetings. There was no secretary present. . . . Many things I saw there I don't see here [in the published record]." Larsen's recantation was a crushing setback for McCarthy and his allies. "In one blow," as historian Robert Griffith put it, "the main prop behind McCarthy's case had been demolished."[46]

In Larsen's latest version of events, it was Andrew Roth—in Indochina, "with Ho Chi Minh," as Larsen put it, at the time and thus not available to tell his side of the story—who emerged as "the principal conspirator in the case." Larsen admitted that he had read Roth's manuscript, which he described as "very ludicrous and poorly written" and reflecting "a very peculiar ideological nature that I did not subscribe to." Nevertheless, it had not dawned on him that Roth and Jaffe were pro-Communist. When he did finally realize this, in March 1945, he and his wife decided to break off their relationships with both men. Finally, Larsen insisted that he had given Jaffe only "eight or ten" documents in all. He had no idea how Jaffe had obtained the rest of the 1,000-plus government papers seized at the time of the arrests.

It did not take an in-depth knowledge of the *Amerasia* case to recognize that Larsen's testimony to the committee was riddled with lies. At one point, Larsen attempted to explain the presence of more than 700 State Department documents in his apartment at the time of his arrest by saying that he was in the habit of bringing material home at night so that he could work on his reports. When a skeptical committee member questioned how anyone could be working on 700 reports in one night, Larsen quickly backed down, conceding that some of the papers in the stash had been at his home for a long time and were not even reports that would normally have crossed his desk. And again, when Senator Lodge pressed him on why he had chosen to collaborate with Jaffe and not some other journalist whose ideological stance he might have found less peculiar, Larsen attempted a lame wisecrack. "Why did you marry your wife and not some other woman?" he asked Lodge, who snapped back, "I am not here to be questioned."

Not only was Larsen's performance unconvincing, but on many points, it contradicted sworn statements he had made a few days earlier to the Loyalty-Security Board that was reviewing Jack Service's case. Larsen waffled on the number of documents he had turned over to Jaffe (the figure "eight or ten" became twenty, still far from the true count), on the subject of his supposed "break" with Jaffe and Roth in the spring of 1945 (which in fact never happened), as well as on numerous other issues.[47]

Nevertheless, the Democratic members of the Tydings Committee seemed content to believe that because Larsen had lied before, he must be telling the truth now when he insisted that the affair had been a simple case of leaking, blown out of proportion by the government's charges. Isaac Don Levine, tipped off that Larsen was blaming him for the contents of the *Plain Talk* article, sent a telegram to Senator Tydings offering to prove that Larsen's story about the Stilwell letter was a clumsy fabrication. The letter Larsen claimed to have been shown happened to be not from Stilwell to his wife but from Mrs. Stilwell to the American Communist Joseph Starobin, in which the general's widow quoted her late husband. Since the letter had not been published in the *Daily Worker* until 1947, Levine noted, he could not possibly have shown a copy of it to Larsen in 1946. Robert Morris passed Levine's complaint on to Senator Bourke Hickenlooper, who proposed that Levine and Ralph de Toledano be invited to appear before the committee to rebut Larsen's story and defend their reputations. The Democratic majority, however, was not interested.[48]

Although Larsen's testimony gave a boost to the Democrats and to Service, his attempt to ingratiate himself with John Peurifoy was an utter failure. There was simply no chance that the State Department, already under fire from the right, would take him back. Larsen's recantation, meanwhile, dealt a severe blow to his struggling news agency. In 1953 he gave up his freelance work to become a desk clerk at the Roger Smith Hotel in Washington, a job he held for the next sixteen years. He survived until 1988, dying in a Chevy Chase, Maryland, retirement home at the age of 90.[49]

Philip Jaffe, the next witness called before the committee, was in a position to expose Larsen's self-serving lies, and there had been hints in the press that Jaffe might be in a mood to tell all. As Murray Kempton reported in the *New York Post* on May 4, 1950, Jaffe was embittered and politically isolated.[50] No sooner had World War II ended than Jaffe's dream that the Communist Party was about to move into the mainstream of American political life was exposed as a delusion. As a result of the Duclos article, his friend, Earl Browder was ousted as party leader in June 1945, and Jaffe's own 1946 book, *New Frontiers in Asia*, was criticized by party organs for the heresy of "Browderism."

Oddly enough, however, it was the Progressive Party campaign of Henry Wallace in 1948 that finally convinced Jaffe that the Communist movement was bankrupt. Noting that the enthusiastic crowds who cheered Wallace's speeches were invariably dominated by Communist supporters and their friends and families, Jaffe had come to the conclusion that predictions that Wallace would win 5 or 10 million votes were wildly inflated. "I and thousands of others believed that we were playing important roles in shaping the future," Jaffe reminisced in his 1975 book, *The Rise and Fall of American Communism*. "We failed to realize that we were 'converting' one another, that our excitement arose from our successes in convincing a captive audience of 100,000 Party members and perhaps another 100,000 fellow travelers."[51]

An article Jaffe wrote for *Amerasia* questioning the party's support for Wallace resulted in his being summoned to appear before the Communist Party Politburo. Jaffe attended the session voluntarily, but for once he refused to amend his views to accommodate the party line, and he soon found himself being attacked regularly in the *Daily Worker* and in the party journal, *Political Affairs*.[52]

Jaffe had hired O. John Rogge, the prominent attorney who had defended numerous disillusioned Communists since his own break with the party in 1947, and he had been having off-the-record discussions with FBI investigators since early 1950. Jaffe hinted to bureau representatives that he would be willing to talk about the *Amerasia* case if only he could be sure he would not be placing himself in legal jeopardy. An FBI memo stated that Jaffe had cooperated "to a certain extent but he has never involved himself."[53]

The one person Jaffe did talk about was Joseph Bernstein, the man who had approached him to set up an espionage ring in the spring of 1945. The FBI had remained interested in Bernstein for several years but finally concluded in 1948 that the investigation "has failed to indicate that the subject is engaged as a Soviet espionage agent," although the consensus was that he once had been an agent.[54]

In March 1949 the bureau once again became interested in Bernstein. A Justice Department employee named Judith Coplon was arrested for espionage and was found to have possession of a few dozen data slips listing the numbers of certain FBI files, among them Bernstein's. When Coplon's case came to trial in April, her attorneys successfully petitioned the court to force the FBI to submit the raw reports corresponding to the data slips. Since Bernstein's report indicated that the FBI had observed him receiving a document from Mary Keeney and then delivering it to a Communist Party official, it was apparent that the FBI had once had him under surveillance. According to former FBI official Robert Lamphere, who worked on the case for a time, the FBI assumed that the public release of the report on Bernstein had destroyed any value he might have had as a Soviet courier. If Jaffe would talk, the bureau might be able to prosecute Bernstein or pressure him to cooperate.[55]

Whether Jaffe would have actually told the whole truth is debatable—like Larsen, he had a bottomless capacity for self-delusion—but he promised to be a more productive witness than an outsider like Louis Budenz. But the committee could not offer him the assurances—and the immunity—he sought. In consequence, he refused to cooperate, taking the Fifth Amendment more than 100 times and refusing to identify a host of government employees with whom he had been in contact during the war. When Edward Morgan reminded the witness that the statute of limitations had expired, Jaffe's attorney, Rogge, retorted that espionage charges could still be filed since there was no statute of limitations on wartime spying. The committee cited Jaffe for contempt, a charge of which he was speedily acquitted when it came to trial in April 1951.[56]

Although Jaffe's role in the Tydings hearings was finished, a coda to the incident would be played out two years later, when the McCarran Committee set out to investigate the Communist infiltration of the IPR. Jaffe,

Philip Jaffe (*right*) and his attorney, O. John Rogge, leaving the U.S. District Court after Jaffe pleaded innocent to contempt of Congress in 1950. (UPI/The Bettmann Archive)

by now, was eager to talk to the McCarran Committee about how he and other party members had set out to dominate the IPR, but he wanted some assurance that his testimony would not prompt the government to file new espionage charges against him. "Jaffe may make a 'right about face,'" staff counsel Robert Morris reported enthusiastically to L. B. Nichols. Jaffe, however, soon changed his mind.[57]

In February 1952, Nichols reported to Hoover that Jaffe had volunteered to talk about the *Amerasia* affair, but only "if the Federal Immunity Act is passed, which could mean only one thing, namely, that he is involved in wartime espionage and is afraid to implicate himself." Nichols recommended assigning an agent to work with Jaffe to "see if we could develop him" as a source. Over the next two months, Jaffe voluntarily gave this agent four long interviews. The full reports of these discussions have never been released by the FBI, but there are indications that Jaffe assisted the bureau with several ongoing investigations but continued to insist that he would never talk fully about the *Amerasia* affair or Bernstein without a promise of immunity. He did admit to the FBI that Bernstein had asked him to furnish summaries of State Department documents but denied that he had claimed to be working for a Soviet principal. Unaware that his conversations had been taped, Jaffe also insisted that he had refused to aid Bernstein. Jaffe was not granted immunity, and he refused to cooperate further with either the McCarran Committee or the FBI.[58]

This time, the FBI actually went so far as to interview Bernstein, who denied having any connection to espionage and insisted that he had only talked to Jaffe in 1945 because he was hoping to be offered a job. Bernstein refused to answer any questions about Communist Party membership. In the words of the FBI, he "specifically denied ever having engaged in espionage activities, ever having acted on behalf of a foreign government, ever having been asked to engage in espionage activities or ever having sought to obtain documents from state or other departments on behalf of Soviet Union. . . . While not hostile appeared to be evasive throughout."[59]

Bernstein was subsequently called before a federal grand jury in New York City that was looking into Soviet espionage activities in 1953. The bureau then combed through the transcripts of the *Amerasia* case, hoping to find some pretext to file perjury charges or to somehow develop an espionage case against him. It was unsuccessful. Over the years, Bernstein worked for a number of Jewish organizations, including the Zionist Organization of America in the late 1940s, and wrote articles for various pro-Communist publications. The FBI kept up a desultory interest in him until 1966, when it finally dropped his name from the Security Index. He died in 1975, taking his secrets to the grave with him.[60]

As for Jaffe, while privately cooperating with the FBI, he complained publicly that during the *Amerasia* case he had been the target of an attempted entrapment by an OSS agent. In his unpublished autobiography, Jaffe charged that Bernstein was an undercover OSS agent and claimed that it was Bernstein who had unlocked *Amerasia*'s offices to allow the OSS to enter the premises back in April 1945. Agnes Jaffe made the same claim in an interview with the authors, adding that she and Philip were suspicious of Bernstein because he had never been called to testify at any of the hearings on the case and, indeed, had been untouched by the whole McCarthy-era witch-hunts. Of course, if there were any truth to this theory, Bernstein would have been available to talk to the Tydings and McCarran panels and the contrast between Jaffe's public assertion of innocence and his private negotiations for immunity would have soon come to light.[61]

The day after the Tydings Committee's unproductive encounter with Jaffe, the *Amerasia* affair once again came up for discussion on the floor of the Senate. Senator Homer Capehart of Indiana, a conservative Republican, introduced a resolution calling on the Judiciary Committee to look into the handling of the prosecution "on behalf of more than 10,000,000 men and women who offered their lives" in the war. Incensed that Philip Jaffe had been allowed to testify in closed session, Capehart wondered aloud whether Tydings was serious about getting to the truth, and he accused Tydings of protecting Jaffe, who had walked away from the charges against him after paying a small fine "when a doughboy would have been shot, or, at least, imprisoned, for revealing to the enemy so much as a one-man foxhole."[62]

In New York City, meanwhile, a federal grand jury had decided on its own authority to look into the *Amerasia* affair. James McInerney went to New York City to testify on June 8 and, bemused, reported to the FBI that the grand jurors had little use for his advice. They wanted to charge various subjects in the case with transmitting information to a foreign power, and though he had done his best to try to convince them that there was no basis for such a charge, "the Grand Jury didn't seem particularly interested in this."[63]

In the end, there were no indictments, largely because the grand jury's term expired on June 15 before it had a chance to finish its discussions. However, the grand jurors did file a presentment, complaining that their investigation had been cut short for lack of time and asking the presiding judge to turn the matter over to another panel. John Brunini, the foreman, sent a copy of the presentment to Senator Hickenlooper, who read it aloud to his colleagues on the Tydings Committee. The next grand jury that was impaneled did express an interest in taking up the *Amerasia* affair, but the U.S. attorney, Irving Saypol, was able to dissuade them.[64]

In the face of this continued pressure to produce some results, the Tydings Committee turned to its last major witness: John Stewart Service.

John Service (*left*) discussing his forthcoming testimony with Senator Millard Tydings in 1950. (UPI/The Bettmann Archive)

Like Owen Lattimore, Service requested an opportunity to defend his reputation by testifying in a public session. Under the sympathetic eye of Tydings, and with the caucus room's spectator seats filled with supporters, Service was sworn in on June 22, 1950, and read a lengthy statement summarizing his background and defending his views on American policy in China.

Service had been publicly slandered by McCarthy and was fighting for his professional life. With the China Lobby crowd waiting to latch onto any chance admission he might make, his public testimony was hardly a good moment to indulge in soul-searching. Nevertheless, in attempting to put the best face on his actions back in 1945, Service gave a version of events that can only be described as lacking in candor.

Calling the *Amerasia* affair a case "in which it was my misfortune to become innocently involved," Service went on to say that he had not had occasion to read Jaffe's magazine very often while he was in China and was not very familiar with its political slant. However, the transcripts of Service's conversations with Jaffe show that he was very well aware of Jaffe's previous work in *China Today* and of his ideological slant in general, and he told the authors in a 1985 interview that he had indeed read an

Amerasia article on the recall of Stilwell and had been very favorably impressed: "As far as I was concerned, it was right down the line—great stuff."[65]

Service's attempt to raise the defense of ignorance was not particularly convincing, and it is little wonder that the Republicans on the committee reacted with skepticism. Pressed on this issue by Morgan, Service admitted that he had made an attempt to discover Jaffe's political views, but, "unfortunately, the man of whom I made the inquiry was Lieutenant Roth, who assured me that Jaffe was not a Communist."[66]

"I did not particularly like Mr. Jaffe after that first meeting," Service elaborated, explaining that he had been irritated when Jaffe told him he did not have time to read the reports that Service had provided and wanted copies that he could take back to New York City. Jaffe then further annoyed him by requesting copies of monitored radio broadcasts that he could have obtained from press officers at the State Department. Rather than let himself be turned into Jaffe's "errand boy," he had asked Jaffe to come back to the department, where he introduced him to the official responsible for providing transcripts to the press. He had continued to see Jaffe and the others because they took the initiative in arranging invitations; even so, the contacts had been innocuous and were "usually in connection with a meal."[67]

One topic that could not be easily sloughed off was Service's May 8, 1945, exchange with Jaffe, during which he had remarked, "What I said about the military plans is, of course, very secret." Following Ladd and Nichols's disclosure of this tantalizing snippet from the FBI surveillance to a closed hearing, Millard Tydings had no choice but to ask Peyton Ford at the Justice Department to produce the complete record of the conversation. Obtaining the transcript, however, was easier said than done. First of all, Ford's office somehow "lost" Tydings's letter, and by the time his request was relayed to Hoover a week later, the director had reconsidered his threat to punish Clark and McGranery by telling all. In the words of a bureau representative who had responded to an earlier query from the Tydings Committee, the director had always regarded the FBI's raw files as "sacred." The release of some raw information during the Coplon trial had only reinforced his concern. To violate that precept now would only expose the bureau to attack and compromise other espionage investigations currently in progress.[68]

The deadlock was finally broken by McCarthy, who, on the evening of June 22, leaked the "military plans" quote to the press, stealing the headlines away from Service's testimony. A few days later, the FBI did send the committee a rather garbled transcript, following it up with the original recording.[69]

Ironically, even once this recording was made available, it did little to amplify Service's remark. The FBI's microphone had caught the tail end of a conversation that began over breakfast in the hotel coffee shop. Questioned about the incident by minority counsel Robert Morris, Service insisted that he could not recall the exchange and that he could not imagine what he had in mind since he had never been privy to military secrets. "I chose my words in what I was saying very unwisely. . . . I think I misspoke," he admitted. In fact, as Service himself speculated, based on a few chance remarks in the transcript, the conversation was almost certainly about Colonel David Barrett's plan for having U.S. troops cooperate with the Red Army in the event that they landed in northern China— confidential information but hardly a "military plan" in the strict sense of the term. If the transcript was damaging, it was primarily because it showed Service enjoying a chummy relationship with Jaffe and boasting about his success at leaking anti-Hurley stories.

J. Edgar Hoover, meanwhile, apparently had not forgotten his threat to get even with James McGranery and Peyton Ford. Someone, either inside the FBI or close to it, had been feeding information to the Republican members of the committee, and just as Service was winding up his testimony, Senator Lodge brought up Lauchlin Currie.

Service said that he knew Currie only "slightly."

"Did he ever tell you to go to any particular place?" Lodge asked.

"On one occasion he asked me to talk to Drew Pearson," Service said.

"Is that the only person he asked you to talk to?"

Service then acknowledged that Currie had advised him to see Thomas Corcoran.

Committee counsel Robert Morris soon followed up on the subject. "Did you go to see Mr. Corcoran after Mr. Currie had recommended it?"

Service: "Yes."

Morris: "What did he say?"

Service: "He recommended that I retain the lawyer I had already provisionally retained."

Morris: "Did he give you any other advice?"

Service: "No."[70]

In a 1986 article in the *New Republic*, the authors characterized this answer as a lie. Service took vigorous exception, defending the response on the grounds that Morris's question referred only to his first meeting with Corcoran. He had been given no advice on this occasion and saw no reason why he should volunteer information about other meetings.[71]

But, in fact, there was more to it than that.

Committee counsel Robert Morris did not let the matter drop. Moments later, he asked Service whether he had been told, before his grand jury appearance, that everything was going to be all right. "Think very carefully, Mr. Service, because it is an important question," he warned.

Service said he could not recall.

Why, then, had Munter, his attorney, changed his mind about allowing him to appear, Morris pressed on.

Service was flustered. "I assume because he thought I was guilty, and therefore I would be all right—I'm sorry, that I was innocent, was not guilty, and would be all right." Service then denied that he had known he would be cleared before he ever went before the grand jury.

Again, after some unrelated testimony, Morris returned to the subject. Had Service been given any reason to believe, before he went to the grand jury, that he would not be indicted, he wanted to know.

Service: "I was confident that I was innocent."

Morris: "Did anyone assure you that you were?"

Service: "I was confident in my own mind."

Morris: "Did you receive any assurances other than from your own conviction?"

Service: "Of course not; none whatsoever sir."

Morris: "And nobody intimated to you that you were going to be cleared?"

Service: "No, sir. I don't see how anyone could."[72]

Given Corcoran's repeated assurances to Service that the case was "double riveted from top to bottom," it is reasonable to suggest that Service was not telling the truth. But, try as he might, Morris was unable to extract the story of the Corcoran connection from the witness.

Morris got little help on this score. Senator Lodge complained repeatedly that it was ludicrous to imagine that the committee was going to learn anything new about security breaches by questioning witnesses in public. Tydings agreed in principle but pointed out that since testimony from the committee's executive sessions was being regularly leaked to the press, just as little could be learned meeting behind closed doors. In any event, Tydings was mainly interested in compiling a record that could be used to rebut McCarthy's charges, while the other Democrats on the committee had retreated into invisibility—either skipping sessions altogether or sitting through them in silence. Petulance and bickering became the order of the day, and at one point, Lodge, on hearing that the American code name for Yenan was "Dixie," interrupted Service's testimony to inquire, "Are the people there called Dixiecrats?"

The examination Service had just received at the hands of the State Department Loyalty-Security Board was more searching. In particular, the board tried to resolve the nagging question of just how many documents Service had passed on to Jaffe. At issue were several reports that Service had hand carried from China and turned in to the State Department after his arrival in Washington. Official State Department ozalid copies had turned up in Jaffe's briefcase at the time of his arrest. The question was, had they been given to Jaffe by Service or by Emmanuel Larsen?[73]

Service adamantly denied that he was the source of the ozalids. But Service's denials were apparently contradicted by the FBI transcript of Jaffe's conversation with Andrew Roth on May 7, 1945, when he boasted, "It's very interesting that Jack Service gave—I have 19 of his reports, including those three or four he had at last. He let me take them to New York, I have made copies. There is not a single one that Jimmy gave me." Roth then responded, "Well, Jack says that they haven't been read around the Department."[74]

On investigation, the FBI had learned that due to the press of business connected with the San Francisco UN conference, ozalid copies of the last batch of Service's reports were not made until April 30. A. S. Chase, the assistant division chief for Chinese affairs, told the FBI in 1945 that Service was aware of the location of the ozalids and had access to them, whereas Larsen probably could not have obtained them. Chase also recalled Service complaining that his material had not been circulated around the department, seemingly confirming Roth's remark. On the other hand, Larsen, in an interview given after the charges against him were dropped, had all but admitted that he could have given the ozalids to Jaffe. As for the taped conversation of May 7, it was possible that Jaffe was lying in order to impress Roth. In any event, all this did nothing to support the claim that Service was sending Jaffe reports directly from China. (The only person he did send reports to was Lauchlin Currie, who said he needed them to brief Roosevelt.) The Loyalty-Security Board was in no position to cross-examine Jaffe, and so the matter was ultimately dropped.[75]

The board's findings on the contents of Service's reports were more conclusive. George F. Kennan, the universally acknowledged expert on the Soviet Union, had been asked by the board to scrutinize Service's reports for evidence that they had been tailored to conform to the Communist line. Kennan concluded that the reports showed no evidence of "ideological preconceptions." On the contrary, as he pointed out, one of Service's criticism's of Chiang's regime was that it was too weak to be useful as a "possible counterweight" to Soviet influence in eastern Asia.

Kennan's defense of Service's political loyalty was echoed by Brooks Atkinson, who appeared as a character witness before the Loyalty-Security Board, and by Joseph Alsop, who wrote to Senator Tydings offering to testify in Service's behalf. The former press assistant to General Chennault and T. V. Soong was still bitterly critical of General Stilwell, who because of his rage at Chiang Kai-shek and "because he so imagined that the Chinese Communists were really fighting the Japs" had come to "wish for and even work for the triumph of Chiang Kai-shek's enemies in China." Nevertheless, as Alsop pointed out in his letter to Tydings, there was a distinction to be made between Stilwell's rash pronouncements and the position of his political advisers, like Service, who "were operating on a more reasoned theory." This group, Alsop noted, had recognized as early as 1944 that the relationship between the Soviet Union and the Chinese Reds was seriously strained. The Soviets, in an effort to preserve their wartime alliance with the United States and hedge their bets on the ultimate outcome of the Chinese civil war, had channeled wartime aid to Chiang Kai-shek while withholding it from Mao. Service and his fellow China Hands had urged the State Department to try to exploit the mood of resentment in Yenan, arguing that in return for American support, "Mao might be induced to declare independence from the Kremlin." Alsop admitted ruefully that this "bold gamble," which he had opposed at the time, "looks better now than it did then."

Although Alsop still believed that Service had "been gravely in error" in his support of Stilwell, he protested that he and the other China experts in the diplomatic corps had labored "with courage and fidelity" and did not deserve to be maligned by the "vulgar" attacks of McCarthy and his allies.[76]

The three-member Loyalty-Security Board, chaired by retired brigadier general Conrad Snow, apparently agreed. Service was ordered reinstated on October 9, although by this time he was so controversial that it was doubtful that he could hold any appointment requiring Senate confirmation.

The Tydings Committee, meanwhile, wrapped up its inquiry with a glancing look at the background of Mark Gayn. Someone had supplied the committee with a memo containing damaging information about Gayn signed by one Charles Allen. The writer of the memo claimed to have known Gayn in Korea in 1946–47. He charged that Gayn had favored the Korean Communists and had been allowed to cross over into Russian-held territory in 1946, a privilege normally denied American journalists. He further said that he had known Gayn in New York City in 1948, during which time they had occasion to discuss the *Amerasia* case. Gayn supposedly admitted that he had left his fingerprints on a number of classified documents and said he wished, in hindsight, that he had burned them.[77]

Charles Allen, Jr., is a well-known left-wing writer. In a telephone conversation with the authors, Allen confirmed that certain biographical details the writer of the memo mentions about himself were consistent with his own background but insisted that he had no memory of ever writing such things about Gayn. Later, after examining a copy of the two-page memo, he dismissed it as a tissue of "concoctions." A stern letter from Allen's attorney followed, warning that the memo should not be attributed to Allen. Was the Allen memo a forgery, cooked up by someone who wanted to keep the investigation from drawing to a close? If not, then the memo represents yet another possible source of information that the committee staff never bothered to pursue.[78]

This was not the only lead left dangling. Frederick Woltman reported that the Democratic majority had refused a Republican request to call Ben Cohen, Tommy Corcoran, and Lauchlin Currie to testify. Instead, they decided to end the hearings. One newspaper editorial, entitled "Smellier and Smellier," demanded that Judge Proctor and Tom Clark be put under oath. But the hearings were over.[79]

To no one's surprise, the Tydings hearings concluded with the committee sharply divided along party lines. The three Democratic members held that not one "shred of evidence" supported the charge that there had been a cover-up in the *Amerasia* case. The majority report, which eventually ran to more than 300 pages, further implied that the Scripps-Howard newspaper chain's charges of "whitewash" were motivated primarily by the need to bolster its defense against Mark Gayn's slander suit.

Senators Hickenlooper and Lodge refused to endorse these findings. Lodge was especially irate, complaining that the committee had refused even to address the "basic question" of why the whole case had been handled in such a "timid, almost apologetic fashion." Tydings attempted to cajole Lodge into supporting the Democrats' findings, even scheduling him for a junket to Europe at the Senate's expense so that he could study security problems overseas. When Lodge still refused to endorse the majority's conclusions, the Democrats inserted language in their draft attacking Lodge and Hickenlooper for their poor attendance at the committee's sessions and for failing to study the State Department files that had been made available to members of the committee.[80]

As for McCarthy, the report compared his tactics to the Fascists' reliance on "the big lie." Although this judgment would be vindicated by time, it was also clear that Tydings had not achieved his goal of ensuring the Wisconsin senator's political isolation. In addition to alienating Lodge, the Tydings report made sweeping statements that seemed calculated to arouse the derision of conservatives and inspire McCarthy's allies to dig in their heels. In the case of Owen Lattimore, for example, the report concluded that "in no instance has it been shown that he knowingly associated with Communists"—a comment that was not only false but quite unnecessary.

At Tydings's instigation, the report also contained a strong attack on Isaac Don Levine and Ralph de Toledano. In spite of finding Emmanuel Larsen's testimony "highly questionable," the report incorporated some of Larsen's more dubious allegations, including accusations that Levine had rewritten Larsen's original essay for *Plain Talk*. "If true," the report concluded, "the action of Levine and his associates . . . is one of the most despicable instances of a deliberate attempt to deceive and hoodwink the American people in its history. Such conduct is beneath contempt." Larsen's article had indeed made unsubstantiated charges of treason against State Department officials, but the words were Larsen's, supposedly based on his insider knowledge of the State Department, and there was simply no basis for the charge that Levine and de Toledano had deliberately perpetrated a hoax.

Finding themselves branded "despicable" in the official proceedings of the U.S. Senate, Levine and de Toledano were outraged. In a long letter to Tydings, de Toledano challenged him to repeat his charges outside the Senate so he could sue him. He also enlisted Senators Bourke Hickenlooper, Owen Brewster, and Henry Cabot Lodge to raise the issue on the Senate floor. In response, counsel Edward Morgan invited de Toledano to submit exculpatory documents that would be printed in the *Congressional Record*, an offer de Toledano dismissed as inadequate.[81]

Levine, meanwhile, had also fired off a letter to Tydings rebutting Larsen's testimony. Tydings and his fellow committee member Brian

McMahon belatedly attempted to placate Levine by inserting the letter into the *Congressional Record*. However, neither senator volunteered to retract their harsh statements about Levine, and when the letter appeared in the *Record*, it turned out to be heavily edited, with Levine's criticisms of the senators omitted.[82]

As a result of Levine and de Toledano's threat to sue, they were largely successful in keeping the Tydings report's complaints against them out of the press. When Robert Strout of the *Christian Science Monitor* dared to repeat the charges, the *Monitor* was forced to apologize by running an editorial on August 18 "recognizing the services of Isaac Don Levine in uncovering subversive activities in the United States."[83]

Levine and de Toledano's fury was minor compared to the emotions that erupted on the Senate floor when the Tydings report came up for debate on July 20. Senator Kenneth Wherry, livid over the discovery that the report included Larsen's charge that Wherry called himself an "expert on homosexualism" in the State Department, led off the debate by demanding that majority counsel Edward Morgan be banned from the Senate floor. Unsuccessful, he called Morgan "a dirty son of a bitch" and punched him.[84]

This was just the warm-up for a day unequaled in Senate history. Tydings's defense of his committee's work was a two-hour performance, complete with oratorical flourishes, nakedly obvious bluffs, and vituperative attacks on Republican colleagues. Releasing his pent-up frustrations after enduring two months of McCarthy's sniping, Tydings resorted to copying his enemy's tactics, even claiming—falsely—to have a recording of McCarthy's Wheeling, West Virginia, speech, which he threatened to play for the benefit of the full Senate. Democratic senators, responding to a passionate plea made by Tydings in the party caucus room, talked loudly among themselves and shuffled papers or moved their chairs whenever a Republican managed to gain the floor.

Senator William Jenner's complaint that the section of the report on the *Amerasia* affair was "a whitewash of a whitewash" prompted an emotional speech from Tydings in which he recalled his own World War I service record and accused Jenner, who had voted against the NATO pact, of being a traitor. "Joe Stalin and the *Daily Worker* and the Senator all vote the same way," he declared. At this, Homer Capehart objected that Tydings was in violation of the Senate rule against impugning the motives of a colleague. Tydings briefly took his seat but was soon back at it, comparing Bill Jenner to the Communist hard-liner William Z. Foster.[85]

The Tydings report was eventually approved by the full Senate in a straight party vote, but it is safe to say that it did not change many people's minds about Joe McCarthy. Coming two days after the arrest of Julius Rosenberg in New York City and during a summer darkened by the fear that the United States was about to fight an atomic war over Korea, the outbreak of mayhem on the Senate floor—described by the *New Republic* as the "most spectacular we've seen in a quarter of a century"—only hardened the ideological battle lines.[86]

Endgame

On the first day of June 1950, Margaret Chase Smith of Maine, the only woman member of the U.S. Senate, took the floor to deliver a "Declaration of Conscience." Smith spoke in defense of freedom of speech—including "the right to hold unpopular beliefs" and "the right of independent thought"—and, without mentioning McCarthy by name, denounced the encroachment of "totalitarian techniques" within the Senate. She also castigated the Democrats for their "complacency to the threat of Communism."

Smith's speech would be remembered as one of the great moments in Senate history, but it did little to slow down McCarthy's campaign of demagoguery. The Tydings Committee had signally failed to lay the groundwork for a coalition of anti-McCarthy moderates. Moreover, Tydings himself—a veteran senator and chairman of the Senate Armed Services Committee—was defeated in his campaign for reelection later that year. Tydings's opposition to McCarthy was by no means the only reason for his political problems in Maryland, but his defeat had the effect of further intimidating the Wisconsin Republican's political opponents.

In part, Tydings's failure was a personal one. Having started out to compile a devastating factual rebuttal of McCarthy's charges against the State Department, he had lost his composure. The Tydings report was neither objective enough for both parties to rally behind nor direct enough to put McCarthy on the defensive. The possibility cannot be dismissed, however, that Tydings had been warned off from delving too deeply into the *Amerasia* affair. Following Ladd and Nichols' testimony to the committee, J. Edgar Hoover had pointedly forwarded copies of the Corcoran-Clark telephone transcripts to Peyton Ford at the Justice Department, and Ford may well have found a way to let Tydings know that he was veering into dangerous territory. Tom Clark had been appointed to the Supreme Court by Truman in 1948, and James McGranery had become a federal judge, so any scandal involving them—particularly one that suggested that they had been "soft" on accused Communist spies—would undoubtedly have had a devastating impact on Truman and the Democratic Party as a whole.

One potentially explosive memo located in the Official and Confidential File of J. Edgar Hoover's aide, L. B. Nichols, strongly suggests that the Democratic administration had frantically tried to cover up a potential scandal. Nichols wrote Clyde Tolson a memo in April 1952 reporting on a conversation with Lee Mortimer, a coauthor of *USA Confidential*, a smarmy, best-selling exposé of crime, sex, and corruption among public officials. Mortimer reported that McGranery, who had just been nominated by Truman to be attorney general of the United States, had been a source for some material for his book and that an unnamed intermediary, an important Washington fixer, had been the go-between with McGranery. This fixer—who may have been Tommy Corcoran—had told Mortimer that "anything Jim McGranery did in the Amerasia case was done on orders from Tom Clark and the President." Nichols warned Mortimer that this was not consistent with the testimony McGranery had given before congressional committees. Mortimer checked with the fixer, who "insisted that what Jim did he did on orders."[1]

Mortimer considered writing an article claiming that the case against John Service had been manipulated on orders from then attorney general,

Assistant Attorney General James McGranery testifying before Congress in 1946. (UPI/The Bettmann Archive)

now Supreme Court justice, Tom Clark and President Truman. Nichols warned him to be sure of his facts and suggested that he show "the intermediary" the story before he published it. If it was Corcoran, he would have done everything possible to suppress it—and no story did appear. Hoover, meanwhile, had other uses for this information than as the basis for an exposé in a newspaper.

Fear of exposure continued to haunt the Truman administration into its final days. A controversial choice for attorney general, McGranery was opposed by HUAC chairman Harold Velde, and during his confirmation hearings, he was, inevitably, asked about allegations that he had helped engineer a whitewash of the *Amerasia* case. "This accusation is entirely without foundation," McGranery declared. "The simple truth is that as the Assistant to the Attorney General, I had no connection with the *Amerasia* case during the investigation, its preparation or its prosecution." By way of elaboration, McGranery added that his entire role in the matter had been limited to a two-minute conversation with James McInerney— "this was my one and only act in relation to the *Amerasia* case."[2]

A few days later, a disgruntled former assistant attorney general named Herbert Bergson attended a Washington cocktail party where he boasted to a friend in the Justice Department that he and Peyton Ford still had copies of the Corcoran phone tap transcripts and were going to use them to "get" McGranery. Word of this threat made its way back to McGranery, who had no choice but to ask the FBI to investigate. Predictably, Ford and Bergson denied the story, but Hoover took the opportunity to remind the new attorney general that the evidence that could now convict him of perjury was safely ensconced in the FBI's files. "In order that you may be apprised of the complete facts of this matter," Hoover added pointedly, "I am also enclosing a memorandum reflecting verbatim conversations had by you with Mr. Thomas Corcoran concerning this case."[3]

The cover-up that began with one attorney general trying to clear away obstacles to his own confirmation thus ended with another lying to a congressional committee during his confirmation hearings and then being threatened with exposure by the director of the FBI.

As for Jack Service, his double exoneration in 1950 by the Tydings panel and the State Department Loyalty-Security Board did him little good. On November 3, 1950, radio commentator Fulton Lewis, Jr., devoted a long segment of his broadcast to airing charges that Corcoran and Lauchlin Currie—who had by now left the country, pursued by allegations of his connection to the Silvermaster spy ring—had collaborated to protect Service from prosecution. Lewis's facts were somewhat garbled, but the broadcast still came as a rude shock to Service, who just a few weeks earlier had received final notice of his clearance by the State Department board. Service was now at the top of the list for a promotion, and no other career officers could be moved forward ahead of him. Realizing his chances for Senate confirmation were nil, he asked to have his name stricken from the promotion list.[4]

McCarthy, meanwhile, continued his barrage of charges against State Department personnel, relying on research compiled by his assiduous assistant, Don Surine—ironically, a compulsive, undiscriminating document hound whose methods were not unlike those of his ideological opposite Philip Jaffe. A number of highly classified documents found their way into Surine's files, along with obvious disinformation concocted by Nationalist secret police officials in Formosa. Jack Service, along with Owen Lattimore, John Carter Vincent, and John Paton Davies, figured prominently in several of the latter variety of documents.

One such report, obtained by Surine from a mysterious source in New York City whom he identified by the code name T-7, charged that Service had indeed been regularly sending secret reports to Philip Jaffe from China and that these reports were then forwarded by Jaffe to Vasili Zubilin, chief secretary of the Soviet embassy in the United States, via Soviet intelligence operative Max Granich. This was a persistent allegation, but one completely refuted by the FBI wiretaps, which show that Service was startled to learn that Jaffe had obtained copies of his reports through other channels. (Service had, however, been writing to Lauchlin Currie from China, and there is no way to be sure that some of this information did not somehow find its way to Soviet agents.)

Still another "secret" report, originally obtained in Formosa by China Lobby ally General Charles Willoughby, recycled old rumors about Service's private life during the years he lived in Chungking. In this version of the story, however, the woman Service was involved with was none other than "the notorious girl spy" Kung P'eng, who was in fact a press agent in the Chinese Communist Party's Chungking Liaison Office.[5]

Both of these documents were obvious forgeries. The names of the principals were misspelled, chronologies were garbled, and some of the targets were not even in China during the periods when they were supposedly taking part in secret assignations and behind-the-scenes dealmaking. "You should have seen her" was Service's terse comment on the charge that he had been Kung P'eng's lover, and other Americans who were in Chungking during the war agreed that this rumor was ludicrous. Ironically, the fact that Service had once lived in the same house as Chi Ch'ao-ting was never brought up in these reports, perhaps because it would have been difficult to attack Service for this connection without explaining how Chi had been able to fool H. H. Kung and other high officials in the Nationalist government.[6]

For several years, versions of the Taiwanese allegations surfaced periodically in the press. Eventually they also provided fodder for the Senate Internal Security Committee hearings, chaired by Senator John McCarran, and for a seemingly endless round of Loyalty-Security Board inquiries into the careers of John Carter Vincent, John Paton Davies, O. Edmund Clubb, and other China Hands.

Jack Service was investigated again by the State Department Loyalty-Security Board in the summer of 1951, his fifth appearance before this group, and once again he was exonerated. A few months later, however, his case was taken up by the Civil Service Commission's Loyalty Review Board, a sort of administrative appeals court empowered to review the reviewers. This group took into account the allegations of Service's affair with his "spy sweetheart"—apparently unaware that the FBI had already labeled the story unfounded.

President Truman had established the loyalty program on March 22, 1947, as a result of pressure created by Republican congressional victories and growing concern in the country at large over Communist expansionism abroad and charges of Communist infiltration of the government at home. Formally inaugurated by executive order 9835, the program required every government agency to convene loyalty boards to investigate charges and render decisions. Accused employees could attend hearings to respond to charges, but they were not told who had accused them, nor were they allowed to cross-examine or confront any accusers or other witnesses. If the board called for dismissal, they could appeal the decision to the head of the agency and then to an overall review board.

The standards for judgment were loosely drawn and extended from treason and sabotage to "affiliation" with groups designated by the attorney general as Communist or Fascist. If there were "reasonable grounds" to believe that the accused was "disloyal" to the government of the United States, the board was enjoined to dismiss the accused. Seth Richardson, a Republican appointed by Truman as the first head of the Civil Service Commission's Loyalty Review Board, explained that government employment was a responsibility and not a right. The burden of proof of innocence was put on the accused; an accuser had only to make a charge and an investigation would be launched. As a result, many anti-Communist liberals, concerned about the lack of protection afforded employees brought before loyalty boards, opposed the boards on civil liberties grounds.

The review board chairman in 1951, Hiram Bingham, was a former U.S. senator who, coincidentally, had once dated Jack Service's mother. Bingham was not entirely unsympathetic—he never believed that Service had actually been a spy—but he and his fellow review board members were frustrated by the State Department's reluctance to cooperate with the loyalty program. Whereas the post office's panel had found a full 10 percent of investigated employees "worthy of separation," and the Department of Commerce approximately 6.5 percent, the State Department had so far failed to recommend a single dismissal.

The review board had informally discussed its unhappiness with the State Department during an executive session in February 1951, nine months before it decided to undertake an official review of Service's case. As a disgruntled board member named L. V. Meloy put it, hearing officers at the State Department were "taking the attitude that they're there to clear the employee, not to protect the government. We've been arguing with them since the program started."[7]

Also, the State Department had been regularly giving employees the option of resigning before their cases were decided upon. This practice irritated another member of the review board, who further complained, "As far as the State Department is concerned, I don't understand their position at all. Because although their board has not held their people ineligible under the loyalty test, who should have been held ineligible under that test, they have plenty of power to remove them as a security risk. Why haven't they exercised it? They haven't exercised it in spite of all the searchlights turned on them."

Chairman Bingham had proposed responding to this problem by unilaterally reinterpreting the review board's mandate. Instead of rubber-stamping the dismissal of employees already found disloyal by department boards, the review board would initiate action on its own. Under its new definition of the rules, employees might be dismissed as long as there was a "reasonable doubt" of their loyalty.

This proposal, however, bothered the board member: "It seems to me that we should decide whether we are going to consider security risks . . . and if we want to stick to loyalty, let's stick to it as it is written down. In the minds of the public, there would be no difference. If there is reasonable doubt of a man's loyalty, it's going to be just as hard on him as if it is believed that he is disloyal, in spite of Webster's dictionary."

As they debated this change of policy, Jack Service was already very much on the minds of the board members. Taking issue with a colleague, board member Robert E. Lee complained: "On this loyalty business— Now, take the Service case, where the record shows that the man was living over there with a Chinese woman who we know and the record shows was under the pay of the Russian government, and he's in love with that woman, and you say that he can be loyal, perfectly loyal to this Government, and he's a safe employee for the State Dept. But we know that he's living with a woman who's under the pay of the Russian government, but we are prohibited from passing on that or finding him disloyal."[8]

Lee's comment demonstrates that the concern of the hearing officers at the State Department for protecting employee rights was not misplaced. Not only did Lee take allegations of the "spy sweetheart" at face value—a version of the facts none of the other board members disputed—but in one fell swoop he had transformed Service's supposed lover from a Chinese Communist into a woman "under the pay of the Russian government."

Later that year, after Service was exonerated by the State Department board, the review board announced that in accordance with its new policy it planned to examine his file. By this time, Lee was no longer a member of the board, and neither Service nor his attorney were ever told that the "spy sweetheart" story figured in the decision to take up his case. As far as they knew, the review board's main concern was with the excerpts of the FBI surveillance transcripts that had come to light as the result of the Tydings hearings.

This was the first time that the review board had been given a glimpse of the friendly relationship that developed between Jaffe and Service during the spring of 1945, and many of Service's offhand remarks—criticisms of Stettinius ("happy as a baboon") and Hurley, as well as effusive praise for *Amerasia*—looked compromising in cold print. Board members were especially disturbed by one conversation that had taken place at the bugged home of T. A. Bisson, during the weekend when Service was a guest in his country house. Jaffe, it seems, went off on a tangent, declaring that there was more freedom of the press in the Soviet Union than in the United States, and Service did not take issue with him, or at least not vehemently enough to suit the board.

After perusing the new evidence, the review board arrived at precisely the decision foretold by its discussion of the previous February: although there was no proof that Service was actually disloyal, to deny that his behavior raised a reasonable doubt as to his loyalty was to "stretch the mantle of charity much too far." A few hours after this finding was forwarded to the State Department, Service was fired by order of Secretary Dean Acheson.[9]

If Service had been fired in 1945, the State Department would have lost a valuable area specialist, one with unique firsthand knowledge of the future rulers of China. But such a decision would have been justified on the grounds that Service was guilty of a major indiscretion: that he had undertaken a covert campaign to undermine his superiors and had gotten mixed up in an abortive spy plot.

Service's dismissal in 1951 raised several troubling issues. During six years of executive department hearings, he had been afforded none of the basic protections routinely enjoyed by accused criminals. The same charges were raked over again and again by panels of administrative officials who were unfamiliar with the evidence and apparently unconcerned with the difference between fact and rumor. Service and his attorney Charles Rhetts were not given the right to examine the transcripts seen by the board or to subpoena witnesses. He was fired, in short, on the basis of false charges when the true ones would have been sufficient. In the mean-

time, Service's reputation was tried in the press. In January 1952, for ex-
ple, Miriam de Haas, a review board attorney, leaked the portions of
minutes of the February 1951 review board executive session in which t...
"spy sweetheart" charges were discussed to Senator McCarthy, who
promptly inserted them into the *Congressional Record*. Suspended and
forced to resign in punishment for this indiscretion, de Haas retaliated by
taking out a three-column, full-page advertisement in the *Washington
Times-Herald* in order to reiterate her contention that the transcript proved
that McCarthy had so far only "scratched the surface" of the problem of
Communist infiltration.[10]

Service had been, at the very least, indiscreet, conniving with a group of
left-wingers to undermine some of his own superiors. When he got caught
up in more than he bargained for, some of his friends had tried to protect
him, in large measure to protect themselves. When he was questioned
about the whole mess, he had not been totally forthright about what had
happened. And, ironically, he was finally fired in large part because of
leaked and inaccurate information spread by his political and ideological
enemies.

Service's dismissal was the signal for a general purge of the China
section of the foreign service. In December 1952, the review board recommended the termination of John Carter Vincent on charges even more
vague than those considered in Service's case. (While neither "expressly
accepting or rejecting" various allegations that Vincent was a pawn of the
Communists, the review board lumped all the unvetted evidence together
and concluded that where there was so much smoke, there must be fire.)
John Paton Davies lost his job in 1954.

The loyalty system was deeply flawed. Having come under fire for its
failure to do a convincing job of prosecuting suspected spies, the Truman
administration had reacted by instituting a program that transferred the
burden of proof onto employees, who found themselves in the position of
having to prove they were innocent of the nebulous sin of disloyalty. In
Service's case, the issues were so garbled, many of the facts so carefully
hidden, and the motivations of so many of the players so complicated that
a satisfactory outcome was impossible.

Charles Rhetts decided to challenge Service's firing on the specific
grounds that the review board had no authority to reverse the State Department board's earlier decision in Service's favor. By considering new
evidence in the form of the FBI transcripts, Rhetts charged, Bingham's
group had gone beyond its function as an administrative appeals body.

With the help of financial contributions from former State Department colleagues, Service was able to take the case all the way to the Supreme Court.

Service's appeal was finally heard in 1957. By a unanimous vote, the Court ruled that the review board had no provenance to reopen Service's case after the State Department board had already ruled in his favor. The ninth justice, Tom Clark, excused himself from the vote.

In the meantime, during his involuntary furlough from government work, Service had worked as an executive in a company that manufactured steam traps. He had mastered the design of the product well enough to become coholder of a patent on an improved design and, through purchasing stock options in the company, had accumulated a sizable nest egg—much of which he used to pay his legal bills. Despite his success in business, Service accepted reinstatement into the foreign service. At Foggy Bottom, it quickly became apparent that he had been cleared but not forgiven. Denied a security clearance, he was assigned to administrative jobs and eventually served three years at the American consulate in Liverpool. In 1962, realizing that he was unlikely ever to work in the area of Chinese affairs again, he resigned to become, at age fifty-three, an M.A. and Ph.D. candidate at the University of California at Berkeley.[11]

When the Eisenhower administration came into office in 1953, the new attorney general, Herbert Brownell, considered reopening the whole *Amerasia* affair once again. Brownell consulted with Hoover, but he soon recognized the folly and futility of reopening the case. The FBI's high command concluded that digging up the truth of the *Amerasia* affair would depend on "Tom Clark, Tom Corcoran, John Stewart Service or Hitchcock making a full disclosure" and that was unlikely. The administration did nothing.[12]

Although he was no longer in public life, Service's name continued to pop up whenever Americans became agitated about Communist China. Beginning in 1955, the Senate Internal Security Subcommittee, chaired by James Eastland of Mississippi, long a staunch supporter of Chiang Kai-shek, took an interest in the *Amerasia* affair and the subject of disloyal employees at the State Department. Eastland demanded the right to examine the exhibits seized in connection with the case, arguing that it was ridiculous to deny his subcommittee the right to examine them when "it is the simplest logic to conclude that [the contents] were transmitted to Soviet intelligence ten years ago." The Justice Department reluctantly agreed to hand over the material.[13]

In early 1970, as the Nixon administration was entering into talks with the Chinese Communists in Warsaw, Eastland's subcommittee saw fit to publish a large number of these exhibits in a two-volume edition entitled *The Amerasia Papers: A Clue to the Catastrophe of China*. The editor of the collection was one Anthony Kubek, a diplomatic historian whose first book was *How the Far East Was Lost: American Policy and the Creation of Communist China, 1941–1949*. Out of 142 documents selected by Kubek for publication, 101 were reports written by John S. Service. In his 113-page introduction, Kubek identified Service as the individual responsible for turning most of the *Amerasia* documents over to Jaffe. In fact, the majority of the reports published, some 69 of them, came from a file seized from Service's desk at the time of his arrest. Neither the FBI nor the prosecutors had ever suggested that these documents were seen by Philip Jaffe.[14]

Kubek's distortion of the record prompted Service to write *The Amerasia Papers: Some Problems in the History of U.S.-China Relations*, which was published in 1971. The time was ripe for rehabilitation, and as a result of the publication of his rebuttal to Kubek, Service was invited by Senator William Fulbright to testify as a friendly witness before the Senate Foreign Relations Committee. John Paton Davies and John Fairbank were also heard during the same session. Six months later, Service and his wife returned to China as honored guests of the government.[15]

Service's 1971 book defended his own record and the accuracy of his wartime reporting in China, but it did not tell the full story of the *Amerasia* affair. To begin with, he chose not to disclose what he knew about the Corcoran-Currie maneuvering. As Service pointed out in a recent letter to the authors, he believed he had done nothing wrong and was not privy to any knowledge of a fix. His discretion on this point was total—even his own wife was unaware that he had accepted advice from Soong's man in Washington. Also, twenty-six years after the fact, he did not admit to having any second thoughts about the possibility that Philip Jaffe was involved in espionage.[16]

Relying in large part on Service's version of events, Joseph Esherick, the editor of a 1975 collection of Service's China dispatches, characterized the *Amerasia* affair as prefiguring the illegal breaking-and-entering tactics of Richard Nixon's "plumbers," who penetrated the Democratic headquarters in the Watergate Hotel as well as the offices of Daniel Ellsberg's psychiatrist. "As in the Ellsberg case," Esherick noted, "the principal fear of the government was that leaked official documents might support the arguments of journalistic critics on the left."[17]

One might think that Philip Jaffe would have been happy with this verdict in the arena of public opinion, but he was not. Jaffe was infuriated by Service's portrait of himself as a premature victim of McCarthyism, a principled public servant who had innocently stumbled into trouble while conducting routine press briefings. In a pamphlet that he published privately in 1979 and circulated on his own behalf, Jaffe took issue with Service's claim that he was a political innocent who had not been reading *Amerasia* in China and was therefore unaware of its political stance. "There is no doubt that Service knew of me and my magazine," Jaffe wrote. "Jack would often march into my office without a prearranged appointment to bring me one of his reports. Although I was very pleased to be the recipient of all his knowledge and reports, he was the activist in our short relationship."

Jaffe portrayed Service as a manipulative careerist who realized that Mao would take power in China and was willing to go out on a limb to promote a policy tilt in his favor because he had ambitions to be the first American ambassador to Communist China. Jaffe even insisted that it was not Service who was the innocent victim of the case but himself. "The trap would not have been so tightly sprung if he had not been on the scene," he complained.[18]

Andrew Roth's comment on reading Jaffe's pamphlet was that Jaffe "should tell the whole truth or forget about it." Roth reflected that he no longer considered himself a victim of Grew and the conservatives at the State Department. What had happened to him was "an unpleasant accident, being pushed under the juggernaut of history by a couple of naive and self-preoccupied middle-aged men, a fellow-traveling businessman and a right-wing, amoral Dane." With no evident malice, he basically agreed with Jaffe's characterization of Service, observing that he was hardly the hero of the case but a bureaucratic infighter who, when the chips were down, had lacked the courage to fight for his convictions.[19]

Roth's and Jaffe's comments reflect the disappointment of many on the left that Service did not immediately take his case to the public, becoming the symbol and spokesman (and no doubt the martyr) for a campaign against U.S. support for the Nationalist Chinese. There are other ways to characterize this decision than careerism and lack of courage. Service's views were complex, his desire for privacy strong. Jaffe and Roth also fail to consider that having been used once, Service might not have been eager to put himself in a position where he might be exploited again.

There is no way to determine what would have happened if the *Amerasia* defendants had gone to trial and Service had tried to use the opportunity to expose the corruption of Chiang Kai-shek's regime and the dubious assumptions underlying America's support for the Nationalists. A highly publicized courtroom battle, with both Stilwell and Service testifying, might well have had a profound influence on the future course of U.S. policy toward China. It would be going too far to say that a thorough thrashing out of the issue would have defused the impulse that culminated in the rise of Senator Joseph McCarthy. However, the whitewash that did occur certainly gave right-wingers a ready-made cause célèbre and deep suspicions about the loyalty of government employees and the willingness of the U.S. government to prosecute betrayals of its secrets.

Even in 1986, after revelations about the Corcoran wiretaps emerged, pro-McCarthy journalists concluded that the new information was a vindication of their much-maligned standard-bearer. M. Stanton Evans noted in an article in *Human Events* that "McCarthy's charges were entirely true—more so than he imagined." Ralph de Toledano, writing in the *Washington Times*, agreed but called the idea, first suggested in the authors' *New Republic* article, that T. V. Soong may have had a hand in the cover-up "the greatest tooth fairy story of the year."[20]

De Toledano simply could not bring himself to let go of his conviction that the left must be responsible for any and all conspiracies. His article even identified Corcoran as a "recruiter of left-wingers for government posts," a characterization that must have caused Tommy the Cork to let go with some belly laughs from the next world. What really riled both de Toledano and Evans, however, was the assertion that Jack Service was never a spy. Evans cited the presence of roughly a thousand government documents in the *Amerasia* offices, implying that if they were there, Service must somehow have been responsible.

Echoing the charges of thirty years ago, the chief "evidence" Evans cited against Service was the fact that he expressed pro-Mao opinions in his China dispatches. Like McCarthy and his allies in the 1950s, Evans seemed not to grasp the concept that political officers had a duty to describe conditions as they saw them. Even a sometime critic of Service like General Joseph Wedemeyer, who thought it "inexcusable that any foreign service officer in the service of our country . . . should recommend that we support the Communists and abandon Chiang," stressed in remarks he made to Joseph Alsop at the time that he had no doubts about Service's true sympathies. All the career diplomats who served on his staff, Wedemeyer emphasized, were "outstanding foreign service officers—keen, analytical and loyal."[21]

Service and some of his colleagues may, as Joseph Alsop once charged, have held an "emotional bias" in favor of the Communists, failing to see that their show of moderation was, in large degree, a temporary expedient and that once in power they would exceed the Nationalists in cruelty and repression. But this "bias," mistaken as it was, was not synonymous with disloyalty. In any case, no objective reader of Service's dispatches could deny that he expressed his views in a forthright and considered manner.

It is true, although sometimes overlooked by liberal critics of McCarthy, that by leaking material unfavorable to Hurley to Atkinson, Jaffe, and others, Service crossed the line between executing and recommending policy and trying to influence it. But such activities, though theoretically improper for career civil servants, are hardly unusual, and few have ever paid more dearly for them than Service and his fellow China experts in the diplomatic corps.

Any lingering doubts about Service's true position are erased by the evidence of the FBI surveillance. If he had been a secret Communist, much less a spy, some better evidence would likely have surfaced in the transcripts. Philip Jaffe would not have been so surprised and overwhelmed by his good luck in securing Service's cooperation—or so bitter in later years over the fact that Service, the liberal, emerged from the affair as a hero in the eyes of many, while the pro-Soviet defendants were either despised or ignored.

The *Amerasia* affair was a proxy for a bitter conflict within the State Department and Congress over the post–World War II foreign policy of the United States toward China and the question of how to deal with Communism. Moreover, it is impossible to ignore the fact that the division of opinion about the case reflected a larger cultural split between liberal intellectuals on one side and conservatives on the other. Indisputably, some unsavory characters climbed aboard the McCarthyite bandwagon. Some were gutter fighters and hard drinkers, like the senator himself. Others, like Congressman George Dondero, were simply none too bright. On the other hand, Emmanuel Larsen, Philip Jaffe, John Service, James McGranery, and Tom Clark, to name just a few of the right wing's enemies, hardly covered themselves with glory either. Several of them broke the law, and others lied or covered up what had happened.

Nevertheless, a certain double standard has been operative. Patrick

Hurley's conviction that the China Hands were plotting against him has invariably been dismissed as evidence of paranoia, even senility and mental incompetence. But Hurley *was* systematically undermined, almost from the day he arrived in China and concluded that Stilwell had to be recalled. Hurley's reaction—and that of Dooman—may have been malicious and inappropriate, but they were hardly wrong in thinking that they had enemies who were willing to engage in unscrupulous activities to undermine them.

Three government employees were meeting regularly with a magazine publisher who had devoted his career to promoting the Stalinist line and who, as it turned out, had cultivated these contacts in the first place because it was his life's ambition to become a full-fledged Soviet agent—and this during wartime. One did not have to be a right-wing crank to find this unacceptable and to feel isolated and suspicious when the whole mess was swept under a rug.

Most importantly, defenders of Service and the other China Hands have erred in their readiness to accept the instant judgment of the press at the time that the *Amerasia* investigation was, from its inception, an attempt to stifle left-wing leakers. Clearly, from the record, the motivation of the Departments of State and the Navy was to search out spies and staunch a massive breach in national security.

Moreover, although it cannot be proven that Jaffe actually turned over data to Soviet agents, he probably did take the opportunity to pass information to representatives of the Chinese Communists. At any rate, by his own admission, his ambition to succeed as a spy was what motivated him to begin collecting documents from Larsen in the first place.

In the spring of 1945, with Germany out of the war and the Soviets increasingly seen as the enemy, the climate of opinion regarding leaking information to pro-Communists was rapidly changing. The *Amerasia* surveillance had already cast suspicion on others not directly related to Jaffe—Harry Dexter White, for one—and Lauchlin Currie, himself enmeshed in relationships with a host of people giving information to Soviet agents, no doubt foresaw that a continuing probe might throw a spotlight on his own activities. As the first step in a remarkably successful effort at damage control, he arranged for Tommy Corcoran, the archetypal Washington insider, to prevent the full story from emerging. Corcoran's intricate maneuvering in turn created new secrets that people labored to hide for years afterward.

Although there is no proof that Corcoran profited financially from his role in the case, he did prevent a full public airing of the unhappiness of many American diplomats with the regime whose commercial interests he represented. Others benefited in more obvious ways from the exchange of favors that Corcoran arranged. Philip Jaffe, a wealthy client of Representative Emmanuel Celler's law firm, got off the hook, escaping from an espionage charge with the legal equivalent of a slap on the wrist. So did Kate Mitchell, assisted by the lawyer arranged for her by her wealthy uncle. Robert Hitchcock, a former Buffalo assistant U.S. attorney and devout Catholic layman, became a partner in a prosperous, politically well-connected law firm.

J. Edgar Hoover watchers have long been fascinated by the rumor that Hoover's secret files contained enough dirty secrets to blackmail all of Washington. Whether or not this was true, Hoover certainly did have the goods on his immediate superiors in the office of the attorney general. Although he was a fervent anti-Communist who favored the jailing of Communist Party officials under the Smith Act, Tom Clark did not mind scuttling a potential espionage case that promised to be troublesome and politically touchy in exchange for help with his own confirmation problems. One of his successors, James McGranery, who did most of the negotiating with Tommy Corcoran over his wiretapped lines, knew from the day he took office that Hoover had evidence of malfeasance and perjury on his part, and this knowledge certainly must have given the FBI director enormous leverage over his boss. Senator McCarthy cynically used the *Amerasia* affair even though he was indifferent to the facts of the case. But so too did Senator Tydings, who preferred to find convenient scapegoats rather than be embarrassed by the truth.

Several conspiracies occurred in the *Amerasia* case. Philip Jaffe and Joseph Bernstein were conspiring to commit espionage on behalf of Joseph Stalin and the Soviet Union with the tacit approval of Andrew Roth and Earl Browder. Philip Jaffe, Andrew Roth, Kate Mitchell, Mark Gayn, Emmanuel Larsen, John Service, and Lauchlin Currie, among others, were conspiring to leak information, both classified and nonclassified, to undermine Patrick Hurley and Chiang Kai-shek. Lauchlin Currie, Ben Cohen, Tommy Corcoran, Tom Clark, James McGranery, James McInerney, Robert Hitchcock, and perhaps T. V. Soong were conspiring to prevent a full public airing of the facts of the case.

If there is a moral to the tangled history of the *Amerasia* affair, it is the triumph of political expediency over ideology. The *Amerasia* affair was a case without heroes, a potential scandal that could have hurt prominent

individuals, both anti-Communists and New Dealers. And at the cru
moment, there was a middle man on the scene, ready and willing to wo
out an arrangement that would protect all concerned.

McCarthyism—smearing opponents by use of false accusations and
guilt by association—is a term of opprobrium in American life. Precisely
because Senator McCarthy was reckless and made false charges, actual
Communists who engaged in and contemplated espionage sought to
claim the status of victims. As the *Amerasia* case ought to teach us, not
everyone accused of disloyalty or espionage was innocent—regardless of
whether the perpetrator could be legally convicted. Even some of the
victims of the case were not entirely innocent—they were drawn into an
espionage conspiracy not out of disloyalty but out of stupidity or greed or
hubris and then they frantically maneuvered for years to avoid the fallout.
While various politicians scrambled to gain political advantage from the
affair and bureaucrats dueled to secure position, the truth was the only
casualty.

Notes

ABBREVIATIONS

In addition to the abbreviations used in the text, the following abbreviations are used in the notes.

Cong. Rec.   *Congressional Record*, Washington, D.C., 1945–52.
IPRH   U.S. Senate Committee on the Judiciary, Subcommittee to
                 Investigate the Administration of the Internal Security Act and
                 Other Internal Security Laws, *Institute of Pacific Relations
                 Hearings*, 82d Cong., 1st and 2d sess., 1951–52, 14 parts.
Jaffe Papers   Philip Jaffe Papers, Special Collections Department, Robert
                 W. Woodruff Library, Emory University, Atlanta, Georgia.
Levine Papers   Isaac Don Levine Papers, in possession of Ruth Levine,
                 Washington, D.C.
SDELI   U.S. Senate Subcommittee of the Committee on Foreign
                 Relations, *State Department Employee Loyalty Investigation*,
                 81st Cong., 2d sess., 1950, 5 parts.
Service Papers   John S. Service Papers, in possession of John S. Service,
                 Berkeley, California.

INTRODUCTION

1. *New York Times*, June 7, 1945, p. 1.

2. Ted Morgan, *FDR: A Biography* (New York: Simon and Schuster, 1985), pp. 737–40.

3. *New York Times*, June 1, 1945, p. 1.

4. *Cong. Rec.*, 81st Cong., 2d sess., 1950, 96, pt. 6:7438.

5. Andrew Roth, "Illegal Search and the Siamese Underground," unpublished typescript, kindly provided by Andrew Roth. A copy is in box 9, folder 2, Jaffe Papers.

6. This information comes from Bielaski's 1946 testimony to the Hobbs Committee, printed in *Cong. Rec.*, 81st Cong., 2d sess., 1950, 96, pt. 6:7438.

7. Bielaski provided the Tydings Committee with a memo he said he had prepared on April 12, 1945, for his own files. The memo first notes that the original of the Wells report was not found but later says that "the original and all of the copies of the secret document which was responsible for our quest had been extracted from the receptacle . . . and these were among the papers delivered to

the security officer." During his questioning, however, Bielaski said that the original was not found. See *SDELI*, pp. 961–62. Bielaski in his testimony also underestimated the number of documents he had taken by about a dozen. The FBI noted that it received twenty-three documents from the OSS on March 13, 1945. The FBI did not make these documents part of its case file because "they were illegally obtained by OSS, could not be used as evidence, and were not part of the case which the Bureau developed against the subjects." They were added to the FBI file in 1950. See to D. M. Ladd from A. H. Belmont, April 20, 1950, FBI File 100-267360-1059, box 125, folder 5, Jaffe Papers.

8. Richard Gid Powers, *Secrecy and Power: The Life of J. Edgar Hoover* (New York: Free Press, 1987), p. 253.

9. *New York Journal-American*, June 7, 1945, p. 1; *New York Herald Tribune*, June 9, 1945, p. 10.

10. David Caute, *The Great Fear: The Anti-Communist Purge under Truman and Eisenhower* (New York: Simon and Schuster, 1978), p. 56.

CHAPTER ONE

1. Barbara Tuchman, *Stilwell and the American Experience in China, 1911–1945* (New York: Macmillan, 1970), pp. 525–26.

2. William F. Buckley, Jr., and L. Brent Bozell, *McCarthy and His Enemies* (Chicago: Henry Regnery, 1954), pp. 147–52.

3. *SDELI*, pp. 1325–26.

4. Ibid., pp. 2067–68.

5. Stanley Hornbeck to secretary of state, July 27, 1944, quoted in Russell D. Buhite, *Patrick J. Hurley and American Foreign Policy* (Ithaca: Cornell University Press, 1973), p. 182.

6. *Current Biography* (New York: H. W. Wilson, 1941), pp. 192–93; report made at New York City, February 8, 1954, FBI File 101-3616-84, and report made at Chicago, May 14, 1954, FBI File 101-3616-143, both at FBI Reading Room, Washington, D.C.

7. Gary May, *China Scapegoat: The Diplomatic Ordeal of John Carter Vincent* (Washington, D.C.: New Republic Books, 1979), p. 75.

8. Joseph Esherick, ed., *Lost Chance in China: The World War II Despatches of John S. Service* (New York: Random House, 1974), pp. 93–96.

9. Ibid., pp. 178–82.

10. Ibid., p. 357.

11. Ibid., p. 268.

12. Ibid., pp. 335–36.

13. On Chi, see Howard Boorman, *Biographical Dictionary of Republican*

China (New York: Columbia University Press, 1967), pp. 293–97, and Donald Klein and Ann Clark, *Biographic Dictionary of Chinese Communism* (Cambridge: Harvard University Press, 1971), 1:160–63. Greg Lewis, "From Polemics to Patriotism: The Transformation of Ji Chao-ding, 1929–1943," Selected Papers in Asian Studies, Western Conference of the Association for Asian Studies, 1993, includes some interesting material. We are also indebted to Minister Ji Chao-zhu of China, a brother of Chi, for agreeing to take part in a telephone interview with Harvey Klehr, March 25, 1985. A third brother was an actor, who, among other roles, played the butler on the popular television show *Falconcrest*.

14. Philip Jaffe, *The Amerasia Case, from 1945 to the Present* (New York: privately printed, 1979), p. 10.

15. John S. Service to Harvey Klehr and Ronald Radosh, November 27, 1985.

16. Joseph Alsop, "The Feud between Stilwell and Chiang," *Saturday Evening Post*, January 7, 1950, p. 16.

17. Tuchman, *Stilwell and the American Experience in China*, p. 494.

18. Buhite, *Patrick J. Hurley and American Foreign Policy*, p. 149.

19. Tuchman, *Stilwell and the American Experience in China*, p. 504.

20. Esherick, *Lost Chance in China*, pp. 161–66, emphasis in original.

21. John S. Service, interview with Harvey Klehr and Ronald Radosh, Berkeley, California, November 12, 1985.

22. E. J. Kahn, Jr., *The China Hands: America's Foreign Service Officers and What Befell Them* (New York: Viking, 1975), pp. 137–38.

23. Ibid., pp. 152–53.

24. Esherick, *Lost Chance in China*, p. 387.

CHAPTER TWO

1. Bradley F. Smith, *The Shadow Warriors: OSS and the Origins of the CIA* (New York: Basic Books, 1983), p. 39.

2. *Cong. Rec.*, 81st Cong., 2d sess., 1950, 96, pt. 6:7438. During his testimony before the Hobbs Committee, Bielaski used the pseudonym Frank Brooks for security reasons.

3. Ibid.

4. William Fairchild and Charles Clift, "The Wiretappers," *Reporter*, December 23, 1952, p. 22. In 1959 Bielaski was linked to influence-peddler Bernard Goldfine in the press but denied any connection to him. Details about Bielaski's life can be found in his obituary in the *New York Herald Tribune*, April 6, 1961, p. 23.

5. *SDELI*, pp. 928–29.

6. Ibid., p. 1187.

7. Ibid. Donovan confirmed the outlines of this scenario in an interview with Lyon Tyler in 1950, printed in *SDELI*, p. 1919.

8. Report made at New York City, August 8, 1944, FBI File 100-267360-6, box 116, folder 1, Jaffe Papers.

9. Bertram D. Wolfe, introduction to *The Rise and Fall of American Communism*, by Philip Jaffe (New York: Horizon Press, 1975), p. 3.

10. Details on Philip Jaffe's background come from his unpublished autobiography, "Odyssey of a Fellow Traveler," in box 1, folder 5, Jaffe Papers, and notes of interviews with Agnes Jaffe conducted by Nancy Remington, April 19, 20, June 15, 19, 1981, in the authors' possession. FBI files differ from these records on some minor details. The bureau listed Jaffe's year of birth as 1897, and FBI records reveal that when Jaffe applied to Columbia University, he claimed he was born in New York City. See report made at New York City, January 22, 1944, FBI File 100-267360-1, box 116, folder 1, Jaffe Papers.

11. Philip Jaffe, *The Amerasia Case, from 1945 to the Present* (New York: privately printed, 1979), pp. 2–10.

12. Jaffe, "Odyssey of a Fellow Traveler," p. 125; to New York City from Baltimore, April 18, 1950, FBI File 100-55714-85, box 131, folder 2, Jaffe Papers.

13. Jaffe, *The Rise and Fall of American Communism*, p. 12, and *The Amerasia Case*, pp. 6–8.

14. Frederick Vanderbilt Field, *From Right to Left: An Autobiography* (Westport: Lawrence-Hill, 1983).

15. Agnes Jaffe, interview with Harvey Klehr and Ronald Radosh, New York City, May 18, 1984.

16. *IPRH*, p. 31.

17. Fred Field to Edward Carter, March 29, 1938, in *IPRH*, pp. 4093–94.

18. *New York World Telegram and Sun*, May 8, 1950, p. 1.

19. Owen Lattimore to Edward Carter, July 10, 1938, in *IPRH*, pp. 39–41. For a favorable biography of Lattimore, see Robert P. Newman, *Owen Lattimore and the "Loss" of China* (Berkeley: University of California Press, 1992).

20. Kenneth Shewmaker, *Americans and Chinese Communists, 1927–1945* (Ithaca: Cornell University Press, 1971).

21. Philip Jaffe, "China's Communists Told Me," *New Masses*, October 12, 1937, pp. 3–10.

22. Stanley Hornbeck to Fred Field, November 5, 1940, Stanley Hornbeck Papers, Hoover Institution on War, Revolution, and Peace, Stanford, California.

23. Background information on Roth is from Andrew Roth, "Pioneer of the Purge," unpublished typescript, in the authors' possession. A copy is in box 9, folder 2, Jaffe Papers.

24. Biographical details on Larsen come from his personality card, box 59, Jaffe Papers, and *SDELI*, pp. 2180–82.

25. *SDELI*, pp. 2180–82; Emmanuel Larsen, "They Called Me a Spy," in ibid., p. 1739.

26. To the director from SAC, Louisville, June 25, 1945, FBI File 100-267360-475, box 120, folder 1; report made at New York City, June 28, 1945, FBI File 100-267360-501, box 120, folder 4; to the director from FBI, Charlotte, July 11, 1945, FBI File 100-267360-540, box 120, folder 3; and to the director from SAC, Charlotte, July 16, 1945, FBI File 100-267360-571, box 120, folder 9, all in Jaffe Papers.

27. *SDELI*, pp. 2180–82; *Washington Post District Weekly*, August 6, 1981, p. 1.

28. Andrew Roth, interview with Harvey Klehr and Ronald Radosh, London, England, September 16, 1985; Roth, "Pioneer of the Purge."

29. Roth, "Pioneer of the Purge."

30. Ibid.

31. Ibid.

32. Memo for the director, March 20, 1945, FBI File 100-267360-45, box 116, folder 1, Jaffe Papers.

33. Report made at New York City, March 20, 1945, FBI File 65-14461-[unrecorded], box 116, folder 2, and memo re. Philip Jacob Jaffe, March 20, 1945, FBI File 100-267360-46, box 116, folder 1, both in Jaffe Papers.

34. Memo for the attorney general from John Edgar Hoover, March 22, 1945, FBI File 100-267360-48, box 116, folder 1; to M. E. Gurnea from [blacked out], March 21, 1945, FBI File 100-267360-88, box 116, folder 3; and report made at Washington, D.C., March 24, 1945, FBI File 100-267360-88, box 116, folder 3, all in Jaffe Papers.

35. Memo for the attorney general from John Edgar Hoover, March 22, 1945, FBI File 100-267360-49, box 116, folder 1, and report made at Washington, D.C., March 24, 1945, FBI File 100-267360-88, box 116, folder 3, both in Jaffe Papers.

36. To the director from M. E. Gurnea, March 21, 1945, FBI File 100-267360-47, box 116, folder 1, Jaffe Papers.

37. Biographical information is from Mark Gayn, *Journey from the Far East* (New York: Knopf, 1944). Other information is found in report made at New York City, May 10, 1945, FBI File 100-267360-214, box 117, folder 1, Jaffe Papers.

38. To Inspector M. E. Gurnea from Guy Hottel, April 30, 1945, FBI File 100-267360-157, box 116, folder 8, Jaffe Papers; Gayn, *Journey from the Far East*, pp. 180, 220, 225.

39. To the director from M. E. Gurnea, March 27, 1945, FBI File 100-267360-75, box 116, folder 2, Jaffe Papers.

40. Report made at New York City, April 2, 1945, FBI File 100-267360-90, box 116, folder 3, Jaffe Papers.

41. Summary of file references, May 2, 1955, FBI File 100-557494-249, box 131, folder 6, Jaffe Papers.

42. Ibid.; report made at Washington, D.C., May 11, 1945, FBI File 100-267360-215, box 117, folder 2, Jaffe Papers.

43. Summary of file references, May 2, 1955, FBI File 100-557494-249, box 131, folder 6, Jaffe Papers.

44. Report made at Washington, D.C., April 19, 1945, FBI File 100-267360-113, box 116, folder 5, Jaffe Papers.

45. To the director from M. E. Gurnea, June 4, 1945, FBI File 100-267360-278, box 117, folder 9, and re. Philip Jacob Jaffe, March 16, 1945, FBI File 65-14461-13, box 128, folder 8, both in Jaffe Papers.

46. Report made at Washington, D.C., April 19, 1945, FBI File 100-267360-113, box 116, folder 5, Jaffe Papers. Although Friedman's name is blacked out in this document, we were able to determine his identity from internal evidence in the files.

47. To Inspector M. E. Gurnea from Guy Hottel, April 30, 1945, FBI File 100-267360-157, box 116, folder 8, and to Inspector M. E. Gurnea from Guy Hottel, May 1, 1945, FBI File 100-267360-158, box 116, folder 8, both in Jaffe Papers.

48. Memo labeled "Top Secret," April 2, 1945, FBI File 100-267360-109, box 116, folder 4, and report made at Cincinnati, Ohio, May 29, 1950, FBI File 100-267360-1111, box 125, folder 5, both in Jaffe Papers.

49. Robert Lamphere and Tom Shachtman, *The FBI-KGB War* (New York: Random House, 1986), p. 101.

50. To the director from D. M. Ladd, April 18, 1945, FBI File 100-267360-105, box 116, folder 4, Jaffe Papers. Additional information from the same memo, which was re-released by the FBI, is in FBI File 100-267360-1285, box 126, folder 7, Jaffe Papers.

51. Report made at Cincinnati, Ohio, May 29, 1950, FBI File 100-267360-1111, box 125, folder 5, Jaffe Papers.

CHAPTER THREE

1. Gary May, *China Scapegoat: The Diplomatic Ordeal of John Carter Vincent* (Washington, D.C.: New Republic Books, 1979), p. 93.

2. E. J. Kahn, Jr., *The China Hands: America's Foreign Service Officers and What Befell Them* (New York: Viking, 1975), p. 165.

3. Attention: Inspector M. E. Gurnea, May 2, 1945, FBI File 100-267360-161, box 116, folder 8, Jaffe Papers.

4. Attention: Inspector M. E. Gurnea, May 4, 1945, FBI File 100-267360-170, box 116, folder 8, and Attention: Inspector M. E. Gurnea, May 5, 1945, FBI File 100-267360-174, box 116, folder 9, both in Jaffe Papers.

5. Attention: Inspector M. E. Gurnea, May 5, 1945, FBI File 100-267360-174, box 116, folder 9, Jaffe Papers.

6. Ibid.

7. Attention: Inspector M. E. Gurnea, May 8, 1945, FBI File 100-267360-184, box 116, folder 9, Jaffe Papers.

8. Ibid.; Attention: Inspector M. E. Gurnea, May 9, 1945, FBI File 100-267360-188, box 116, folder 9, Jaffe Papers.

9. Attention: Inspector M. E. Gurnea, May 9, 1945, FBI File 100-267360-188, box 116, folder 9, Jaffe Papers.

10. Ibid.

11. Kahn, *The China Hands*, p. 165.

12. Andrew Roth, interview with Harvey Klehr and Ronald Radosh, London, England, September 16, 1985. The Foner brothers were fired from the faculty at CCNY in 1941 for being members of the Communist Party.

13. John S. Service, interview with Harvey Klehr and Ronald Radosh, Berkeley, California, November 12, 1985.

14. Attention: Inspector M. E. Gurnea, May 9, 1945, FBI File 100-267360-188, box 116, folder 9; report made at Washington, D.C., May 11, 1945, FBI File 100-267360-215, box 117, folder 2; Attention: Inspector M. E. Gurnea, May 17, 1945, FBI File 100-267360-221, box 117, folder 4; and report made at Washington, D.C., May 26, 1945, FBI File 100-267360-237, box 117, folder 6, all in Jaffe Papers.

15. Report made at New York City, May 2, 1945, FBI File 100-267360-211, box 116, folder 10; Attention: Inspector M. E. Gurnea, May 17, 1945, FBI File 100-267360-221, box 117, folder 4; and report made at Washington, D.C., May 26, 1945, FBI File 100-267360-237, box 117, folder 6, all in Jaffe Papers.

16. Report made at New York City, May 2, 1945, FBI File 100-267360-211, box 116, folder 10, Jaffe Papers.

17. Ibid.

18. To SAC, New York City, from [blacked out], May 20, 1954, FBI File 100-267360-1562, box 127, folder 7, Jaffe Papers.

19. Attention: Inspector M. E. Gurnea, May 17, 1945, FBI File 100-267360-221, box 117, folder 4, and report made at Washington, D.C., May 26, 1945, FBI File 100-267360-237, box 117, folder 6, both in Jaffe Papers.

20. Attention: Inspector M. E. Gurnea, May 17, 1945, FBI File 100-267360-221, box 117, folder 4, and report made at Washington, D.C., May 26, 1945, FBI File 100-267360-237, box 117, folder 6, both in Jaffe Papers.

21. Ibid.

22. Andrew Roth, interview with Harvey Klehr and Ronald Radosh, London, England, September 16, 1985.

23. Information about Bernstein is from report made at New York City, July 9, 1952, FBI File 100-343242-76, box 129, folder 5, Jaffe Papers.

24. On the collaboration between Katz and Bernstein, we are indebted to Stephen Koch for information from his interview (New York City, June 26, 1991) with Rae Bernstein, Joseph's widow, who refused our request for an interview.

25. Stephen Koch, *Double Lives* (New York: Free Press, 1994), pp. 75–95.

26. Karel Kaplan, *Report on the Murder of the General Secretary* (Columbus: Ohio State University Press, 1990), p. 278; Theodore Draper, "The Man Who Wanted to Hang," *Reporter*, January 6, 1953, pp. 26–30.

27. Alan Weinstein, *Perjury: The Hiss-Chambers Case* (New York: Knopf, 1978), p. 128.

28. Report made at New York City, June 28, 1945, FBI File 100-267360-501, box 120, folder 4, and memo re. Joseph Milton Bernstein, November 8, 1946, FBI File 100-343242-23, box 129, folder 3, both in Jaffe Papers.

29. Robert Lamphere to Harvey Klehr, June 10, 1986; report made at New York City, July 9, 1952, FBI File 100-343242-76, box 129, folder 5, Jaffe Papers. Trachtenberg claimed that the envelope contained the will of a German politician who had been murdered by the Nazis.

30. To SAC, New York City, from the director, May 3, 1946, FBI File 100-343242-14, box 129, folder 2, Jaffe Papers.

31. Details about Soviet espionage in the United States can be found in David Dallin, *Soviet Espionage* (New Haven: Yale University Press, 1955). A full discussion of Baker's secret apparatus can be found in Harvey Klehr, John Haynes, and Fridrikh Firsov, *The Secret World of American Communism* (New Haven: Yale University Press, 1995). Although we have gained access to the FBI file entitled "The Comintern Apparatus in the United States," it is so heavily blacked out that it is useless in confirming whether Bernstein was involved.

32. Excerpts from the Nelson-Zubilin conversation, in U.S. Senate Subcommittee to Investigate the Administration of the Internal Security Act and Other Internal Security Laws, *Interlocking Subversion in Government Departments* (Washington, D.C.: Government Printing Office, 1953), part 15, pp. 1050–51; Elizabeth Bentley, *Out of Bondage* (New York: Devin-Adair, 1951), pp. 242–57.

33. Klehr, Haynes, and Firsov, *The Secret World of American Communism*, pp. 232–43.

34. Attention: Inspector M. E. Gurnea, May 17, 1945, FBI File 100-267360-221, box 117, folder 4, Jaffe Papers.

35. Ibid.

36. John S. Service to Harvey Klehr and Ronald Radosh, November 27, 1985.

37. Attention: Inspector M. E. Gurnea, May 24, 1945, FBI File 100-267360-231, box 117, folder 4, and report made at Washington, D.C., May 26, 1945, FBI File 100-267360-237, box 117, folder 6, both in Jaffe Papers; Earl Latham, *The Communist Conspiracy in Washington: From the New Deal to McCarthy* (Cambridge: Harvard University Press, 1966).

38. Attention: Inspector M. E. Gurnea, May 24, 1945, FBI File 100-267360-231, box 117, folder 4, and report made at Washington, D.C., May 26, 1945, FBI File 100-267360-237, box 117, folder 6, both in Jaffe Papers.

39. Attention: Inspector M. E. Gurnea, May 24, 1945, FBI File 100-267360-231, box 117, folder 4; report made at Washington, D.C., May 26, 1945, FBI File 100-267360-237, box 117, folder 6; and to SAC Guy Hottel from SA Lewis Glenn, March 21, 1945, FBI File 100-267360-717, box 122, folder 3, all in Jaffe Papers.

40. Report made at Washington, D.C., May 26, 1945, FBI File 100-267360-237,

box 117, folder 6, and to SAC, New York City, from [blacked out], May 20, 1954, FBI File 100-267360-1562, box 127, folder 7, both in Jaffe Papers.

41. Report made at Washington, D.C., May 26, 1945, FBI File 100-267360-237, box 117, folder 6, Jaffe Papers.

42. Report made at New York City, May 26, 1945, FBI File 100-267360-236, box 117, folder 5; to SAC, New York City, from [blacked out], May 20, 1954, FBI File 100-267360-1562, box 127, folder 7; and to M. E. Gurnea from SA Floyd Jones, June 27, 1945, FBI File 100-267360-468, box 119, folder 5, all in Jaffe Papers.

43. Report made at New York City, May 30, 1945, FBI File 100-267360-247, box 117, folder 7; Attention: Inspector M. E. Gurnea, May 23, 1945, FBI File 100-267360-229, box 117, folder 4; and report made at New York City, May 26, 1945, FBI File 100-267360-236, box 117, folder 5, all in Jaffe Papers.

44. Report made at New York City, May 17, 1945, FBI File 100-267360-218, box 117, folder 3, Jaffe Papers.

45. Ibid.

46. Report made at Washington, D.C., June 6, 1945, FBI File 100-267360-288, box 117, folder 9, and to the director from SAC Guy Hottel, June 14, 1945, FBI File 100-267360-531, box 120, folder 6, both in Jaffe Papers.

47. To the director from SAC Guy Hottel, June 14, 1945, FBI File 100-267360-531, box 120, folder 6, Jaffe Papers.

48. Ibid.

49. Ibid.; report made at Washington, D.C., June 6, 1945, FBI File 100-267360-288, box 117, folder 9, Jaffe Papers.

50. To the director from SAC Guy Hottel, June 14, 1945, FBI File 100-267360-531, box 120, folder 6, Jaffe Papers.

51. Report made at Washington, D.C., June 6, 1945, FBI File 100-267360-288, box 117, folder 9, Jaffe Papers.

52. Ibid.

53. Emmanuel Larsen, "The State Department Espionage Case," *Plain Talk*, October 1946, p. 36.

CHAPTER FOUR

1. William Fairchild and Charles Clift, "The Wiretappers," *Reporter*, December 23, 1952, p. 10.

2. Ibid., p. 12.

3. Ibid.; Richard Gid Powers, *Secrecy and Power: The Life of J. Edgar Hoover* (New York: Free Press, 1987), p. 237.

4. Fairchild and Clift, "The Wiretappers," p. 13.

5. To D. M. Ladd from A. H. Belmont, June 12, 1950, FBI File 100-267360-1339, box 125, folder 6; report made at Washington, D.C., June 6, 1945, FBI File

100-267360-288, box 117, folder 9; to the director from M. E. Gurnea, May 28, 1945, FBI File 100-267360-260, box 117, folder 8; and memo for D. M. Ladd, M. E. Gurnea, and Clyde Tolson from J. E. H., May 29, 1945, FBI File 100-267360-245, box 117, folder 7, all in Jaffe Papers.

6. To the director from M. E. Gurnea, May 23, 1945, FBI File 100-267360-217, box 117, folder 2, and memo from [blacked out], May 26, 1945, FBI File 100-267360-235, box 139, folder 1, both in Jaffe Papers.

7. To the director from M. E. Gurnea, May 29, 1945, FBI File 100-257360-283, box 117, folder 9, Jaffe Papers.

8. Ibid.

9. To the director from M. E. Gurnea, June 4, 1945, FBI File 100-267360-279, box 117, folder 9, and memo for D. M. Ladd, M. E. Gurnea, and Clyde Tolson from J. E. H., May 29, 1945, FBI File 100-267360-245, box 117, folder 7, both in Jaffe Papers.

10. To the director from M. E. Gurnea, May 30, 1945, FBI File 100-267360-284, box 117, folder 9, Jaffe Papers.

11. To the director from M. E. Gurnea, June 5, 1945, FBI File 100-267360-320, box 118, folder 2, Jaffe Papers.

12. "For Immediate Release," June 6, 1945, FBI File 100-267360-289, box 118, folder 1, and to Clyde Tolson from L. B. Nichols, June 5, 1945, FBI File 100-267360-299, box 118, folder 1, both in Jaffe Papers.

13. To the director from M. E. Gurnea, May 30, 1945, FBI File 100-267360-284, box 117, folder 9, Jaffe Papers.

14. To the director from M. E. Gurnea, June 4, 1945, FBI File 100-267360-279, box 117, folder 9, Jaffe Papers; *SDELI*, p. 2107.

15. "Report of the Department of Justice in Connection with the Amerasia Case," FBI File 100-267360-1512, box 127, folder 3, Jaffe Papers.

16. Walter Millis, ed., *Forrestal Diaries* (New York: Viking, 1951), pp. 65–66; memo for the director, May 29, 1945, FBI File 100-267360-244, box 117, folder 7; to the director from M. E. Gurnea, May 29, 1945, FBI File 100-267360-282, box 117, folder 9; to A. H. Belmont from C. E. Hennrich, June 12, 1950, FBI File 100-267360-1219, box 126, folder 4; and to the director from D. M. Ladd, June 14, 1950, FBI File 100-267360-1322, box 126, folder 10, all in Jaffe Papers.

17. To the director from M. E. Gurnea, May 31, 1945, FBI File 100-267360-285, box 117, folder 9, Jaffe Papers.

18. Memo from M. E. Gurnea, May 31, 1945, FBI File 100-267360-276, box 117, folder 9, Jaffe Papers.

19. To the director from M. E. Gurnea, June 2, 1945, FBI File 100-267360-277, box 117, folder 9, and to the director from D. M. Ladd, June 14, 1950, FBI File 100-267360-1322, box 126, folder 10, both in Jaffe Papers; Joseph Grew, Department of State Memorandum of Conversation, June 2, 1945, State Department Files, 111.74/6-245, RG 59, box 492, National Archives and Records Administra-

tion, Washington, D.C. A note with Grew's memo indicates that a copy of it was sent to Secretary Stettinius in San Francisco on June 4.

20. To the director from M. E. Gurnea, June 2, 1945, FBI File 100-267360-277, box 117, folder 9; to the director from D. M. Ladd, June 14, 1950, FBI File 100-267360-1322, box 126, folder 10; and to Herbert Brownell from James Vardaman, December 3, 1953, FBI File 100-267360-1552, box 127, folder 6, all in Jaffe Papers. In 1950 McInerney told the Tydings Committee that he had discovered a note, dated May 29, in his own handwriting that said, "Matters may be held up by Navy. Mr. Forrestal called Mr. Clark." This suggests that Forrestal, whose diary entry indicated that he was concerned about the diplomatic impact of the arrests, may have been responsible. See *SDELI*, p. 1059.

21. Report made at New York City, June 12, 1945, FBI File 100-267360-471, box 119, folder 6, and to M. E. Gurnea from SA G. K. Allen, October 18, 1945, FBI File 100-267360-718, box 123, folder 1, both in Jaffe Papers.

22. Report made at New York City, June 12, 1945, FBI File 100-267360-471, box 119, folder 6, and to the director from Guy Hottel, June 15, 1945, FBI File 100-267360-471X, box 120, folder 1, both in Jaffe Papers.

23. Report made at New York City, June 12, 1945, FBI File 100-267360-471, box 119, folder 6, Jaffe Papers.

24. Ibid.

25. Ibid.

26. Report made at Washington, D.C., June 13, 1945, FBI File 100-267360-407, box 119, folder 2, Jaffe Papers.

27. Ibid.

28. Ibid.; Andrew Roth, interview with Harvey Klehr and Ronald Radosh, London, England, September 16, 1985.

29. Report made at Washington, D.C., June 13, 1945, FBI File 100-267360-407, box 119, folder 2, Jaffe Papers.

30. Ibid. Lee was named by Elizabeth Bentley as one of the sources for her espionage group. He admitted knowing her but denied that he had ever given her information.

31. Ibid.

32. *SDELI*, p. 1323.

33. Emmanuel Larsen statement, "To Whom It May Concern," March 20, 1950, box 11, General Files of the Tydings Committee, RG46, Sen. 81A-F8, State Department Employee Loyalty Investigation, National Archives and Records Administration, Washington, D.C.

34. To the file, July 17, 1945, FBI File 100-267360-580, box 120, folder 9, Jaffe Papers.

35. Report made at Washington, D.C., June 13, 1945, FBI File 100-267360-407, box 119, folder 2, Jaffe Papers.

36. To SAC Guy Hottel from SA Lewis Glenn, March 21, 1945, FBI File 100-267360-717, box 122, folder 3, Jaffe Papers.

37. *New York Post*, June 12, 1945, p. 6.

38. *Daily Worker*, June 8, 1945, p. 2; *New York Journal-American*, June 7, 1945, p. 1.

39. *PM*, June 8, 1945, p. 2. For additional comments on the case by Stone, see "Arrest of the Six," *Nation*, June 16, 1945, pp. 666–67.

40. Grew's statement is quoted in *New York Times*, June 8, 1945, p. 1.

41. *New York Herald Tribune*, June 8, 1945, p. 1; *New York Daily Mirror*, June 8, 1945, p. 3; *New York Journal-American*, June 8, 1945, p. 1.

42. *New York Times*, June 8, 1945, p. 1.

43. *SDELI*, pp. 1180–84.

44. To the director from SAC, Philadelphia, July 27, 1945, FBI File 100-267360-622, box 121, folder 2, Jaffe Papers; Philip Jaffe, *The Amerasia Case, from 1945 to the Present* (New York: privately printed, 1979), p. 19.

45. Gary May, *China Scapegoat: The Diplomatic Ordeal of John Carter Vincent* (Washington, D.C.: New Republic Books, 1979), p. 248.

46. *New York Post*, June 8, 1945, p. 3.

47. *New York Herald Tribune*, June 9, 1945, p. 10.

48. For the guild resolution, see to M. E. Gurnea from L. Whitson, July 2, 1945, FBI File 100-267360-513, box 120, folder 5, and "Twohey Analysis of Newspaper Opinion," box 44, folders 8, 17, both in Jaffe Papers.

49. Harvey Klehr is writing a biography of Karr. For McCarthy's statement, see *Cong. Rec.*, 81st Cong., 2d sess., 1950, 96, pt. 12:16640–46, 16744–47. For the charge that he was a KGB agent, see *Izvestia*, June 24, 1992, p. 4.

50. Andrew Roth, "Pioneer of the Purge," unpublished typescript, in the authors' possession; a copy is in box 9, folder 2, Jaffe Papers; Andrew Roth, interview with Harvey Klehr and Ronald Radosh, London, England, September 16, 1985. For Jaffe's version, see "Memo dictated December 27, 1945," interview with Philip Jaffe by Robert Hitchcock, box 44, folder 13, Jaffe Papers.

51. Andrew Roth, interview with Harvey Klehr and Ronald Radosh, London, England, September 16, 1985.

52. Quoted in *Department of State News Digest*, June 11, 1945, in the authors' possession; *San Francisco Chronicle*, June 15, 1945, in box 44, folder 14, Jaffe Papers.

53. *SDELI*, p. 1180; *New York Post*, June 12, 1945, p. 24; Freda Utley, *The China Story* (Chicago: Henry Regnery, 1951), p. 116.

54. To the director from SAC E. E. Conroy, June 14, 1945, FBI File 100-267360-420, box 119, folder 3, Jaffe Papers.

55. Ibid.; I. F. Stone, "Not a Secret Document," in FBI File 100-267360-365, box 118, folder 3, and memo for Clyde Tolson and D. M. Ladd from J. Edgar Hoover, June 12, 1945, box 118, folder 3, both in Jaffe Papers.

56. *New York Post*, June 11, 1945, p. 3; *Washington Post*, June 17, 1945, p. 3.

57. To the director from M. E. Gurnea, June 11, 1945, FBI File 100-267360-490,

box 120, folder 2, and to Clyde Tolson from J. A. Sizoo, June 11, 1951, FBI File 100-267360-1434, box 126, folder 13, both in Jaffe Papers. A number of widely ranging figures have been cited as the "total" number of documents involved in the case. The figure 1,722 includes handwritten and typed copies of official papers, as well as material that no one claimed had been misappropriated, such as Service's personal file of dispatches, taken from his desk.

58. To the director from M. E. Gurnea, June 11, 1945, FBI File 100-267360-490, box 120, folder 2, Jaffe Papers.

59. Ibid.; to Clyde Tolson from J. A. Sizoo, June 11, 1951, FBI File 100-267360-1434, box 126, folder 13, Jaffe Papers.

60. The personality cards are in boxes 59, 60, Jaffe Papers.

61. Ronald H. Spector, *Eagle against the Sun* (New York: Free Press, 1985), pp. 451–52.

62. To M. E. Gurnea from SA George Allen, September 14, 1945, FBI File 100-267360-681, box 121, folder 4, and to the attorney general from Neil Dalton, acting director, OWI, October 8, 1945, FBI File 100-267360-709, box 122, folder 2, both in Jaffe Papers.

63. To the director from D. M. Ladd, July 23, 1945, FBI File 100-267360-597, box 121, folder 1; to L. Whitson from M. E. Gurnea, July 31, 1945, FBI File 100-267360-626, box 121, folder 2; to M. E. Gurnea from F. L. Jones, August 1, 1945, FBI File 100-267360-628, box 121, folder 2; and teletype to Washington, D.C., from New York City, August 2, 1945, FBI File 100-267360-631, box 121, folder 2, all in Jaffe Papers.

64. To M. E. Gurnea from SA George Allen, July 3, 1945, FBI File 100-267360-524, box 120, folder 5, Jaffe Papers.

65. Report made at San Francisco, July 13, 1945, FBI File 100-267360-537, box 120, folder 7, Jaffe Papers. Given the press's perception that the case involved a crackdown on journalists, making the Phillips letters the centerpiece of the case against Roth might have created problems.

66. Friedman testified on this matter before the McCarran Committee. See *IPRH*, pp. 4294–316.

CHAPTER FIVE

1. E. J. Kahn, Jr., *The China Hands: America's Foreign Service Officers and What Befell Them* (New York: Viking, 1975), p. 169.

2. John S. Service to Joseph Stilwell, July 27, 1945, box 30, #303, Joseph Stilwell Papers, Hoover Institution on War, Revolution, and Peace, Stanford, California.

3. John S. Service, interview with Harvey Klehr and Ronald Radosh, Berkeley, California, November 12, 1985.

4. U.S. House Committee on Un-American Activities, *Hearings Regarding*

Communist Espionage in the United States Government, 80th Cong., 2d sess., 1948, p. 533.

5. Ted Morgan, *FDR: A Biography* (New York: Simon and Schuster, 1985), p. 425.

6. Allen Lichtman, "Tommy the Cork: The Secret World of Washington's First Modern Lobbyist," *Washington Monthly*, February 1987, p. 44. For additional background information on Thomas Corcoran and Ben Cohen, see Katie Louchheim, *The Making of the New Deal: Insiders Speak* (Cambridge: Harvard University Press, 1983), pp. 20–25, 114–18.

7. Transcripts of the Corcoran wiretap are in to the director from D. M. Ladd, June 30, 1952, FBI File 100-267360-1516, box 127, folder 4, Jaffe Papers.

8. Sterling Seagrave, *The Soong Dynasty* (New York: Harper and Row, 1985), pp. 366–68, 397–98.

9. Memo written by John S. Service in Washington, D.C., November 1–3, 1950, Service Papers, copy kindly provided by John S. Service.

10. To the director from D. M. Ladd, June 30, 1952, FBI File 100-267360-1516, box 127, folder 4, and to the director from M. E. Gurnea, June 27, 1945, FBI File 100-267360-485X, box 120, folder 2, both in Jaffe Papers.

11. To D. M. Ladd from A. H. Belmont, June 12, 1950, FBI File 100-267360-1220, box 126, folder 4, Jaffe Papers.

12. Ibid. Wadmond told Mitchell on June 21 that "there is just the possibility that Hitchcock may return the indictment and have it filed," but he thought that Clark had "instructed him to keep it sealed until at least next Monday."

13. Ibid.; *SDELI*, pp. 1015–19.

14. To D. M. Ladd from A. H. Belmont, June 12, 1950, FBI File 100-267360-1220, box 126, folder 4; to M. E. Gurnea from SA A. E. Ostholthoff, June 28, 1945, FBI File 100-267360-488, box 120, folder 2; and to M. E. Gurnea from SA A. E. Ostholthoff, June 29, 1945, FBI File 100-267360-503, box 120, folder 5, all in Jaffe Papers.

15. To D. M. Ladd from A. H. Belmont, June 12, 1950, FBI File 100-267360-1220, box 126, folder 4, Jaffe Papers.

16. Ibid.

17. To the director from M. E. Gurnea, June 30, 1945, FBI File 100-267360-505, box 120, folder 5, and to D. M. Ladd from M. E. Gurnea, July 16, 1945, FBI File 100-267360-570, box 120, folder 9, both in Jaffe Papers.

18. Memo written by John S. Service in Washington, D.C., November 1–3, 1950, Service Papers. Throughout this memo, Service refers to himself in the third person.

19. To the director from D. M. Ladd, June 30, 1952, FBI File 100-267360-1516, box 127, folder 4, Jaffe Papers.

20. Ibid. The transcripts are replete with incriminating statements. For example, on July 26 McGranery pledged to "take care of it for you. Your man is Service.

I got it." The next morning Tom Clark told Corcoran that Service would have trouble before a grand jury only if his staff was "antagonistic." Usually prosecutors tried to "tie them down, but in this case . . . they don't have any such idea."

21. To D. M. Ladd from M. E. Gurnea, August 1, 1945, FBI File 100-267360-643, box 121, folder 3, Jaffe Papers.

22. To the director from D. M. Ladd, June 30, 1952, FBI File 100-267360-1516, box 127, folder 4, Jaffe Papers.

23. John S. Service, interview with Harvey Klehr and Ronald Radosh, Berkeley, California, November 12, 1985; John S. Service to Harvey Klehr and Ronald Radosh, November 25, 1985.

24. Memo written by John S. Service in Washington, D.C., November 1–3, 1950, Service Papers.

25. John S. Service, interview with Harvey Klehr and Ronald Radosh, Berkeley, California, November 12, 1985.

26. Paul Jones to Harvey Klehr, January 20, 1985. Although the letter in which Stilwell indicated his desire to testify has apparently been lost, Service's reply to Stilwell on July 27, 1945, clearly indicates that such an offer was made.

27. "Report of the Department of Justice in Connection with the Amerasia Case," FBI File 100-267360-1512, box 127, folder 3, Jaffe Papers.

28. Seagrave, *The Soong Dynasty*, pp. 379–80.

29. William S. Youngman, telephone interview with Harvey Klehr, January 25, 1986.

30. Lauchlin Currie to Harvey Klehr, January 17, 1986. For the June 14, 1945, resignation letter, see report made at Washington, D.C., January 14, 1954, FBI File 100-3616-72, FBI Reading Room, Washington, D.C.

31. Lauchlin Currie to Harvey Klehr, January 17, 1986.

32. Lichtman, "Tommy the Cork," pp. 41–49.

33. *New York Times*, July 13, 1945, p. 19.

34. John S. Service, interview with Harvey Klehr and Ronald Radosh, Berkeley, California, November 12, 1985.

35. Niccolò Machiavelli, *The Prince and Discourses* (New York: Modern Library, 1950), p. 68.

36. To D. M. Ladd from M. E. Gurnea, July 25, 1945, FBI File 100-267360-605, box 121, folder 2, Jaffe Papers.

37. To M. E. Gurnea from W. Albert Stewart, August 1, 1945, FBI File 100-267360-627, box 121, folder 2, Jaffe Papers.

38. To the director from M. E. Gurnea, August 10, 1945, FBI File 100-267360-650, box 121, folder 4, Jaffe Papers.

39. To D. M. Ladd from M. E. Gurnea, July 25, 1945, FBI File 100-267360-606, box 121, folder 2; to the director from D. M. Ladd, July 25, 1945, FBI File 100-267360-668, box 121, folder 4; and to the director from M. E. Gurnea, August 6, 1945, FBI File 100-267360-646, box 121, folder 4, all in Jaffe Papers.

40. Memo for the attorney general from John Edgar Hoover, August 4, 1945, FBI File 100-267360-615, box 121, folder 4, Jaffe Papers.

41. To the director from M. E. Gurnea, August 10, 1945, FBI File 100-267360-650, box 121, folder 4, Jaffe Papers.

42. Ibid.

43. Ibid.

44. Memo for the attorney general from John Edgar Hoover, August 29, 1945, FBI File 100-267360-671, box 121, folder 4, Jaffe Papers.

45. *New York Post*, June 25, 1945, p. 2. Roth also charged that he had been held incommunicado for eight hours by the FBI. Hoover requested a report on this charge, to which Gurnea replied that Roth had never requested an attorney despite being asked several times if he had one. See from Office of Director, n.d., FBI File 100-267360-486, box 120, folder 2, Jaffe Papers.

46. Report made at New York City, July 13, 1945, FBI File 100-267360-552, box 120, folder 8, and report made at New York City, June 28, 1945, FBI File 100-267360-501, box 120, folder 4, both in Jaffe Papers.

47. Memo for the attorney general from John Edgar Hoover, August 29, 1945, FBI File 100-267360-671, box 121, folder 4, Jaffe Papers.

48. To the director from D. M. Ladd, May 11, 1950, FBI File 100-267360-1206, box 126, folder 3, Jaffe Papers. The affidavit is in *SDELI*, pp. 1928–32. Larsen claimed that the fact that the agents who arrested him had seemed familiar with the layout of his second apartment had made him suspect that the FBI had previously entered it. These agents had not been involved in placing the bug, however, and were probably unaware of its existence. On this basis, Hoover insisted that Larsen had lied in his sworn statement.

49. *SDELI*, pp. 1020–23. Since Larsen had suspected for some time that his apartment had been illegally entered, it would, moreover, have been surprising if Jaffe had not heard the news beforehand.

50. The transcript of the hearing is in *SDELI*, pp. 1933–37. A copy of "The U.S. v. Philip Jacob Jaffe et al." is also in FBI File 100-267360-992, box 125, folder 3, Jaffe Papers.

51. Albert Arent to Philip Jaffe, October 1, 1945, box 44, folder 13, Jaffe Papers.

52. Ibid.

53. Robert Hitchcock, for the file, December 12, 1945, FBI File 100-267360-765, box 124, folder 2, Jaffe Papers; *SDELI*, pp. 1937–39.

54. To D. M. Ladd from M. E. Gurnea, October 30, 1945, FBI File 100-267360-730, box 124, folder 1, Jaffe Papers.

55. *SDELI*, pp. 1020–23.

56. Robert Hitchcock, for the file, December 12, 1945, FBI File 100-267360-765, box 124, folder 2, Jaffe Papers. See also "Memo dictated December 27, 1945," interview with Philip Jaffe by Robert Hitchcock, box 44, folder 13, Jaffe Papers.

57. *Washington Post*, February 18, 1946, p. 15.

58. Philip Jaffe to Mark Gayn, July 18, 1949, box 114, folder 10, Jaffe Papers. For Gayn's troubles in Japan, see the letters in box 114, folder 2, Jaffe Papers.

59. Mark Gayn to Philip Jaffe, September 5, 1949, box 114, folder 11, Jaffe Papers.

60. *New York World Telegram and Sun*, January 4, 1951, p. 1.

61. Subject: Andrew Roth, 3 January 1947, FBI File 100-267360-931, box 124, folder 8, Jaffe Papers.

62. *SDELI*, pp. 2347–48.

63. Hurley's resignation letter to President Truman, November 26, 1945, is reprinted in Don Lohbeck, *Patrick J. Hurley* (Chicago: Henry Regnery, 1956), pp. 428–32.

CHAPTER SIX

1. *Cong. Rec.*, 79th Cong., 1st sess., 1945, 91, pt. 7:9552–53.

2. Memo for the director from Edward Tamm, November 20, 1945, FBI File 100-267360-755, box 124, folder 2; to the director from Edward Tamm, October 26, 1945, FBI File 100-267360-734, box 124, folder 2; to the director from Edward Tamm, October 31, 1945, FBI File 100-267360-727, box 124, folder 1; and to the director from D. M. Ladd, December 4, 1945, FBI File 100-267360-758, box 124, folder 2, all in Jaffe Papers.

3. *Cong. Rec.*, 79th Cong., 1st sess., 1945, 91, pt. 8:11150–51. See to the director from D. M. Ladd, November 30, 1945, FBI File 100-267360-750, box 124, folder 2, Jaffe Papers, for the FBI's summary of the documents mentioned by Dondero, and to the director from D. M. Ladd, May 22, 1946, FBI File 100-267360-825, box 124, folder 3, Jaffe Papers, for the description of the OSS memo.

4. To the director from D. M. Ladd, March 19, 1946, FBI File 100-267360-797, box 124, folder 3, and to the director from D. M. Ladd, June 30, 1952, FBI File 100-267360-1516, box 127, folder 4, both in Jaffe Papers.

5. To Edward Tamm from D. M. Ladd, October 10, 1946, FBI File 100-267360-909, box 124, folder 7, Jaffe Papers.

6. *Cong. Rec.*, 79th Cong., 2d sess., 1946, 92, pt. 3:4006–12.

7. E. J. Kahn, Jr., *The China Hands: America's Foreign Service Officers and What Befell Them* (New York: Viking, 1975), p. 132, emphasis in original.

8. *Cong. Rec.*, 79th Cong., 2d sess., 1946, 92, pt. 3:4006–12.

9. Memo for the director from Edward Tamm, November 20, 1945, FBI File 100-267360-755, box 124, folder 2, and memo for the attorney general from John Edgar Hoover, December 6, 1945, FBI File 100-267360-759, box 124, folder 2, both in Jaffe Papers.

10. To the director from D. M. Ladd, March 8, 1946, FBI File 100-267360-796X1, box 124, folder 3, Jaffe Papers.

11. To M. E. Gurnea from SA G. E. Allen, September 4, 1945, FBI File 100-267360-678, box 121, folder 4, and memo from J. E. Hoover, March 12, 1946, FBI File 100-267360-791, box 124, folder 3, both in Jaffe Papers.

12. For the Hobbs Committee transcript, see *Cong. Rec.*, 81st Cong., 2d sess., 1950, 96, pt. 6:7428–68.

13. Ibid. Shortly after testifying, Larsen wrote to Jaffe pleading for a $300 loan and assuring him that in his testimony to the Hobbs Committee he had taken care to "give them no information about you or anyone else." See Emmanuel Larsen to Philip Jaffe, June 10, 1946, box 1, folder 1, Jaffe Papers.

14. To the director from D. M. Ladd, June 1, 1946, FBI File 100-267360-854, box 124, folder 5, Jaffe Papers.

15. To the director from D. M. Ladd, July 25, 1946, FBI File 100-267360-890, box 124, folder 6, Jaffe Papers.

16. *Cong. Rec.*, 81st Cong., 2d sess., 1950, 96, pt. 6:7431.

17. Emmanuel Larsen, "They Called Me a Spy," reprinted in *SDELI*, pp. 1739–53.

18. *SDELI*, pp. 1116–23, 2199–207.

19. The original typescript of Larsen's article is located in the Levine Papers.

20. *SDELI*, pp. 1120–23, 2205–8.

21. For background on Isaac Don Levine, see his autobiography, *Eyewitness to History* (New York: Hawthorn Books, 1973).

22. On Levine's connections with Chambers, see Alan Weinstein, *Perjury: The Hiss-Chambers Case* (New York: Knopf, 1978), pp. 329–30.

23. For an admiring view of Kohlberg, see Joseph Keeley, *The China Lobby Man: The Story of Alfred Kohlberg* (New Rochelle: Arlington House, 1959).

24. Memo re. Jaffe case, May 20, 1946, Levine Papers.

25. Emmanuel Larsen, "The State Department Espionage Case," *Plain Talk*, October 1946, pp. 27–39.

26. *SDELI*, pp. 1116–23.

27. Isaac Don Levine to Millard Tydings, August 8, 1950, Levine Papers.

28. Memo re. *Amerasia* case, August 9, 1946, Levine Papers.

29. Emmanuel Larsen to Isaac Don Levine, September 11, 1946, Levine Papers.

30. Emmanuel Larsen to Isaac Don Levine, September 25, 1946, Levine Papers.

31. Emmanuel Larsen to Kenneth Watson, November 13, 1946, Levine Papers.

32. Emmanuel Larsen to Isaac Don Levine, December 16, 1946, and Emmanuel Larsen to *Plain Talk*, December 21, 1946, both in Levine Papers.

33. Emmanuel Larsen to Isaac Don Levine, April 26, 1947, Levine Papers.

34. Emmanuel Larsen to Isaac Don Levine, February 11, 1947, Levine Papers.

35. Emmanuel Larsen to Alfred Kohlberg, February 14, 1947, Levine Papers.

36. Emmanuel Larsen to Isaac Don Levine, April 15, 1947, Levine Papers.

37. Gary May, *China Scapegoat: The Diplomatic Ordeal of John Carter Vincent* (Washington, D.C.: New Republic Books, 1979), p. 120.

38. Emmanuel Larsen to Alfred Kohlberg, February 14, 1947, Levine Papers.

39. May, *China Scapegoat*, p. 166.

40. Emmanuel Larsen to Isaac Don Levine, August 29, 1947; Isaac Don Levine to Emmanuel Larsen, September 5, 1947; and Isaac Don Levine memo, November 14, 1947, all in Levine Papers.

41. Emmanuel Larsen to Isaac Don Levine, January 12, December 18, April 6, May 5, 1949, Levine Papers.

42. Emmanuel Larsen statement, "To Whom It May Concern," March 20, 1950, box 11, General Files of the Tydings Committee, RG46, Sen. 81A-F8, State Department Employee Loyalty Investigation, National Archives and Records Administration, Washington, D.C. The last piece of correspondence between Larsen and Levine in the Levine Papers dates from two months earlier, January 27, 1950.

43. Weinstein, *Perjury*, p. 570; to H. B. Fletcher from L. L. Laughlin, March 22, 1949, FBI File 100-267360-982, box 125, folder 1, Jaffe Papers. The Chambers documents were not in the *Amerasia* haul.

44. Elizabeth Bentley, *Out of Bondage* (New York: Devin-Adair, 1951). A thorough discussion of Bentley's charges, based on extensive use of FBI files by Hayden Peake, is in a reissued edition of Bentley's book, published by Ballantine Books in 1988.

45. *New York Times*, August 1, 1948, p. 1.

46. Ibid.

47. Report made at New York City, November 13, 1949, FBI File 101-3616-4, FBI Reading Room, Washington, D.C.

48. Report made at New York City, January 13, 1956, FBI File 101-3616-238; report made at New York City, February 8, 1954, FBI File 101-3616-84; and report made at Washington, D.C., January 14, 1954, FBI File 101-3616-72, all in FBI Reading Room, Washington, D.C.

49. Lauchlin Currie to Harvey Klehr, January 17, 1986; *New York Times*, December 30, 1993, p. B6.

50. Thomas Reeves, *The Life and Times of Joe McCarthy* (New York: Stein and Day, 1982), p. 228.

CHAPTER SEVEN

1. Stephen Ambrose, *Rise to Globalism: American Foreign Policy since 1938*, 6th ed. (New York: Penguin Books, 1991), p. 112.

2. Emmanuel Larsen statement, "To Whom It May Concern," March 20, 1950, box 11, General Files of the Tydings Committee, RG46, Sen. 81A-F8, State De-

partment Employee Loyalty Investigation, National Archives and Records Administration, Washington, D.C.

3. Thomas Reeves, *The Life and Times of Joe McCarthy* (New York: Stein and Day, 1982), pp. 238–39.

4. David Oshinsky, *A Conspiracy So Immense: The World of Joe McCarthy* (New York: Free Press, 1983), p. 111.

5. Ibid.

6. Robert Morris, *No Wonder We Are Losing* (New York: Bookmaker, 1958).

7. *SDELI*, p. 1161; Fred Cook, *The Nightmare Decade: The Life and Times of Senator Joe McCarthy* (New York: Random House, 1971), pp. 250–51.

8. Larsen, "To Whom It May Concern."

9. Ibid.

10. *SDELI*, pp. 1229–48, 2227–78.

11. Oshinsky, *A Conspiracy So Immense*, p. 128; *SDELI*, pp. 114–48.

12. One source unavailable to McCarthy was Louis Gibarti, one of Willi Munzenberg's chief Comintern lieutenants for much of the 1920s and 1930s. Gibarti briefly cooperated privately with a Senate committee in 1951, while living in France. Under questioning, he asserted that in 1934 and 1937 American Communist officials steered him to Lattimore for assistance on several conferences he was arranging. Gibarti had assumed that Lattimore was at least close to the Communist Party. He also said that he had met John Carter Vincent together with Agnes Smedley and believed their views to be similar. To D. M. Ladd from A. H. Belmont, October 8, 1951, FBI File 61-6629-119, FBI Reading Room, Washington, D.C. We are grateful to Stephen Koch for providing us with this material from Gibarti's FBI file.

13. *SDELI*, p. 1681.

14. Ibid., pp. 1874–76.

15. Louis Budenz, "The Menace of Red China," *Collier's*, March 19, 1949, p. 23.

16. *SDELI*, pp. 490–627.

17. Ibid., pp. 669–735.

18. Ibid., pp. 429–76, 1895.

19. Ibid., pp. 870–93.

20. *Washington Daily News*, May 1, 1950, p. 1.

21. *SDELI*, pp. 996–97, 1025–26, 1045.

22. Memo re. *Amerasia* case, August 9, 1946, Levine Papers.

23. *SDELI*, pp. 2228–30.

24. *Washington Evening Star*, May 4, 1950, p. 1; *SDELI*, pp. 931–32, 956. See also *New York Times*, May 5, 1950, p. 1, and Robert Griffith, *The Politics of Fear* (Lexington: University Press of Kentucky, 1970), p. 96.

25. *Washington Post*, May 22, 1950, p. 1.

26. To the director from D. M. Ladd, May 22, 1950, FBI File 100-267360-1117,

box 126, folder 1, Jaffe Papers; *Washington Post*, May 25, 1950, p. 1; report made at New Haven, June 9, 1950, FBI File 100-267360-1165, box 120, folder 2, Jaffe Papers; *SDELI*, pp. 930–31. In a memo to Hoover dated May 4, 1950, Mickey Ladd characterized the "a bomb" testimony as baseless. See FBI File 100-267360-1032, box 124, folder 4, Jaffe Papers.

27. *SDELI*, pp. 974, 990.

28. Ibid., p. 991; to the director from D. M. Ladd, June 5, 1950, FBI File 100-267360-1179, box 126, folder 2, Jaffe Papers; *New York Herald Tribune*, June 3, 1950, p. 1. McInerney explicitly denied that some sensitive material being written about in the press had been seized during the arrests, but he was forced to concede that he had been wrong and that some sensitive material was found.

29. *SDELI*, pp. 986–87.

30. To Clyde Tolson from L. B. Nichols, May 22, 1950, FBI File 100-267360-1080, box 125, folder 5, Jaffe Papers.

31. *SDELI*, pp. 1029, 1048.

32. *Cong. Rec.*, 81st Cong., 2d sess., 1950, 96, pt. 6:7428–68. For McCarthy's original remark, see ibid., p. 4437.

33. E. J. Kahn, Jr., *The China Hands: America's Foreign Service Officers and What Befell Them* (New York: Viking, 1975), pp. 215–16.

34. *SDELI*, p. 2307.

35. Ibid.

36. To John Peurifoy from Peyton Ford, May 8, 1950, FBI File 100-267360-1209, box 126, folder 4, Jaffe Papers.

37. To Clyde Tolson from L. B. Nichols, May 22, 1950, and to the attorney general from the director, May 23, 1950, both in FBI File 100-267360-1209, box 126, folder 4, Jaffe Papers.

38. To Clyde Tolson from L. B. Nichols, June 1, 1950, FBI File 100-267360-1173, box 126, folder 2, Jaffe Papers.

39. Memo for Clyde Tolson, L. B. Nichols, and D. M. Ladd from J. Edgar Hoover, May 11, 1950, FBI File 100-267360-1115, box 126, folder 1, Jaffe Papers.

40. To the director from D. M. Ladd, April 7, 1952, FBI File 100-267360-1495, and to the director from L. B. Nichols, June 1, 1950, FBI File 100-267360-1186, box 126, folder 3, both in Jaffe Papers.

41. To the director from L. B. Nichols, June 1, 1950, FBI File 100-267360-1186, box 126, folder 3; to Clyde Tolson from L. B. Nichols, June 1, 1950, FBI File 100-267360-1173, box 126, folder 2; and to Clyde Tolson from L. B. Nichols, June 2, 1950, FBI File 100-267360-1143, box 126, folder 1, all in Jaffe Papers; *SDELI*, pp. 1066–67.

42. *Cong. Rec.*, 81st Cong., 2d sess., 1950, 96, pt. 6:7885–94; *Washington Daily News*, June 1, 1950, p. 1; to the director from D. M. Ladd, June 5, 1950, FBI File 100-267360-1179, box 126, folder 2, Jaffe Papers.

43. To Clyde Tolson from L. B. Nichols, June 2, 1950, FBI File 100-267360-1143,

box 126, folder 1; to Clyde Tolson from L. B. Nichols, June 2, 1950, FBI File 100-267360-1174, box 126, folder 2; and to Clyde Tolson from L. B. Nichols, June 1, 1950, FBI File 100-267360-1132, box 126, folder 1, all in Jaffe Papers.

44. To Clyde Tolson from L. B. Nichols, June 2, 1950, FBI File 100-267360-1174, box 126, folder 2; to Clyde Tolson from L. B. Nichols, June 1, 1950, FBI File 100-267360-1132, box 126, folder 1; and to the director from D. M. Ladd, June 5, 1950, FBI File 100-267360-1142, box 126, folder 1, all in Jaffe Papers; *SDELI*, pp. 1064–65.

45. *SDELI*, p. 1116.

46. Griffith, *The Politics of Fear*, p. 98.

47. *SDELI*, pp. 1077–78, 1086, 1092, 1095, 1105, 1108, 1139, 1144, 2281–83.

48. Emmanuel Larsen to Isaac Don Levine, August 29, 1947, and Isaac Don Levine to Emmanuel Larsen, September 5, 1947, both in "Notes by E. S. L.," Levine Papers.

49. For an interesting portrait of Larsen, see *Washington Post District Weekly*, August 6, 1981, p. 1. His obituary is in *Washington Post*, May 4, 1988, p. B7.

50. *New York Post*, May 4, 1950, p. 8.

51. Philip Jaffe, *The Rise and Fall of American Communism* (New York: Horizon Press, 1975), pp. 12–13.

52. Ibid., pp. 87–97.

53. To D. M. Ladd from A. H. Belmont, December 11, 1951, FBI File 100-267360-1450, box 127, folder 1, Jaffe Papers.

54. Report made at New York City, November 24, 1948, FBI File 100-343242-58, box 129, folder 4, Jaffe Papers.

55. Robert Lamphere to Harvey Klehr, June 10, 1986; U.S. House Committee on Un-American Activities, *The Shameful Years: Thirty Years of Soviet Espionage in the United States*, report no. 1229, 82d Cong., 2d sess., January 8, 1952.

56. *SDELI*, pp. 1213–27. Material on Jaffe's contempt trial is in box 1, folders 6–9, Jaffe Papers.

57. To Clyde Tolson from L. B. Nichols, September 14, 1951, FBI File 100-267360-1440, box 127, folder 1; to Clyde Tolson from L. B. Nichols, November 24, 1953, FBI File 100-267360-1529, box 127, folder 5; and to the director from SAC, New York City, May 17, 1956, FBI File 100-267360-1579, box 127, folder 9, all in Jaffe Papers.

58. To Clyde Tolson from L. B. Nichols, February 8, 1952, FBI File 100-267360-1466, box 127, folder 1; to D. M. Ladd from A. H. Belmont, February 13, 1952, FBI File 100-267360-1465, box 127, folder 1; to the director from D. M. Ladd, March 7, 1952, FBI File 100-267360-1474, box 127, folder 2; and to SAC, New York City, from [blacked out], May 20, 1954, FBI File 100-267360-1562, box 127, folder 7, all in Jaffe Papers.

59. FBI teletype, June 16, 1952, FBI File 100-343242-73, box 129, folder 4, Jaffe Papers.

60. Report made at New York City, June 29, 1953, FBI File 100-343242-89, box 129, folder 6; to A. H. Belmont from W. A. Brannigan, September 14, 1954, FBI File 100-343242-124, box 129, folder 8; and to the director from SAC, New York City, March 7, 1966, FBI File 100-343242-[unrecorded], box 129, folder 11, all in Jaffe Papers. See also Bernstein's obituary in *New York Times*, July 12, 1975, p. 28.

61. Philip Jaffe, "Odyssey of a Fellow Traveler," box 1, folder 5, Jaffe Papers; Agnes Jaffe, interview with Harvey Klehr and Ronald Radosh, New York City, May 18, 1984.

62. *Cong. Rec.*, 81st Cong., 2d sess., 1950, 96, pt. 6:8486–87.

63. To the director from D. M. Ladd, June 9, 1950, FBI File 100-267360-1184, box 126, folder 3, Jaffe Papers.

64. *Cong. Rec.*, 81st Cong., 2d sess., 1950, 96, pt. 6:8778–80; to the director from D. M. Ladd, June 15, 1950, FBI File 100-267360-1222, box 126, folder 5, and to D. M. Ladd from A. H. Belmont, November 3, 1950, FBI File 100-267360-1396, box 126, folder 12, both in Jaffe Papers. An often inaccurate account of the grand jury's investigation is found in an unpublished memoir by the foreman, John Brunini, supplied to us by his son. Among other memories, Brunini recalled that all six of the *Amerasia* defendants were originally indicted, that Jaffe and Mitchell were found guilty, and that the *Amerasia* papers were subsequently burned. Brunini was also associated with Elizabeth Bentley in producing her book, *Out of Bondage.* His dual role as Bentley's aide and the grand jury foreman considering evidence she supplied was, to put it mildly, a conflict of interest. See Herbert Packer, *Ex-Communist Witnesses: Four Studies in Fact Finding* (Stanford: Stanford University Press, 1962), pp. 85–90.

65. John S. Service, interview with Harvey Klehr and Ronald Radosh, Berkeley, California, November 12, 1985.

66. *SDELI*, p. 1285.

67. Ibid., p. 1303. In his testimony to the State Department Loyalty-Security Board, which was eventually included in the Tydings Committee transcripts, Service elaborated on his reasons for disliking Jaffe, saying that he "was perplexed by Jaffe's aggressive nosy manner." On this occasion, however, he recalled that he *had* received a warning about Jaffe. Sometime in late April, Harold Isaacs, a former Trotskyist whom Service had known as a correspondent in China, had told him that Jaffe was "bad medicine." See ibid., pp. 2296, 2315, 2326.

68. To J. Edgar Hoover from Peyton Ford, June 15, 1950, FBI File 100-267360-1300, box 126, folder 10, Jaffe Papers.

69. To the director from D. M. Ladd, June 26, 1950, FBI File 100-267360-1372, box 125, folder 7, and to Peyton Ford from the director, June 27, 1950, FBI File 100-267360-1292, box 126, folder 9, both in Jaffe Papers; *SDELI*, p. 1403.

70. *SDELI*, pp. 1423–26.

71. Harvey Klehr and Ronald Radosh, "Anatomy of a Fix," *New Republic*, April 21, 1986, pp. 18–21; John S. Service to Harvey Klehr and Ronald Radosh, June 22, 1986.

72. *SDELI*, pp. 1428–29.

73. Ibid., pp. 1958–2509, contains the transcript of the hearings before the Loyalty-Security Board.

74. To M. E. Gurnea from L. Whitson, July 3, 1945, FBI File 100-267360-659, box 121, folder 4, and to D. M. Ladd from A. H. Belmont, April 19, 1950, FBI File 100-267360-1048, box 125, folder 5, both in Jaffe Papers.

75. To M. E. Gurnea from L. Whitson, July 3, 1945, FBI File 100-267360-659, box 121, folder 4, and to D. M. Ladd from A. H. Belmont, April 19, 1950, FBI File 100-267360-1048, box 125, folder 5, both in Jaffe Papers.

76. Joseph Alsop to Millard Tydings, n.d., box 64, Stewart and Joseph Alsop Papers, Manuscript Division, Library of Congress, Washington, D.C.

77. Statement by Charles R. Allen, Jr., box 10, General Files of the Tydings Committee, RG 46, Sen. 81A-F8, State Department Employee Loyalty Investigation, National Archives and Records Administration, Washington, D.C.

78. Charles R. Allen, Jr., telephone interview with Harvey Klehr, October 18, 1985; Charles R. Allen, Jr., to Harvey Klehr, December 4, 1985; Harvey Klehr to Charles R. Allen, Jr., December 27, 1985; Stanley Faulkner to Harvey Klehr, April 16, 1986.

79. *Washington Daily News*, June 26, 1950, p. 6.

80. Oshinsky, *A Conspiracy So Immense*, pp. 168–69.

81. Ralph de Toledano to Millard Tydings, July 16, 1950; Edward Morgan to Ralph de Toledano, July 27, 1950; and Ralph de Toledano to Edward Morgan, August 3, 1950, all in Levine Papers.

82. *Cong. Rec.*, 81st Cong., 2d sess., 1950, 96, pt. 6:13925–27.

83. Gale, Bernays, Falk, and Eisner to trustees of the *Christian Science Monitor*, August 15, 1950, and *Christian Science Monitor*, August 18, 1950, both in Levine Papers.

84. Oshinsky, *A Conspiracy So Immense*, pp. 166–70.

85. *Cong. Rec.*, 81st Cong., 2d sess., 1950, 96, pt. 6:10706–15.

86. *New Republic*, July 31, 1950, pp. 3–4.

CHAPTER EIGHT

1. Memo for Clyde Tolson from L. B. Nichols, April 15, 1952, Nichols Official and Confidential File, FBI Reading Room, Washington, D.C.

2. Hearings before the U.S. Senate Committee on the Judiciary, *Nomination of James P. McGranery*, 82d Cong., 2d sess., 1952, p. 3.

3. To the attorney general from the director, July 1, 1952, FBI File 100-267360-1513, box 127, folder 4, Jaffe Papers; memo for Clyde Tolson, D. M. Ladd, and A. H. Belmont from John Edgar Hoover, June 30, 1952, FBI File 100-267360-1514, box 127, folder 4, Jaffe Papers.

4. To Clyde Tolson from L. B. Nichols, November 3, 1950, FBI File 100-267360-1397, box 126, folder 12, Jaffe Papers.

5. Robert Newman, "Clandestine Chinese Nationalist Efforts to Punish Their American Detractors," *Diplomatic History* 7 (Summer 1983): 205–22.

6. John S. Service, interview with Harvey Klehr and Ronald Radosh, Berkeley, California, November 12, 1985.

7. Typed excerpts from the February 13–14 executive session of the review board were eventually provided to Service by Murray Marder. Service kindly allowed us to see them.

8. Ibid.

9. Opinion of the Loyalty Review Board, December 12, 1951, in *Service v. Bingham et al.*, Complaint for Declaratory Judgment and Mandatory Order, Service Papers.

10. *Cong. Rec.*, 82d Cong., 2d sess., 1952, 98, pt. 1:192–93. On Miriam de Haas, see *New York World Telegram*, November 3, 1952, p. 3.

11. E. J. Kahn, Jr., *The China Hands: America's Foreign Service Officers and What Befell Them* (New York: Viking, 1975), pp. 267–68.

12. Memo for the director from L. B. Nichols, February 12, 1953, Nichols Official and Confidential File, FBI Headquarters, Washington, D.C.

13. To the director from F. Tompkins, April 28, 1955, FBI File 100-267360-1564, box 127, folder 7, Jaffe Papers.

14. U.S. Senate Committee on the Judiciary, Subcommittee to Investigate the Administration of the Internal Security Act and Other Internal Security Laws, *The Amerasia Papers: A Clue to the Catastrophe of China*, 2 vols. (Washington, D.C.: Government Printing Office, 1970).

15. John S. Service, *The Amerasia Papers: Some Problems in the History of U.S.-China Relations* (Berkeley: University of California Press, 1971).

16. John Service to Harvey Klehr and Ronald Radosh, June 22, 1986.

17. Joseph Esherick, ed., *Lost Chance in China: The World War II Despatches of John S. Service* (New York: Random House, 1975), p. xvi.

18. Philip Jaffe, *The Amerasia Case, from 1945 to the Present* (New York: privately printed, 1979), pp. 15–17.

19. Andrew Roth to Ronald Radosh, March 3, 1985; Andrew Roth, interview with Harvey Klehr and Ronald Radosh, London, England, September 16, 1985.

20. M. Stanton Evans, "The Vindication of Joe McCarthy," *Human Events*, February 14, 1987, pp. 7–8; Ralph de Toledano, "Cover-up of a Bygone Cover-up?," *Washington Times*, April 25, 1986; Harvey Klehr and Ronald Radosh, "Anatomy of a Fix," *New Republic*, April 21, 1986, pp. 18–21.

21. Joseph Wedemeyer to Joseph Alsop, October 3, 1951, Stewart and Joseph Alsop Papers, Manuscript Division, Library of Congress, Washington, D.C.

Bibliographical Essay

The *Amerasia* case has been the subject of considerable attention by writers interested in the post–World War II controversies in American political life. The confusion that enveloped the entire affair and the absence of hard evidence, however, have meant that no one has been able to get at more than a small portion of the truth.

The first serious scholarly examination of the *Amerasia* case appeared in Earl Latham, *The Communist Controversy in Washington: From the New Deal to McCarthy* (Cambridge: Harvard University Press, 1966). Latham's discussion of the case was set in the context of an overview of the entire era and, in particular, of the Tydings Committee hearings. He relied heavily, almost exclusively, on the hearings themselves and public testimony about the case, concluding that "although it seemed to be virtually impossible to establish espionage by courtroom standards, there is the silent testimony of the documents themselves. There was either espionage in the *Amerasia* case or the security procedures of the Department of State were so grotesquely lax that the responsible officials should have been disciplined" (p. 216).

Although Latham suspected espionage, most academics and journalists, critical of Senator Joseph McCarthy, have suggested that the case was a red herring. In her classic *Stilwell and the American Experience in China, 1911–1945* (New York: Macmillan, 1970), the late Barbara Tuchman suggested that John S. Service's arrest marked the first step of McCarthy's "tawdry reign of terror" (p. 671). In *The Great Fear: The Anti-Communist Purge under Truman and Eisenhower* (New York: Simon and Schuster, 1978), David Caute argued that neither Philip Jaffe nor his associates "had in mind to pass information to a foreign power" (p. 56) and that the whole episode involved the leaking of government documents, not spying. The *Amerasia* case has also been discussed in most of the major scholarly works on McCarthyism, where the dominant interpretation is similar to that of David Oshinsky in *A Conspiracy So Immense: The World of Joe McCarthy* (New York: Free Press, 1983), which suggests that even though Service's actions showed poor judgment, his obvious intention was not espionage but "rather to publicize an alternative position on China through a news leak" (p. 128). Defenders of McCarthy, most notably William F. Buckley, Jr., and L. Brent Bozell in *McCarthy and His Enemies* (Chicago: Henry Regnery, 1954), have singled out the *Amerasia* case as proof of the existence of a far-reaching conspiracy in the higher realms of government.

The literature on McCarthyism is voluminous. Interested readers should consult one of the most complete overviews of the era, Richard Fried's *Nightmare in Red: The McCarthy Era in Perspective* (New York: Oxford University Press, 1990), which also contains a complete bibliography of books, monographs, and articles dealing with the McCarthy phenomenon. The best book on J. Edgar Hoover is Richard Gid Powers, *Secrecy and Power: The Life of J. Edgar Hoover* (New York: Free Press, 1987).

In addition to Latham's book, several accounts of Communist espionage in America have been written. The most recent is Harvey Klehr, John Haynes, and Fridrikh Firsov, *The Secret World of American Communism* (New Haven: Yale University Press, 1995). Elizabeth Bentley told her story in *Out of Bondage* (New York: Devin-Adair, 1951).

Several books deal specifically with the travails of the China Hands. In addition to Tuchman's account of Stilwell, a sympathetic account can be found in E. J. Kahn, Jr., *The China Hands: America's Foreign Service Officers and What Befell Them* (New York: Viking, 1975). Two academic accounts are Gary May, *China Scapegoat: The Diplomatic Ordeal of John Carter Vincent* (Washington, D.C.: New Republic Books, 1979), and Robert P. Newman, *Owen Lattimore and the "Loss" of China* (Berkeley: University of California Press, 1992).

American policy in China during and after World War II remains a contentious issue. One of the best general accounts remains Michael Schaller, *The U.S. Crusade in China, 1938–1945* (New York: Columbia University Press, 1979). A scathing and unfair critique of Service's views can be found in Anthony Kubek, *How the Far East Was Lost: American Policy and the Creation of Communist China, 1941–1949* (Chicago: Henry Regnery, 1963). Service defends his policy advice in *The Amerasia Papers: Some Problems in the History of U.S.-China Relations* (Berkeley: University of California Press, 1971), which also contains Service's incomplete and inaccurate account of his role in the *Amerasia* case.

Philip Jaffe gave a brief and selective chronicle of the case in *The Amerasia Case, from 1945 to the Present* (New York: privately printed, 1979). A valuable source was Jaffe's unpublished autobiography, "Odyssey of a Fellow Traveler," box 1, folder 5, Philip Jaffe Papers, Special Collections Department, Robert W. Woodruff Library, Emory University, Atlanta, Georgia. Of the other defendants, Mark Gayn wrote an autobiography, *Journey from the Far East* (New York: Knopf, 1944), and Emmanuel Larsen told his many different versions of the story to various congressional committees. Andrew Roth has written of his involvement in the *Amerasia* case in several unpublished papers, copies of which Roth kindly provided to us. Copies are also in box 9, folder 2, Jaffe Papers.

We depended very heavily on the transcripts of congressional hearings held on matters pertaining to the *Amerasia* case. The most important of these hearings include those conducted by the Hobbs Committee, whose original report was sealed but eventually printed in the *Congressional Record*, 81st Cong., 2d sess., 1950, 96, pt. 6:7428–68; the Tydings Committee hearings, U.S. Senate Subcommittee of the Committee on Foreign Relations, *State Department Employee Loyalty Investigation*, 81st Cong., 2d sess., 1950, 5 parts; and the McCarran Committee hearings, U.S. Senate Committee on the Judiciary, Subcommittee to Investigate the Administration of the Internal Security Act and Other Internal Security Laws, *Institute of Pacific Relations Hearings*, 82d Cong., 1st and 2d sess., 1951–52, 14 parts. In addition to the published hearings, we examined the General Files of the Tydings Committee, RG 46, Sen. 81A-F8, State Department Employee Loyalty Investigation, National Archives and Records Administration, Washington, D.C.

The most valuable information for this book was gathered from the enormous FBI files on the *Amerasia* case, which include the extensive wiretaps of Mark Gayn, Philip Jaffe, Emmanuel Larsen, Kate Mitchell, and Andrew Roth. Included in these files are the wiretap transcripts of Thomas Corcoran revealing his involvement in the case and files on Joseph Bernstein and Lauchlin Currie. These FBI files are now available to researchers in the Philip Jaffe Papers, Special Collections Department, Robert W. Woodruff Library, Emory University, Atlanta, Georgia. Other FBI files released to us under the Freedom of Information Act are available at the FBI Reading Room, Washington, D.C.

We were also fortunate to have access to a number of collections of personal papers, either located in libraries or in the possession of individuals connected with the case. Through the courtesy of these libraries and individuals, we consulted the following collections:

Stewart and Joseph Alsop Papers, Manuscript Division, Library of Congress, Washington, D.C.
Tom Clark Papers, University of Texas Library, Austin, Texas
George Dondero Papers, Detroit Public Library, Detroit, Michigan
Stanley Hornbeck Papers, Hoover Institution on War, Revolution, and Peace, Stanford, California
Philip Jaffe Papers, Special Collections Department, Robert W. Woodruff Library, Emory University, Atlanta, Georgia
Isaac Don Levine Papers, in possession of Ruth Levine, Washington, D.C.
James P. McGranery Papers, Manuscript Division, Library of Congress, Washington, D.C.
Andrew Roth Papers, in possession of Andrew Roth, London, England
John S. Service Papers, in possession of John S. Service, Berkeley, California
Joseph Stilwell Papers, Hoover Institution on War, Revolution, and Peace, Stanford, California

We also conducted a number of personal interviews. Even when not specifically cited in the notes, these interviews provided invaluable background and context for this book. The following people were interviewed:

Charles R. Allen, Jr., by telephone, October 18, 1985
Ralph de Toledano, Washington, D.C., May 30, 1985

Frederick Vanderbilt Field, Minneapolis, Minnesota, April 19, 1985
Agnes Jaffe, New York City, May 18, 1984
Minister Ji Chao-zhu, by telephone, March 25, 1985
Robert Lamphere, by telephone, June 20, 1986
Robert Morris, Harvey Cedars, New Jersey, October 17, 1984
Andrew Roth, London, England, September 16, 1985
John S. Service, Berkeley, California, November 12, 1985
Karl Wittfogel, New York City, May 17, 1986
William S. Youngman, by telephone, January 25, 1986

In addition, we corresponded with Charles R. Allen, Jr., Lauchlin Currie, Stanley Faulkner, Paul Jones, Robert Lamphere, Mrs. Emmanuel Larsen, Andrew Roth, and John S. Service.

Index

Acheson, Dean, 102, 135, 155; Red-baiting attacks on, 103, 137, 143, 152, 157; firing of Service, 210

Adler, Solomon, 21, 22, 59, 60, 150, 158, 159

Allen, Charles, Jr., 199

Alsop, Joseph, 20, 22, 198, 215–16

Ambrose, Stephen E., 164

Amerasia magazine: Jaffe as editor of, 3, 6, 38, 41, 42, 43, 44, 59, 135; Mitchell as editor of, 3, 44, 61, 135; Wells report on Thailand plagiarized in, 3–4, 6, 29, 30, 31, 44, 54, 107, 155, 221–22 (n. 7); classified documents found at offices of, 5–6, 30, 49–50, 90–91, 105–6, 177, 185; founding of, 38–39, 40; contributors to, 40–41, 43–44, 59; circulation of, 41–42; financing of, 43; Service's knowledge of, 58, 61, 62, 79, 193–94, 214; attacks on Grew, 99

Amerasia Papers: A Clue to the Catastrophe of China, 213

Amerasia spy case, 9–10, 218–19; arrests of suspects, 3, 7, 89–97, 145; OSS investigation of, 5–6, 29, 30, 31, 146, 178; and Soviet espionage, 7, 8, 9, 67–68, 139, 217, 218; FBI investigation, 7, 32, 49–50, 52–53, 78, 107, 108, 155, 212; collapse of prosecution's case, 7, 127, 133, 136, 218; "whitewash" of, 8, 136–37, 172, 201, 205, 218; McCarthy and, 8, 173, 179, 181, 215, 218; and China policy, 9, 11, 12, 216; contribution to McCarthyism, 9, 219; Service's role in, 11, 12, 55, 213–15; FBI's illegal searches and seizures in, 88, 104–5,

110, 130, 132–33, 141, 144, 146, 177–78, 185; news media reactions to, 97–99, 100, 102, 103–4; State Department blamed for mishandling of, 103–4, 140, 146, 150, 151; Hitchcock appointed prosecutor of, 105, 118–19; Chinese Nationalists and, 114, 123–24, 125; political influence and, 115, 118, 123, 125, 218; grand jury indictments, 117, 129; FBI blamed for mishandling of, 131, 141, 144, 177–78, 180; Dondero resolution and, 137–38, 139–40, 141, 145; Justice Department blamed for mishandling of, 139, 140, 144, 145, 178; Hobbs Committee hearings on, 142–46; Hobbs Committee report on, 146–47, 179–80; Tydings Committee hearings on, 169, 170–71, 172–74, 175–79, 183–85, 186–87, 192–97, 198–99; second grand jury investigation, 192, 243 (n. 64); Tydings Committee report on, 199–202, 204; Eastland subcommittee investigation, 212–13; Service's *The Amerasia Papers* on, 213

American China Policy Association, 156

American Civil Liberties Union, 103

American Council of Learned Societies, 47

American Friends of the Chinese People, 35, 37

American Peace Mobilization (American People's Mobilization), 43

Arent, Albert, 130–31, 132

"Asiaticus" (Hans Müller; Heinz Shipper), 41, 43